P9-AQT-699

Alexander Fodor

TOLSTOY
and the
RUSSIANS

Reflections on a Relationship

Ardis, Ann Arbor

The author wishes to thank the Faculty of Graduate Studies and Research of McGill University for its help in preparing the manuscript of this book for publication.

Alexander Fodor, *Tolstoy and the Russians*
Copyright © 1984 by Ardis Publishers

Ardis Publishers
2901 Heatherway
Ann Arbor, Michigan 48104

Library of Congress Cataloging in Publication Data

Fodor, Alexander.
 Tolstoy and the Russians.

 Includes bibliographical references.
 1. Tolstoy, Leo, graf, 1828-1920—Appreciation—
Soviet Union. 2. National characteristics, Russian.
I. Title.
PG3409.5.F6   1984   891.73'3   83-25800
ISBN 0-88233-891-9

To the Russian people, in the hope of a new Tolstoy

Contents

Introduction   *11*

I.   The High-Born and the Peasants   *15*

II.   Tolstoy and the Twilight of Tsardom   *33*

III.   Russia Rediscovers Tolstoy   *55*

IV.   Russia's Giant   *75*

V.   Tolstoy's New Readers   *105*

VI.   Novels Revived by History   *123*

Conclusion   *145*

Notes   *149*

Biographical Notes   *159*

Preface

An extraordinarily strong bond must exist between Leo Tolstoy and the Russian people, for he is still read and sincerely loved by them even after the many years which have elapsed since his death in 1910. Although Russia has undergone fundamental social, political and cultural changes Tolstoy remains a colossus in his country. To the Russians, Tolstoy's greatness is the greatness of Russia herself. To be ignorant of Tolstoy or to lack regard for his work is to be gravely at fault in the eyes of his compatriots—it is tantamount to being alien to the very spirit of Russia.

Tolstoy's accepted and firmly established presence in Russia is a reassuring fact. As long as his works are published there by the million, as long as he figures prominently in the curricula of schools and universities, as long as the population continues to flock to his birthplace, decency and purity will exist in Russian society.

To know Tolstoy is to understand the Russians, and no one can really understand Tolstoy without understanding the Russians. It is to those who share this view that the present work is addressed.

Introduction

As the year 1941 drew to a close, Russia's very existence was at stake, with the German army pushing ever deeper into the country in a seemingly unstoppable march. Leningrad, already besieged, lacking adequate means of defense, its food supplies largely destroyed, seemed to face the stark choice of surrender or a fight to the end.

The speeches due to be made in the Palace Square of the former imperial capital during the celebrations to mark the twenty-fourth anniversary of the October Revolution in November of that first year of war were expected to be the most passionate ever. Only oratory of such a kind, it was supposed, could be equal to the task of rallying the whole population to the defense of "the cradle of the Revolution" and endowing it with the strength to endure the ordeal ahead.

The awaited speeches were never delivered. Zhdanov, the city's all-powerful party secretary, was silent, as were other party and military leaders; and, when the moment came, it was Leo Tolstoy whose words were heard by the people of Leningrad. From street loudspeakers came forth excerpts from the great writer's tales of heroism during the Crimean War of 1854-56. "Nowhere can the strength of the Russian people be shattered" came the declaration, and there were eulogies to the heroes "who in that period of trial never lost courage, and joyfully prepared for death"[1] for Russia.

Allowing Tolstoy's stories to be heard on that fateful anniversary of the Revolution was a brilliant inspiration on the authorities' part. Not only did the descriptions of Russian patriotism in times past strengthen Leningrad's will to resist, but the very fact that Tolstoy's tales were publicly broadcast at the city's hour of mortal danger was deeply gratifying to the populace, to whom Tolstoy personified a beloved Russia with all its greatness and contradictions.

As the war was drawing to a close in 1945, Boris Pasternak, later to achieve world renown as the author of *Doctor Zhivago,* looked back at the years of trial and observed that he found it impossible to be critical of Tolstoy, since Russia and Tolstoy were one.[2] And Konstantin Simonov, Russia's most popular writer during the wartime years, declared that the Russians' attitude towards Tolstoy is "more than love; it is more because it is unthinkable and impossible to imagine Russia without Tolstoy."[3]

Konstantin Fedin, a Soviet writer who was held in high regard by his country's literary establishment and headed the Writers' Union during the last years of his life, maintained—and his novel *Bonfire* is based on the idea—that the psychological turning point of the war for Russia was not the victorious battle at Stalingrad, but rather the German occupation of Tolstoy's birthplace, Yasnaya Polyana. This event and the effrontery of the Germans in burying their dead next to Tolstoy's grave, according to Fedin, aroused the Russians to a state of patriotic fury which might have been a decisive factor in the winning of the war.

With the return of peace, allusions to Tolstoy's ability to portray the soul of Russia not only continued to be made but, if anything, became more frequent. In 1960, the writer Leonid Leonov declared at a meeting of persons prominent in all walks of Russian life, held in the Bolshoi Theater in Moscow to mark the fiftieth anniversary of Tolstoy's death:

> Pushkin revealed to us the wondrous music of our native tongue. Tolstoy, with its assistance, expressed as none other has ever been able to express the deeds, the joys and sorrows, of the Russian people...Pushkin's poetic achievements affected our national character...On the other hand, the sweep, the persistence, the depth, and other qualities of the Russian character were manifested in Tolstoy's work...Whatever the wealth of our forbears, who created our history and our language, and laid the foundation of our material being—we are richer than they; for in each of us there is some fragment of Tolstoy.[4]

Such an affirmation is quite remarkable when one considers that the leaders of the Bolshevik revolution proudly declared that event to be international, and evoked neither the name of Tolstoy nor his special place in the hearts of the Russian people. In the civil war that followed the revolution, both the Whites and the Reds were silent about the great writer; the former regarded him as a progenitor of the Bolsheviks and the latter detested his philosophy of non-violence. It is paradoxical that Tolstoy, wealthy landowner, aristocrat and man of deep religious faith, is more honored today in the atheist Soviet state than writers such as Gorky and Mayakovsky, whose contributions to the creation of the new order were immeasurably more significant.

The transformation of Tolstoy from a socially alien writer into one whose name is synonymous with Russia herself constitutes a fascinating episode in the cultural history of Soviet Russia. This transformation has not been examined before and it is hoped that the present study, although not exhaustive, will in some measure throw light on those aspects of Tolstoy's personality and life's work that are cherished by that nation even today. This book is written for the Western reader and it is offered in the sincere desire that it will stimulate interest in comprehending cultural values held dear by the Russians.

The transliteration of Russian words and titles follows the British Standard System. However, since many Russian names have acquired fixed spelling in English (Dostoevsky, Gorky etc.), the "ii" and "yi" endings in all Russian names are transliterated as "y" in the main text. Dates throughout the study are given according to the New Style, i.e., the Gregorian calendar, which the Russians adopted in February 1918.

The High-Born and the Peasants

Apart from being a literary genius, Tolstoy was also an organic part of his nation's history. Therein, perhaps, lies the reason why foreign studies of Tolstoy, no matter how brilliantly written or what their ideological standpoints, attract little attention in Russia. Of the scores of such studies which have been published in socialist countries, and likely been cited in Soviet books and journals as evidence of the renown of Tolstoy abroad, not a single one has been translated into Russian or reissued in Russia. The dozens of books which have been written on Tolstoy in the West since his death have been largely ignored in his homeland—with the possible exception of one by Romain Rolland* which has become fairly popular there. The Russians simply cannot believe—perhaps quite justifiably—that foreigners, who must as such lack intimate knowledge of the unfolding drama of Russian social history, can have any real conception of who and what Tolstoy was. There is a certain similarity between the Russians' attitude towards Tolstoy and the respect the Americans have for their flag. One has to be a Russian to know that Tolstoy was much more than just a writer, and an American to know that "Old Glory" is much more than a piece of cloth.

Contemporaries of Tolstoy in the West were nonetheless aware of the special place the writer occupied in the hearts of the Russians and wrote a great deal about it. Henry Norman, a British author and traveler who visited Tolstoy in 1901, observed: "The name of Moscow will always bring back to my mind, before anything else, my visit to Tolstoy. Indeed, he is as much part of Russia, as significant of Russian character, as prophetic of Russian development, as the Kremlin itself."[1] Edward A. Steiner, an American, who also knew Tolstoy personally, wrote in 1904: "Tolstoy's coming and his growing into such prominence were not the trick of genius, were not the striking of a golden vein which brought fame and wealth to the lucky finder, but were as truly an historic event as they were 'historic necessity'."[2] For his part, the renowned Austrian writer, Stefan Zweig, wrote of Tolstoy: "He has no face of his own; he possesses the general face of the Russian folk, because in him the whole of Russia lives and breathes."[3]

The family of Tolstoy's mother were of very ancient Russian lineage, claiming descent from Prince Rurik, traditionally regarded as the founder, in the year 862, of the Russian state. Whether or not such ancestry can be

---

* Entitled *Vie de Tolstoi*/The life of Tolstoy/, it was published in France in 1911 and translated into Russian in 1933.

15

proved, the Russians have an awesome reverence for the part played by Tolstoy and his family in their country's past, which equals in intensity their unstinted admiration of the writer's literary masterpieces. This fact—the very key to a true understanding of what Tolstoy means to the Russians—has been almost completely overlooked in the majority of studies published outside his homeland. In the brief historical survey which follows mention is therefore made of ancestors of Tolstoy who participated in critical events of their country's history. It should be noted that Tolstoy's own participation in Russia's defence is an important chapter in his life.

In 1237, the Tartars invaded Russia and burned Moscow and a multitude of other towns and villages. After destroying and massacring for several more years they withdrew to the lower Volga region, from whence they governed their state, known as the Golden Horde. In order to retain their titles all the Russian princes were obliged to visit the Horde and pay tribute to it, including military contingents. The latter were often thrown into battle against their Russian kin. Any disobedience of Tartar rule resulted in swift and extremely cruel retribution.

One of the most glorified events in Russian history is the battle which was fought on the plains of Kulikovo, near the Don river, in 1380. In that encounter Grand Prince Dmitry of Moscow, subsequently styled "Donskoi", defeated the Tartars. In doing so he destroyed the myth of the invaders' invincibility, although another two hundred years were to elapse before the Russians were free of the Tartar yoke. In the battle of Kulikovo the Tartars lost about 100,000 men and the Russians almost as many. Among the dead was Prince Fedor Volkonsky, an ancestor of Tolstoy's on his mother's side.

Ivan the Terrible died after a bloody reign in 1584 without leaving an heir fit to be tsar, for he had killed his eldest son in a fit of rage and left his throne to his feeble-minded son Fedor. During Fedor's reign the country was in reality ruled by the ambitious regent, Boris Godunov, who himself became tsar upon Fedor's death in 1598. Russia by this time was full of rumors that Godunov had killed Dmitry, Ivan's infant son (by his seventh wife), the legitimate heir to the throne after Fedor. Godunov was deposed by an impostor claiming to be Dmitry. From Godunov's death in 1605 until the election of the first Romanov in 1613 ensued the "Time of Troubles", the most confused period in Russian history. During this time there occurred numerous riots and peasant uprisings, and more attempts by persons who claimed to be Ivan's son, Dmitry, to be acknowledged tsar. These impostors, backed by Russia's enemy Poland, in turn moved an army against Moscow with the intention of capturing the Kremlin, its citadel. During the last of these expeditions, in 1610, the invaders' path was blocked by a fortified monastery in Borovsk, near Moscow. Inside a small force was stationed, commanded by the governor of Moscow province, whose intention it was to resist the approaching army. However, his men, on perceiving its overwhelming size, capitulated and opened the monastery's gates. The governor, who drew his sword and fought alone until cut down in the monastery's chapel, was Prince Mikhail Volkonsky, another of Tolstoy's ancestors.

In the end of the seventeenth century, Peter the Great began to modernize Russia and increase its military strength by ruthless, and often barbarous, means. At the same time, however, he sought to introduce into the country all the refinements of European civilization. To that end he induced engineers, architects, artists and tradesmen to come from France, England, Holland, Germany and other countries, and made his subjects adopt Western dress and manners. To those foreigners who made outstanding contributions to the advancement of his plans he accorded most of the distinctions and privileges of the Russian aristocracy. A select number of native Russians (referred to by Alexander Pushkin as "Peter's eaglets"), whom the tsar appointed to the highest offices of state, were the most accomplished and dedicated group of individuals ever to serve imperial Russia. Many of them bore venerable aristocratic names such as Dolgoruky and Galitsyn, while others, like Alexander Menshikov, who later became a field marshal, were of plebeian origin.

Peter the Great was well aware of the opposition to his reforms which existed among his subjects, and he mercilessly stamped out all real or imaginary plots through the agency of his Secret Chancellery. This scourge of the tsar's enemies even interrogated Peter's own son, Alexei, after his arrest on charges of conspiracy, and the young man died in mysterious circumstances two days after he had been sentenced to death. Since the Secret Chancellery was pivotal to the achievement of Peter's ambitions, only his most trusted supporters became heads of it. One of them, appointed to this position in 1718—rewarded by the title of count a year before Peter died—was Peter Tolstoy, classical scholar,* former ambassador to Turkey and first bearer of the title that Lev Tolstoy later inherited.

In the summer of 1812, Napoleon invaded Russia with his Grande Armée of over 600,000 men, the most formidable force then in existence. Leaving behind large detachments of soldiers to protect his supply lines, he pursued the retreating Russian army as far as Borodino, about seventy miles from Moscow. There the Russian commander, Kutuzov, decided to fight what turned out to be the decisive battle of the war. It took place on the 7th of September. Of the 120,000 men committed to battle by Kutuzov 40,000 became casualties, while Napoleon's force of 130,000 was depleted by 30,000. After the engagement the Russian army retreated again and abandoned Moscow to Napoleon. The French emperor spent thirty-five days in the city, large parts of which were ravaged by fire, before shortage of food and concern about the approach of winter caused him to retreat

---

* He was the first to translate Ovid's *Metamorphoses* into Russian.

westwards. In its march home the French army was constantly harassed by regular units of the Russian army, by guerilla bands and also by individual peasants who attacked with everything which could serve as a weapon. With the advent of November the weather became severe and caused sickness to vie with Russian ambushes in destroying the Grande Armée as an effective force.

While the French army was disintegrating, the Russian army was being reinforced with volunteers eager to join in pursuing Napoleon all the way back to France. Among those volunteers was a dashing eighteen-year-old hussar who displayed a contempt for all danger while bearing the standard of his regiment. He fell into the hands of the French, but was liberated when the victorious Russian army entered Paris in March 1814. The hussar was Count Nicholas Tolstoy, father of the great writer.

During the nineteenth century it was the constant aim of imperial Russia to penetrate the Balkans, eliminate Turkish power and influence there and establish new states under tsarist protection. In 1853, in furtherance of this aim, Russian troops were dispatched to the Danubian principalities of Moldavia and Wallachia, then Turkish protectorates, as part of an intended drive towards the Bosphorus. The Russian plan was from the very beginning vigorously opposed by the Western powers, primarily France, Great Britain and Austria. The Russian troops were withdrawn, but not before armed clashes occurred which led to the outbreak of the Crimean War. In September 1854, French, British and Turkish troops landed in the Crimea and, after defeating the Russians at the Alma river, advanced towards the key fortress of Sevastopol.

Count Leo Tolstoy, a subaltern in the Russian army and veteran of the Danubian campaign of the previous year, reacted with profound shock to the allied landing. He immediately petitioned to be sent to Sevastopol where he arrived in November 1854, just as the seige was beginning. At the outset of the seige he was attached to an artillery brigade near the fortifications, but in January 1855 he was transferred, much to his frustration, to a location seven miles from the fortress. In April, however, Tolstoy received the chance he had long awaited to prove that he was ready to sacrifice his life for Russia.

His battery was ordered to take up position in a very exposed bastion less than two hundred yards from the French lines. There under heavy round-the-clock bombardment he commanded his battery for a month and a half. Although casualties in the bastion were very heavy, Tolstoy himself escaped injury. After becoming adjusted to discomfort and fear, he found the constant presence of danger and death so spiritually rewarding that when he was transferred to a new location thirteen miles from Sevastopol he again felt frustrated.* His desire to be in the fortress for the final struggle

---

* There is a popular legend often mentioned in connection with the Crimean War that the tsar, moved by Tolstoy's story, *Sevastopol in December,* arranged his transfer. It is likely that

18

was, however, realized. He was in charge of five guns when, on the 8th of September 1855, he witnessed twelve successive allied assaults. The Russians beat back all of these except the last, mounted by a French force, which succeeded in capturing a strategic redoubt. Thereupon the Russian commander, Prince Gorchakov, a relative of Tolstoy's, realizing that further resistance would be useless, ordered the evacuation of the fortress and the city. Tolstoy wept when he saw the city in flames and French flags on the bastions. He was decorated for his brave behavior* under bombardment and left the army in November 1856. After brief but intense contacts with the Russian literary world and a visit to Western Europe, he settled down in August 1857 at Yasnaya Polyana, the country estate where he was born.

Yasnaya Polyana was a portion of the real estate holdings of Princess Maria Volkonsky. It passed to the Tolstoy family in 1822 when she married Count Nicholas Tolstoy. She died after a happy married life in 1830, and her husband survived her by only seven years. The orphaned Leo Tolstoy, his three brothers and his sister were placed under the guardianship of relatives. In 1847 Leo received Yasnaya Polyana as his share of the family holdings. It was 2,100 acres in extent and had a male working force of 233 serfs.

The estate is located about nine miles south of Tula, and some 125 miles from Moscow, near the ancient road from the capital to Kiev. The house itself is set in undulating terrain densely wooded with silver birches—the Russians' favorite tree. In winter they are hoary, and, standing with their snow-laden branches against blue skies, create a veritable fairy-tale world. It is a world dear to the Russians and Tolstoy continues to inhabit it in their imagination. Indeed, it is safe to assert that the writer would never have entered so much into the hearts of his compatriots had he chosen to live in a treeless and snow-free part of the imperial domains.

Yasnaya Polyana is a very beautiful place name in Russian.** Its first

the legend originated from the work of Tolstoy's well-known German biographer, Raphael Löwenfeld, published in 1896. Löwenfeld names Nicholas I as having given the order,[4] overlooking the fact that the emperor died before the story was completed, let alone published. Tolstoy's most reliable Russian biographer, Nicholas Gusev, proved that it was the emperor, Alexander II, who read the story but only after Tolstoy's transfer from Sevastopol. There is evidence, however, that the tsar ordered the story to be translated into French. Entitled, *Une journée à Sevastopol,* it appeared in *Le Nord* (1855, No. 7), a Brussels publication subsidized by the Russian government.

* During his military service Tolstoy had had some differences with his superiors over certain aspects of army life, particularly the treatment of soldiers. This might be the explanation for a rather modest decoration that Tolstoy received: the order of Ste. Anne, 4th class.

** Tolstoy's son, Ilya, in his book published in Moscow in 1969, begins his reminiscences about his family with the following words: "Yasnaya Polyana! Who gave you this beautiful name? Who first fell in love with this wonderful corner of the world, who first blessed it tenderly with his labor?"[5]

word means "clear"* and its second, "glade", and so the very utterance of it evokes a sunlit clearing in a deep forest. Even to the foreign ear the three successive soft "ya" sounds make the name very sonorous and musical. (One shudders at the thought of Tolstoy's having chosen to reside permanently on his Buzuluk estate in the Province of Samara. "Great man of Buzuluk" would have sounded ridiculous!)

Another aspect of Yasnaya Polyana that the Russians can easily associate themselves with is its sheer size. The estate as a whole is very extensive, the park is enormous, the house is spacious, and the library could serve a sizeable town. In consequence, millions of Russians have become convinced that Tolstoy himself was a giant of a man. This belief is reinforced by the fact that public statues of him are generally larger than life size. In reality, Tolstoy was not a tall man, and most of his contemporaries found him stocky or short.**   He was, however, very strong and agile.*** In his prime he could lift a man with his palms while lying on his back, and he was an indefatigable horseman.****

On settling down in Yasnaya Polyana Tolstoy began a fight against social injustice that was to occupy his entire life. He strove in particular to better the lot of the peasants who in his time formed the overwhelming majority of the Russian people. The historian Nicholas Riasanovsky has supplied the following data concerning that peasant mass:

> Nineteenth-century Russia was a land of peasants. Population statistics for 1796 indicate that then 34,700,000, or 96.4 per cent, of its inhabitants were rural and only 1,300,000, or 3.6 per cent, were urban. A hundred years later, in 1897, the countryside

---

* In a few cases translators have decided that the adjective was derived from the word "yasen'" which is "ash tree" in Russian. Thus the name "Ash Glade" also denotes Tolstoy's birthplace.

** Ilya Repin, Russia's famous painter, referred to Tolstoy in 1880 as a thickset man with a large head. The English journalist, Emile Dillon, who visited Tolstoy in 1890 thought that Tolstoy looked like a stocky peasant. Maxim Gorky described Tolstoy in 1902 as having a small, angular figure.

***The Austrian writer, Stefan Zweig was very impressed by Tolstoy's vitality and he made the following comparison to some other great men of letters:

> Goethe at sixty had begun to grow stout, and, being nervously afraid of chills, was careful in winter time to exclude every breath of fresh air from his study. Old Voltaire, lean and bony, looks more like a plucked fowl than a human being, as he sits at his desk covering ream after ream of paper with his scribbling. Kant in old age, a mechanical mummy, hobbles stiffly and toilsomely along Königsberger Allee. But Tolstoy as an octogenarian breaks the ice for his daily tub, digs vigorously in the garden, prances over the tennis court . . . at eighty-two, when death was already beckoning, he would make his riding whip sing in the air over his mare's ears when, after a twenty-verst gallop, she halted or stumbled.[6]

****A recent Russian source has calculated that Tolstoy spent a total of seven years in the saddle at Yasnaya Polyana.[7]

contained 112,700,000, or 87.4 per cent, of the total population, while the towns sheltered the remaining 16,300,000, or 12.6 per cent. With a minor discount for the gentry and the clergy, this rural sea of people consisted of peasants ... To say that in the nineteenth century Russian peasants were not represented in proportion to their numbers in the government, administration, politics, social life, education or culture of their country would be euphemistic to the point of nonsense.[8]

On the basis of Riasanovsky's estimate that the peasants accounted for well over eighty per cent of Russia's population in 1897 one may conclude that at the time of the Bolshevik revolution, twenty years later, the percentage was not significantly lower, since the growth of industrialization, with the huge demand for new labor which it stimulated, attained its peak before the turn of the century. During the period of revolution and civil war, from 1917 to 1921, the aristocracy, the military, the clergy, and intellectuals of the old regime were either caught up in the armed conflicts and perished or left the country. The industrial working class was small and an unproportionately high number died in the civil war, since the Bolsheviks drew their shock troops and commissars from them. Thus, the proportion of peasants in the population sixty years ago may be safely taken to have been on the order of eighty per cent. The great majority of Russians living today are therefore descended from the oppressed peasants of earlier centuries. Even though a high proportion of them lead urban lives, peasant characteristics such as love of land and open spaces and stoic endurance of calamity are still manifest.

The esteem in which Tolstoy is held by the Russians of today is in some measure attributable to the passionate zeal with which he endeavored to secure a better life for their forbears. It is a point which has not attracted due attention in the West. In Soviet Russia, on the other hand, the compilation of a detailed work on Tolstoy and the peasants would be a politically hazardous undertaking. Some of the demands made in the nineteenth century by Tolstoy for a better and freer life for peasants would sound embarrassingly contemporary in the land of collective and state farms. Any Soviet scholar would be venturesome indeed if he mentioned Tolstoy's indignation at the fact that the tsarist authorities did not issue internal passports to the peasants after their release from serfdom. In consequence they severely limited the peasants' freedom of movement, for persons caught without passports in imperial Russia were liable to be fined, deported or exiled. The internal passport system, which Lenin called "shameful", was abolished after the Revolution but reinstated under Stalin in 1932. Until the end of the 1970s farm workers were not supplied with passports, and so were in the same situation as the peasants before 1917.

A number of measures adopted in the course of Russian history served to transform free peasants gradually into serfs and they remained so for well over two centuries. During the first several hundred years of Russia's existence serfdom was practised only in a few isolated parts of the country, and on such a small scale that it could not have been called a social institution. Peasants generally belonged to a commune (*mir*) which was subject to a protecting noble to whose military requirements it had to contribute. The same peasants nevertheless regarded themselves as the true proprietors of the land they tilled, and they were free to move elsewhere and form communes under the protection of other nobles if they wanted to.

It was in 1597, during the reign of Ivan the Terrible's son, Fedor, and the actual rule of Boris Godunov, that the first law forbidding peasants to move from one estate to another was enacted. The reasons for depriving them of their freedom were too numerous to be listed here. Suffice it to state that Godunov needed the support of the small landowners who supplied almost all the cavalry contingents for his army. These same landowners had been losing peasants to princes who could offer greater privileges and protection. Godunov did not want the princes, who were in opposition to his rule, to become too powerful, so he stopped the movement of the peasants. Russia's social structure was given a violent jolt, since many peasants vented their resentment at losing their freedom by starting bloody uprisings and by running away to Cossack settlements. The peasants never regained their freedom and remained tied to their communes for an increasingly compelling reason: it was the need of the Russian state, which was becoming more and more complex in structure, to secure for itself a permanent and constant basis for taxation. Needless to say, bondage to the land soon developed into bondage to particular landowners, and this regime of what amounted to slavery endured until the middle of the nineteenth century.

The suppression of the peasants became especially severe during the reign of Peter the Great, considered by slavophile historians to have been the real creator of serfdom, the Russian people's "Antichrist." Other social historians have pleaded historical necessity for the harsh measures Peter adopted. The eminent philosopher, Nicholas Berdyaev, considered that without the reforms of Peter the Russian state itself would have been incapable either of self-defence or of development, and that the views the slavophiles put forward could not survive critical examination.[9] The fact remains that it was the Russian peasants who bore the burden of Peter's reforms, of his military expenditures and of the extravagances of their masters. Furthermore, it was Peter who obliged those peasants who were recruited into the army to serve for twenty-five years, under conditions even worse than those prevalent on the estates of the landowners. The peasants never willingly put up with such double slavery, and time and again manifested their discontent in bloody riots. It was only towards the end of the eighteenth century that these disorders ceased to endanger the very existence of the Russian state.

It was during the reign of Catherine the Great that a protest against the inhumanity of serfdom was made in the form of a work of literature.

Written by a nobleman, Alexander Radishchev, and printed privately in 1790, *Journey from St. Petersburg to Moscow* served to actualize the human misery and degradation which were so widespread. It also demonstrated to what extent the functioning of the Russian state depended at the time on the unquestioned acceptance of the institution of serfdom that caused the evil. The reaction to this work was immediate and harsh. Radischev was condemned to be beheaded, but he was reprieved and sent into exile in Siberia. He was allowed to return from there after Catherine's death and committed suicide in 1802, despairing of his efforts on behalf of the serfs. The reprinting of *Journey* by a Russian emigré press in 1858 greatly helped to speed up the process of emancipating the serfs.

Although the institution of serfdom had become a national shame by the nineteenth century, no statesman or influential person was prepared to run the considerable risk of actually advocating its abolition. The need for fundamental change was once again expressed in literary form. Pushkin, Gogol,* Grigorovich, Turgenev and others published works which were understood by their countrymen to be condemnations of serfdom. Acceptance of the need for reform by the highest authorities was at last made evident in March 1856. Tsar Alexander II himself suggested to an assembly of marshals of the nobility in Moscow that it would be far more advantageous, even to the nobility, for serfdom to be abolished from above than to wait for it to be abolished from below. As Russia's richest landowner the tsar was in a better position to understand how matters stood than the average nobleman. He was aware that, although Russia had not been engulfed in the revolutionary disturbances of 1848-49, its peasant masses were so disaffected that serious disorders could be set off at any time. He also knew that his country's defeat in the Crimean War had in large measure been due to the backwardness of a society fettered by serfdom. He perceived that should Russia again become involved in a military conflict with other leading European powers before reform had taken place, she would be certain to suffer another defeat. The oppressed peasants represented an unpredictable, explosive force; of the fifty or so million of them more than half lived and worked on properties owned directly by the Russian state or the imperial court. The remainder—over twenty-two million—were on the estates of about 104,000 landowners.

> Gather the peasants and explain to them . . . that you are the landowner not because you want to dominate and be a landowner, but because you are already a landowner because you were born a landowner, because God will punish you if you were to exchange this social position for any other . . . Tell them that you compel them to labor because God ordered man to earn his bread in labor and sweat.[10]

---

* Although Gogol's *Inspector-General* and *Dead Souls* were understood as satire on the corruption in the Russian society and the denunciation of the institution of serfdom, this writer was also capable of giving the most conservative suggestions to the landowners:

In 1860 Alexander II realized from data compiled for him by his security advisers that peasant disturbances necessitating the use of police or army units were becoming so numerous that radical action could not safely be delayed any longer. He accordingly signed, in February 1861, a manifesto proclaiming the abolition of serfdom. Deliberately written in an elevated and archaic style for liturgical effect,* it was read in every church and published in every newspaper in Russia in the course of the following month. The long-awaited measure was not, however, an emancipation in any real sense. Certainly the peasants were freed from bondage to their masters, but whether or not they succeeded eventually in acquiring individual title to a piece of land they remained members of their *mir* with all their numerous obligations to it. Among other things they had to pay heavy taxes and had to supply recruits for the army. If they ran away they did so without obtaining their travel documents from the community or rural authorities. Since the strict internal passport system was enforced by a huge police apparatus, they were caught in a short time.

Within two years after the emancipation, land charters were to be prepared for the "liberated" peasants according to specific rules.** Once the charters were drawn up, the peasants were to pay money or offer labor toward the eventual purchase of plots of land from landowners. The government was empowered to make long-term loans at low interest towards such purchase. Former household serfs (dvorovye), not being entitled to eventual ownership of land, had either to remain with their masters or to seek employment elsewhere.

Spokesmen for the Russian government extolled the historical significance of the emancipation in extravagant terms, but the peasants themselves were, of course, greatly disappointed. What they had always regarded as their rightful property, albeit usurped by landowners, was not distributed among them as they had hoped, and their economic lot did not improve. Frequent riots and ever-present fear was the price the privileged classes had to pay for the perpetuation of the social injustice under which they were permitted to retain huge estates. Millions of peasants who actually cultivated the land could acquire, if they were lucky, only small plots. During 1861 alone there occurred more than 1,800 peasant riots which had to be put down by military forces.*** Underground terrorist organizations sprung up, dedicated to the belief that only through violence could social justice be achieved. Alexander II, the "Tsar Liberator", was himself assassinated twenty years after the emancipation—ironically, on

---

* The manifesto was composed by the Metropolitan Filaret.

** In more than half of Russia's provinces numerous peasants refused to accept the land charters. They were under the illusion that the "promised hour" (slushnyi chas) would come within two years and would give them liberty with free land. Many peasants lost their lives in clashes with the authorities because of this misconception.

*** In May 1861, Sir Francis Napier, the British envoy in St. Petersburg wrote this in his

the very day that he agreed to sign a decree providing for the creation of a representative national assembly. Later another tsar, Nicholas II, was murdered with his entire family when the Empire collapsed as a result of failing to respond to the elementary needs of millions of its inhabitants.

One of the greatest merits of Tolstoy in the eyes of the Russians is that, having had sufficient time and opportunity to observe the tragic consequences of the unsolved land problem in his country, he became—and remained for the rest of his life—an uncompromising opponent of all acts of injustice to the peasantry. The mature Tolstoy dismissed the officials of the Russian landowners' establishment as parasites, thieves and murderers—a sentiment that was shared by many of his contemporaries—and he did not want to have anything to do with them. The well-known Tolstoy scholar, Nicholas Apostolov,* compared the writer's demeanor towards the Russian autocracy with that of the other great literary figures of his time. He asserts that whereas Pushkin, Gogol, Dostoevsky and Turgenev all begged and received favors from the tsarist authorities, Tolstoy never stooped to such behavior.[12]

At the time he inherited Yasnaya Polyana, Tolstoy had an attitude to serfdom then common among liberal landowners. He saw nothing wrong in owning peasants and living off their labor—after all, he had been born to do just that—as long as he acted responsibly. He therefore sought sincerely to improve the lot of his serfs. His efforts to that end are reflected in a novel started in 1852, in which he portrayed the relationship between an aristocratic landowner and his serfs. Only the first part of the work, entitled *A Landowner's Morning,* was completed; it was published in 1856. In it, the landowner, a nineteen-year-old youth who has abandoned university studies in order to devote himself to the management of his estate, makes tragicomic attempts to become the benefactor of his serfs. He abolishes corporal punishment on his estate, provides schooling for his peasants, and goes from hut to hut telling them how to live better. Confronted by mistrust, greed and stupidity on their part, the young landowner finally abandons his efforts, realizing that he has been wasting his time.

Tolstoy made his first acquaintance with the lot of the peasant class in the idyllic surroundings of Yasnaya Polyana. A completely different aspect

---

dispatch to London:

> ...In various parts of the Empire outbreaks accompanied by acts of personal vengeance have occurred. In districts where people are particularly miserable and oppressed, and on estates previously administered with severity, the Manifesto has been received with incredulity, disappointment, and in a moody spirit.[11]

* Apostolov, who changed his name to Ardens in 1934, was one of the most prolific Tolstoy scholars in the 1920s. In 1928 alone, when the one hundredth anniversary of Tolstoy's birth was celebrated, three books of his[13] were published.

of their plight opened up to him when he served in Sevastopol during its seige. There he saw peasant soldiers performing heroic deeds and dying in thousands in the defense of a country which treated them like subhumans. He marvelled at them, observing in a letter to his brother, Sergei, that "there was less heroism in ancient Greece." But his enthusiasm soon turned to anger when he saw these soldiers being sent into battle with inefficient firearms and hardly any combat training and being beaten by the very officers who stole their provisions. This, and the sight of Russian officers shot by their own soldiers, made a deep impression on Tolstoy.

Before the abolition of serfdom the ordinary soldiers of the imperial army came almost without exception from the peasant class. The length of service was twenty-five years—reduced about the middle of the nineteenth century to fifteen for exemplary conduct. It was a terrible calamity for a man to be made to serve in the army; harsh conditions apart, he was unlikely to see his family again after enlistment. If one considers the fact that landowners and village communities had the right to decide which serfs should serve in the ranks, the hatred of the peasants for the prevailing social order is easy to understand. Life in the army was brutal and dehumanizing. The beatings and floggings which occurred daily were the principal means of training the soldiers and maintaining discipline. Tolstoy witnessed such brutality during his army years and never forgot it. He was seventy-five years old when he wrote the story *After the Ball,* in which a soldier is made to run the gauntlet and is literally beaten to death by his comrades-in-arms.

After the Crimean War the length of service was reduced to seven years—nine for soldiers without good records—and, in 1863, flogging and running the gauntlet were officially abolished. However, army life still remained repugnant to the peasant recruits, since the authorities used the armed forces frequently to quell riots of land-hungry former serfs. Tolstoy maintained to the end of his life that it was criminal to force peasants into the army to oppress other peasants. He was especially outspoken on this matter after the suppression of the 1905 revolution, when army units were rounding up peasants who had joined in disturbances, frequently to be shot or hanged.

Upon leaving the army, Tolstoy resolved to emancipate his serfs. He had originally thought of distributing his land among them, but after making a careful study of his financial situation he realized that he could not afford to do so. During his military service he had lost large sums of money in gambling, and he had debts to settle. He made an extremely generous offer: to free all his peasants of the obligation to work for him, and at the same time to give each of them one acre of land free and ten more acres at a very low cost which would be amortized over the following thirty years.

To Tolstoy's amazement the peasants did not accept the offer. They had apparently heard rumors that the date set for the coronation of Alexander II was also to be that of their own liberation, when the land they tilled would become theirs free of charge. Tolstoy was shocked to realize that his peasants considered him to be a cheat who was seeking to sell land which he would soon be required to surrender to them without any compensation. He had never expected to find so much distrust among his peasants, and interpreted the whole episode as a manifestation of the deep-seated hatred serfs felt for their landowners. Knowing of estates where the peasants were treated far worse than his, Tolstoy began to speculate about the possibility of serious peasant uprisings in Russia. He even expressed the view, in a letter—which he never actually sent—to a high-ranking government official, that if the peasants were not freed within six months there would be a holocaust. Tolstoy had every reason to believe that the peasants would one day take terrible revenge for their long bondage. His own father was rumored to have been murdered by two of his serfs in 1837 and the large sum of money that he had been carrying was never recovered.* Tolstoy's daughter Alexandra makes it clear in her memoirs that thoughts about the possibility of that murder were never absent from the minds of the Tolstoys.[14]

The rebuff that Tolstoy suffered after offering to sell his land did not deter him from his efforts to improve the lot of his peasants. Upon realizing that they were too ignorant to even recognize where their own interests lay, he resolved to provide them with some basic education. He estimated that only one per cent of Russia's population was literate, and he knew that villages whose peasants could read and write were hard to find. Such instruction as was provided by the authorities for the peasantry took place in an atmosphere of strict and stifling discipline considered appropriate to their place in the existing social order.

In the fall of 1859 Tolstoy opened a school in Yasnaya Polyana for peasant children.** Their parents were naturally suspicious of his motives, since it was unheard of for a landowner to educate the children of his serfs. Especially without compensation, for such village priests as were willing to teach a few children always made some charge. However, the parents were reassured by the accounts of Tolstoy's teaching methods that their children brought home. Instruction was carried out in a very relaxed atmosphere, with not even a hint of corporal punishment for breaches of discipline or not knowing lessons. There was no homework and the children could leave

_____

* The father of another great Russian writer, Dostoevsky, was known to have been murdered by his serfs in 1839.

** It should be noted that Tolstoy had a school for a brief period at Yasnaya Polyana as early as 1849. He closed it when he left his estate to join the army. Although Tolstoy often appeared in the class-room, it was really his servant, Foka Demidych, a serf with musical training, who was the teacher. There were twenty peasant boys in the class.

the classroom and go home whenever they wanted to. They were encouraged by Tolstoy to be informal in their approach to him. This they did not find difficult, for the peasant garb he chose to wear made him look much like their fathers. Twelve subjects were taught in the school: reading, writing, calligraphy, grammar, the history of religion, the history of Russia, drawing, design making, singing, mathematics, elementary natural science, and God's law. By March 1860 the number of pupils had reached fifty, and Tolstoy was opening other schools in the villages surrounding Yasnaya Polyana. At the peak of Tolstoy's pedagogical activity, in 1862, there were thirteen schools, staffed for the most part by young men expelled from Russian universities for participating in radical activities.*

Since the teaching in Tolstoy's schools was not based on government-approved textbooks, he soon found himself in conflict with both the secular and the ecclesiastical authorities. Whereas they wanted the officially approved patterns of teaching to be adhered to, Tolstoy considered that peasant children required methods of instruction suited to their special needs, and that it was he as their teacher who should decide what to do. Tolstoy had not managed to conduct his classes to his own complete satisfaction, therefore, he accepted the authorities' contention that he was not qualified to teach, and he proceeded with the plans he had already made to remedy his shortcomings. Having appointed a deputy, he departed for Western Europe in July 1860 to study the latest pedagogical methods. After visiting a number of schools in various countries, discussing methods of instruction with eminent teachers and buying a whole library of books on education, Tolstoy returned to Yasnaya Polyana in April of the following year with a young German teacher of mathematics who had accepted a post in his school.

Tolstoy learned about the abolition of serfdom from newspapers while he was abroad. Upon his return he did his best to explain the manifesto of emancipation to his peasants, as it was a difficult document for simple people to understand. They evinced little interest, since they had already understood that they would not be really free for at least two more years, and that they would have to pay for such land as they might receive. The bitterness of Tolstoy's peasants concerning the manifesto lessened considerably, however, when they realized that the terms on which they were being liberated were the best in the whole province of Tula. They were offered the land which they knew and had been cultivating before the emancipation as well as larger arable lots than elsewhere in the province

---

* Tolstoy issued a monthly journal, *Yasnaya Polyana,* in which he described his teaching activities and elaborated on his educational ideas, many of them regarded by the authorities and fellow landowners as subversive. Between February 1862 and March 1863 twelve numbers of this journal appeared, where, along with Toltoy's contributions, the writings of other teachers and pupils were published.

(ranging between five and ten acres). The other landowners were allocating to their peasants small lots of such poor quality that, after paying their taxes and putting aside money for purchase of the land, those peasants would hardly have been able to avoid living in dire poverty. In Yasnaya Polyana things were different and Tolstoy's peasants became the envy of the liberated serfs on neighboring estates.

Tolstoy's network of schools continued to funtion well, but trouble was in store for him. His persistence in providing the children of his peasants with a free liberal education was regarded with some apprehension by neighboring landowners. Tolstoy's practice of appointing young people with radical inclinations to teaching posts in his schools served to increase that apprehension considerably. But what finally established Tolstoy in the eyes of his neighbors as a black sheep in the flock of landowners was the liberation of his peasants on terms which they regarded as needlessly generous. Not surprisingly, conflict occurred fairly soon.

It had been laid down in the manifesto of liberation that the implementation of its provisions was to be overseen by "arbiters of the peace" chosen from the ranks of the nobility in each district. When Tolstoy was appointed as an arbiter by the governor of Tula province, the other nobles in his district immediately protested. They were afraid he would champion the peasants' rights to the detriment of their interests—and with justification. Tolstoy made himself enormously unpopular among them by exposing their swindles and acts of cruelty against their peasants. He received obscene and insulting letters, and even threats of beating. Besides being extremely annoyed, Tolstoy's neighbors were most puzzled that a fellow landowner, an aristocrat to boot, could initiate legal proceedings against members of his own class on behalf of miserable creatures who had not long before been their slaves. Their reaction to Tolstoy's conduct may be likened to what might have been said and done by plantation owners in a southern state in the U.S.A. just after the Civil War if a neighbor had championed the rights of the newly liberated black slaves to the impairment of the owners' interests.

So many complaints were registered against Tolstoy that, in February 1862, he requested that an investigation be made so that his name might be cleared. It is fitting to observe in this connection that Tolstoy never deliberately sought to annoy other landowners. Indeed, he considered himself to be quite unbiased, since he had, on a number of occasions, curbed the excessive demands made by some peasants and shown their landowners to have acted within their rights. It cannot be doubted that he did perform his duties as an arbiter with dedication, and the investigation he had asked for absolved him of any blame. However, he was becoming weary and dispirited as a result of the endless bickering with other landowners, and when some of his rulings were reversed by higher

29

authority without explanation or justification he began to have serious doubts about the usefulness of his office. The duties it entailed included a great deal of administrative drudgery, which he hated even more than the clashes with other landowners. Furthermore, his health was failing, so in April 1862 he submitted his resignation and soon departed for Samara province, where he sought relief for his weak lungs in the sunny, open steppes roved by the Bashkir nomads.*

It was during Tolstoy's absence that the tsarist authorities made their first move against him on the basis of a file the secret police had assembled. This contained carefully recorded information about the contacts he had established with opponents of tsardom while abroad, about the staffing of his schools for peasant children with radical students, and about his activities as an arbiter of the peace. The conclusion the authorities had drawn from this dossier was that Tolstoy was a potential danger to the existing order. Therefore, when an informer reported from Yasnaya Polyana that Tolstoy had set up an underground printing press on his estate, it was decided to take overt action. A police detachment headed by a colonel of the gendarmerie from St. Petersburg descended on Yasnaya Polyana in July 1862. It conducted a very thorough search which lasted two days. Taking complete possession of Tolstoy's home, the policemen ransacked his study and read his private correspondence and diaries. They tore up stable floors, dragged ponds, insulted Tolstoy's sister and terrified the servants. They left the frightened household empty-handed, but with a warning that they might return.

Tolstoy was in Moscow when he was informed about the search, and he became furious. He dispatched a letter to his first cousin once removed, Alexandra, who was a maid of honor to the Grand Duchess Maria, daughter of the late tsar, Nicholas I. He informed her that the "filthy colonel" in charge of the police search had risked his life while on the estate. "It was lucky for me and for that friend of yours that I was not there; I would have killed him."[15] Tolstoy added that until then he had been completely indifferent to the government in St. Petersburg, but his feelings had changed to anger and revulsion. Tolstoy returned to Yasnaya Polyana in August 1862. After becoming aware of every detail about the police raid, he observed in his letter to the tsar, Alexander II:

> Apart from the insult and the suspicion of having committed a crime, apart from the disgrace in the eyes of society and the feeling of everlasting menace under which I have to live and work, this visit has altogether injured the people's opinion of me, which I value, which I have earned over the years, and which is indispensable to me in my chosen

---

* At that time Tolstoy was very worried about his lungs. He believed that he was ill with tuberculosis. His brothers died from that disease a few years earlier: Dmitry in January 1856, and Nicholas in September 1860. Their deaths, especially Nicholas', left a profound mark on Tolstoy.

30

vocation—the founding of schools for the people.[16]

Tolstoy knew that the other landowners in his district were rejoicing over the raid. "They gave moans of rapture", as he put it. His main concern, however, was not what his neighbors thought but the possibility that the peasants, not knowing exactly what had taken place, might think that he had been engaged in criminal activities. He complained to his cousin that his reputation among the peasants as an honest man, which he had built up over many years, was ruined. It remains a matter for speculation whether the peasants would in fact have forbidden their children to attend the schools of a man who had narrowly escaped the handcuffs. Tolstoy made no attempt to find out; after marrying in September he began to dismantle his schools. By the end of 1862 the last class had been dissolved and all the teachers had departed.

Still upset about the police raid, Tolstoy believed at that time he had given up teaching for ever.* However, ten years later, in January 1872, he opened a school for about thirty-five peasant children. It lasted for only three months, with Tolstoy, his wife, his son Sergei and his daughter Tatyana conducting the classes. The textbook they used was Tolstoy's own *Azbuka* (ABC), which he published in the same year. It actually comprised a set of four books for primary education. Only the first of them was, strictly speaking, an ABC, the others being a book of arithmetic and two readers. Tolstoy did an immense amount of work in the preparation of these volumes, contributing 629 written items, 133 of them on scientific subjects. Nevertheless, the project was a failure. Published in 1,600 copies, the four volumes were too bulky and expensive and were received unfavorably by the critics. Furthermore, and contrary to Tolstoy's expectations, the state educational authorities declined to accept them for use in schools. When, later, Tolstoy reedited the first part of *Azbuka* and published it under the title *Novaya azbuka* (New ABC) in 50,000 copies at a modest price, it was an instant success. Officially recommended for schools, it was reissued twenty-eight times in a total of over two million copies during Tolstoy's lifetime. Stories from *Novaya azbuka* continue to

---

* In a letter to his cousin, Countess Alexandra Tolstoy, in October 1863 Tolstoy called his school "his last mistress" and was wondering about his great attachment to the peasants:

> I must confess that my views on life, on the people and on society are now quite different from what they were when we last met. One can be sorry for them but it is difficult for me to understand how could I have loved them so much. Nevertheless, I am glad that I had the school; this last mistress of mine was a great formative influence on me.[17]

The fact that Tolstoy returned to his "last mistress" three more times, and his subsequent activities on behalf of "the people" indicate that his love for them did not diminish at all.

be published today in the U.S.S.R., not only in Russian but in other languages as well.

Tolstoy taught children of the peasantry on two subsequent occasions. In 1890, when his daughters Tatyana and Marya opened a school for the children in Yasnaya Polyana, he assisted with the teaching. The school was closed by the authorities after only a few months for operating without their permission. The other period was from the end of 1906 to June 1907 when Tolstoy taught about fifteen children in Yasnaya Polyana, this time limiting the curriculum to religious and moral instruction.

Tolstoy and the Twilight of Tsardom

The first years of Tolstoy's marriage were also those of his greatest happiness. He adored his wife, found great satisfaction in running his estate and resumed the literary activities he had ceased some three years previously. He was at the height of his creative powers in the writing of his masterpiece, *War and Peace*. Understandably, he was extremely reluctant while so engaged to become involved in any matter arising outside the confines of Yasnaya Polyana. Yet in 1866 he put everything aside in a strenuous effort to save the life of an army sergeant of peasant origin, Vasily Shibunin, who while under the influence of alcohol had struck his commanding officer who had been tormenting him. According to the strict disciplinary code of the imperial army the death penalty could be imposed for such an act. Since Shibunin was stationed near Yasnaya Polyana, Tolstoy undertook his defence and made a passionate plea for clemency at the court-martial.* Unmoved by Tolstoy's entreaties, the court pronounced the death sentence. The writer at once addressed to the tsar a letter of appeal in which, in his haste, he failed to mention the number of Shibunin's regiment. The omission was used by the government officials concerned as a pretext for not placing the appeal before the tsar. By coincidence it so happened that, unbeknownst to Tolstoy, a soldier in St. Petersburg had, at almost the same time, also been sentenced to die for the very same offence that Shibunin had committed. The appeal on Shibunin's behalf was therefore doomed even before it was made. Needless to say, by the time Tolstoy had supplied the missing detail it was already too late.

Shibunin was executed publicly in front of the assembled peasants of several villages, perhaps as an example to the young men among them who were soon to become soldiers. The peasants were shocked at the imposition of sentence of death for a single blow, when members of their own families who were serving in the army were systematically beaten by their officers. They felt deep gratitude towards the master of Yasnaya Polyana, the only person who had tried to prevent the atrocity. The whole episode made an indelible impression on Tolstoy,** and till the end of his days he remained indignant about it and harbored feelings of guilt for his oversight when

---

* Tolstoy's speech in Shibunin's defence is reprinted in the jubilee edition of his work. His main point was that Shibunin was mentally too unbalanced to be responsible for his action.[1] It could also be mentioned here that many Russian and foreign sources spell the soldier's name as Shabunin.

**In 1908, two years before he died, Tolstoy mentioned Shibunin in a letter to his biographer, Paul Biryukov, and remarked that the soldier's execution made him realize for the first time that a state organization was inconceivable without murder.[2]

appealing to the tsar.

On returning to the writing of *War and Peace,* the chronicle of several Russian aristocratic families, Tolstoy did not forget the peasants. In fact, one of the most memorable characters in the novel is the peasant Platon Karataev. Manifestly symbolic of the spiritual strength of the Russians, he was a soldier in Kutuzov's army. He became ill with fever and fell into the hands of the French in Moscow. Karataev managed to remain calm and cheerful and took delight in relating stories about his past life in the country to his fellow prisoners, among whom he was very popular. Without becoming closely attached to any person in particular, he displayed affection to all those with whom he came in contact, his captors included. When he became so ill that he could no longer march with the rest of the Russian prisoners the retreating French shot him. He faced death serenely: "His face, instead of the look of joyful emotion it had worn yesterday while telling the tale of the merchant who suffered innocently, now bore an expression of quiet solemnity."[3]

In *War and Peace* Karataev exercised great influence on Pierre Bezukhov, one of the principal characters of the novel. Pierre underwent a profound spiritual transformation while listening to Karataev's stories and philosophy of life. He became convinced that ordinary peasants could have greater dignity and wisdom than many members of the upper classes. When he recalled the days of his captivity in the hands of the French he could remember only Karataev "who always remained in his soul a most vivid and precious memory and the personification of everything Russian, kind and round."[4] Literary scholars have noted that in *War and Peace,* and to some degree in other works of his, Tolstoy associated roundness with being Russian, while often attributing the quality of angularity to foreigners. Platon Karataev must therefore be the most Russian character that Tolstoy ever created—he is so round that he nearly rolls away.* "Platon's whole figure—in a French overcoat girdled with a cord, a soldier's cap, and bast shoes—was round. His head was completely round, and his back, chest, shoulders, and even his arms, which he held as if always ready to embrace something, were rounded. His peasant smile and his large gentle brown eyes were also round."[5]

---

* There are theories which suggest that Karataev's roundness might be a key to something more profound than his nationality. Professor George Krugovoy of Swarthmore College has observed that from time immemorial in various cultures, roundness, as the most perfect geometrical figure, has been used to portray divinity. Thus Karataev becomes spiritually universal, says Krugovoy, and in his description, like in that of Prince Myshkin in *Idiot,* resemblance with Christ becomes apparent.[6] Professor Boris Sorokin in his book *Tolstoy in Prerevolutionary Russian Criticism* refers to sources according to which Karataev's roundness suggests "the function of a perfectly round opening through which the message of life flowed undistorted and unimpeded."[7]

In spite of Tolstoy's emotions and sympathy in the portrayal of Karataev, this peasant figure was looked upon with disfavor by Russian literary critics for many years after the Revolution. He was regarded as an abstraction,* a submissive person who had very little in common with real Russian peasants. Although as early as 1937 Karataev had been represented favorably in an article in *Pravda* as "a simple, peace-loving peasant and Russian soldier who could at the same time be a formidable foe to any invader,"[8] the authoritative *Literaturnaya entsiklopediya* (Literary Encyclopedia) was in 1939 still describing him as a "false character." It observed that Tolstoy took for granted the "ignorance and submissiveness of the serfs as a result of centuries of slavery."[9] The Tolstoy scholar, Sergei Bychkov, remarked in 1949 that the weak points of Tolstoy's ideological standpoint were particularly manifest in his portrayal of Karataev whom, he added, American critics regarded as the embodiment of Russian national character.[10] Sofya Leusheva, a Soviet critic devoted to the study of *War and Peace,* emphasized in 1957 that Karataev was not a typical Russian peasant but rather an artistic personification of aspects of Tolstoy's developing philosophy of not resisting evil with evil.[11] This could have been the last critical remark concerning Karataev for he is today generally viewed as a "positive" character by Soviet literary experts. They do not dwell on his passivity or meekness any more, but instead stress his patriotism and his firm conviction that Russia was invincible.

When Tolstoy was writing *War and Peace* he could not foresee that like his character Pierre Bezukhov, he himself would be in great need of peasant wisdom. Tolstoy, unlike Pierre, was not captured by the enemy; he was in the grip of a deep spiritual crisis which began to manifest itself toward the end of the 1870s. Here was a famous writer, a wealthy landowner and the head of a devoted family, enjoying excellent health, who suddenly resolved to make radical changes in his way of life. He entertained the idea of becoming a monk or giving away all his possessions to the poor, became gloomy and dissatisfied with himself, and even contemplated suicide on a number of occasions.

It has long been the belief of many persons familiar with the life and writings of Tolstoy that he began to be obsessed by the subject of death at about the age of fifty. (This belief was shared by some members of his own family.) In support of it, it has been pointed out that Tolstoy lost both of his parents in his formative years, and a number of relatives to whom he was greatly attached. He lost his brothers later on, and three of his children died

---

* The Russian literary historian, Prince Mirsky, in his writings first published in 1926, found it difficult to be enthusiastic about Karataev. He declared: "In spite of his quintessential importance for the idea of the novel, he jars. He is not a human being among human beings, as are the other two ideally natural characters, Natasha and Kutuzov. He is an abstraction, a myth, a being with different dimensions and laws from those of the rest of the novel. He does not fit in."[12]

in the 1870s, two—Nicholas and Varvara—in the same year, 1875. Frequent visitations of the "grim reaper," it is said, reminded Tolstoy that he himself could not look forward to anything but old age, sickness and agonizing death.

Some scholars, in going back to the diaries which Tolstoy kept when he was in his twenties, have discovered passages which, they claim, indicate that he was even then thinking of giving up mundane things and founding "a new religion, a religion of Christ but divested of dogma and mysteries." The changes observed in Tolstoy's behavior in middle life have, therefore, been explained simply as manifestations of thoughts and attitudes which he had harbored throughout his adult life. In this regard three stages may be discerned in the development of Tolstoy's attitude to religion during his spiritual crisis. During the first, the writer evinced an increased interest in the rituals of the Orthodox Church, to which he belonged. During the second, he was becoming critical of, and bewildered by, some of the articles of dogma of that church. At the third stage, after declaring many parts of those articles incompatible with his own conscience and reason, he embarked upon a revision of his religious beliefs on the basis of extensive studies of the Gospels.

Whatever the original cause of Tolstoy's spiritual unrest might have been, one thing was obvious: he was endeavoring to discover the true meaning of life. In his perception, no one in his social circle knew what that meaning was. Only the peasants seemed to know. Tolstoy observed that they regarded themselves as participants in nature's eternal cycle, and therefore looked at the world with much more tranquility than did members of the propertied classes. He began to have long conversations with peasants on spiritual matters, and was amazed at their wisdom and their ability to supply answers to the agonizing questions he posed. Once he had arrived at the conclusion that the peasants possessed spiritual strength of the highest order, his old passion to fight for a better life for them was rekindled and burned fiercely. Now, however, Tolstoy needed the peasants more than they needed him. In his extreme alienation from his family, religion and class, the only real contact he had with the world was through the peasants.

In his search for a satisfying ethical and religious system Tolstoy was given considerable assistance by an emancipated serf named Vasily Syutaev. This peasant had once run a stone-cutting business, but had given it up after realizing that hard work on the land accorded more with his religious views. When he was persecuted by the authorities of the church for refusing to baptize his child, he assembled a congregation of his own devoted to a doctrine of brotherhood, love, and life. Syutaev was particularly opposed to war and refused to pay taxes for fear that the money might be used to finance killing. His own son was imprisoned for refusing military service, and his daughter was married without a priest

36

being present. Unlike Tolstoy, therefore, he was fortunate in having a family who shared his convictions. In 1881 Tolstoy visited Syutaev and was greatly impressed by him. In the following year Syutaev came to Moscow where Tolstoy received him warmly and introduced him to many of his friends. It was Syutaev who implanted in Tolstoy's mind the idea of distributing the poor among the rich so that the underprivileged might start new and productive lives. Although delighted with the possibilities of the idea, the writer never took any definite steps to implement it.

The tendency which exists to regard Tolstoy's predilection for Syutaev and other peasants as purely emotional in origin cannot be reconciled with the facts. Tolstoy was an exceptionally intelligent person who examined everything through a prism of critical analysis. He became drawn closer and closer to the peasants after perceiving that they had great strength of character and were a repository of considerable wisdom. There is every reason to believe that, had he discerned a nobility of spirit in the Russian aristocracy, he would not have hesitated to extoll their virtues and associate himself with them. Tolstoy concluded, however, that they were spiritually dead and far less worthy than the peasants they exploited and abused. Thereafter he campaigned unceasingly for an improvement in the lot of Russia's largest social class.

Tolstoy made a clean break with his past, abandoning all pessimism and thoughts of suicide, and admitting that he had up to then been leading a spiritually dead existence. In his *Confession,* written between 1879 and 1882, he examined critically the development of his religious beliefs. He described how he had gradually lost faith in the Orthodox Church and its dogmas, and had come to realize that in adhering to them he had not been following Christ at all. He also related how, after coming previously to the conclusion that life had no meaning, he had rediscovered one during his communion with the peasants:

> I turned to the simple Russian people and to their meaning of life. This meaning, if one can put it into words, was the following: each man appears in this world by God's will. God created men in such a way that they can damn their souls or save them. The main task of a person in life is to save his soul, to live according to God's will. In order to live according to God's will one has to deny all pleasures in life. One has to work, humble oneself, suffer and be kind.[13]

With a purified faith and a personal identification with the "simple Russian people", Tolstoy became an antagonist of the tsarist regime. *Confession* contained several attacks on the ruling classes and the Orthodox Church; therefore, it was banned in Russia. It was eventually published in 1884 in Geneva, whence copies were smuggled back to Russia. It was not until 1906 that the full Russian text was published in the writer's homeland. With the appearance of *Confession* the tsarist authorities became confirmed in their opinion that Tolstoy was a threat to the established order. They therefore considered that they had been fully justified when, in 1882, they had ordered a secret surveillance of the writer's every move, an order which remained in effect until the end of his life. Instructions were also given for stricter rules of censorship to be applied to Tolstoy's writings, and most of his non-literary works were banned for a time in Russia.*

Tolstoy was not very perturbed about the banning of many of his works. What did appall him was the total absence of low-cost, wholesome literature for members of the poorer classes. Although there were at the time quite a few distinguished writers of Russian literature, their books simply did not reach the ordinary people. The widespread illiteracy and, above all, poverty which existed prevented the masses from becoming acquainted with literature. Furthermore, even literate peasants, having as they did a very limited vocabulary, would have found it difficult to read existing works of any literary quality. Most of the literature that reached the Russian peasants at the time, apart from booklets on the lives of the saints distributed by the church, was written by semi-literate authors in a vulgar style.

With great determination Tolstoy set out to remedy the situation. With the collaboration of Vladimir Chertkov he established, in 1884, the publishing house *Posrednik* (Intermediary) for the sole purpose of making available to the masses cheap editions of booklets by reputable Russian and foreign authors. The venture was a great success. According to Paul Biryukov, another associate of Tolstoy's who participated in the editorial work of *Posrednik,* its booklets were seldom printed in less than 24,000 copies each, and over the first four years of the organization's existence about three million copies of them were sold annually. Since authors did not copyright their writings for *Posrednik,* other publishing houses were able to bring out reprints of the booklets and sell them in immense numbers.[14] The activities of *Posrednik* amounted to a veritable cultural revolution in Russia. For the first time in the nation's history literature for

* Unfortunately, at that time the quality of Tolstoy's writings abroad was greatly reduced by poor translations. Tolstoy's English friend and translator, Aylmer Maude, commented that

> For non-Russian readers the heaviest blow to Tolstoy's reputation as a clear and sane thinker, was struck, not by Censor, or by editor, but by translators who, if perhaps capable of dealing with his stories, were incompetent to render his philosophy. Versions of his most serious work appeared, containing much absolute nonsense. A comparison with the original shows that the usual Russian double negative was sometimes mistaken for the affirmative, and that the translations contained other almost incredible blunders. They appeared at a time when readers, surprised that a novelist should attempt philosophical work, were wondering whether they ought to take Tolstoy seriously in his new role; and they caused many people to conclude that, as a philosopher, Tolstoy must not be taken seriously. Such a prejudice, once created, is not easily broken down, and his subsequent works have not received the serious study they deserve.[15]

the masses was being printed in great quantity by responsible, honest people whose basic purpose it was to widen the mental and spiritual horizons of their compatriots.

In spite of the worthiness of its mission, *Posrednik* was being subjected to much harassment by the end of the 1880s. Publication of quite innocuous items was being either forbidden or else held up on the grounds that they contained "allusions" to revolutionary ideas. Tolstoy's wife made a complaint to Tsar Alexander III about the harassment in the course of a private audience in 1891. She was indignant about the pettiness of the censors for, as she informed the tsar, her husband and Chertkov were rendering a great service to the ordinary people of Russia by weaning them away from stupid and immoral books. The tsar made no comment. Regardless of the difficulties caused by the censors, *Posrednik* continued to be a success. After the transfer of its editorial offices from Chertkov's country estate to Moscow in 1893, books intended for the educated classes began to be published in addition to those for the general masses. *Posrednik* was so popular and well-managed that it outlasted not only its founder but the tsarist regime as well. Its merits were recognized by the revolutionary leaders of 1917, and it was one of the few private publishing houses allowed to function during the early years of Soviet rule.

In addition to combating cultural deprivation, Tolstoy strove to alleviate physical poverty. While in Moscow during the winter of 1881-82, he was dismayed at the very large numbers of destitute people, many of them physically or mentally handicapped, who were living in crowded, unsanitary dwellings in the poor districts of the city. When the decennial census was taken in January 1882, Tolstoy became an enumerator in a Moscow slum and urged his colleagues to register all those poor who were in need of immediate help. His ultimate aim was the elimination of chronic poverty in the city, and he approached a number of wealthy people with the object of obtaining the necessary financial resources for its achievement. However, Tolstoy soon realized that the conditions prevailing could not be remedied by charity alone. Most of the poor accepted their fate, albeit grudgingly, and had neither the strength nor the willpower to alter it. Tolstoy shelved his philanthropic plans and started working on a pamphlet which he entitled *What Then Must We Do?*

This pamphlet, which appeared in 1886, was probably Tolstoy's most eloquent protest against the social injustice prevailing in Russia. Whereas *Confession* was directed in the main against the established church, the new work constituted an attack on the organs of the state. In it, Tolstoy characterized the social order in Russia as one where the state bureaucracy and the ruling classes were supported by the labor of virtual slaves, and protected by a huge police force and an army into which large numbers of the slaves were pressed. The writer believed that property was the root of all evil, serving in particular to perpetuate the slavery against which he was inveighing. He was wholeheartedly on the side of the poor and against the rich who, he pointed out, impoverished themselves morally by tolerating all the poverty around them. As to the question which he had chosen as the title of his pamphlet, Tolstoy asserted that nobody should exploit the labor of others. A person, he considered, should look after his own needs and live in the main like a peasant—tilling the land, building his own house and making the articles he required. Such advice, as has of course been pointed out over the ages, is impractical and naive. Nevertheless, Tolstoy's diagnosis of the sickness of the society he lived in was realistic and accurate. He warned his countrymen that the hatred of the people living in poverty grew with every passing day, and that, unless remedial measures were taken very soon, Russia would become engulfed in a revolution with all its destruction and bloodshed. He admonished that:

> However much we may try to hide from ourselves the plain and most obvious danger of exhausting the patience of those men whom we oppress; however much we may try to counteract this danger by all sorts of deceit, violence and flattery, it is still growing with each day, with each hour . . . The workman's revolution, with the terrors of destruction and murder, not only threatens us, but we have been already living upon its verge during the last thirty years, and it is only by various cunning devices that we have been postponing the crisis.[16]

After the publication of *What Then Must We Do?* Tolstoy made radical changes in the management of his property. He was unwilling to preach to others the evils of owning property while he himself remained a landowner with several hundred peasants serving him on his estates. In 1884 he gave his wife power of attorney over his property and withdrew from the management of it.* He continued to live in Yasnaya Polyana but after a rather unpleasant incident he began to contemplate the idea of leaving home. In the fall of 1890 several peasants of Yasnaya Polyana were taken into custody after being caught felling trees in its park. Tolstoy wanted them to be set free since, in his opinion, the park belonged to the peasants anyway. His wife, however, insisted on the culprits being punished. They were imprisoned for a month and a half and fined heavily— twenty-seven rubles each. (The Countess' cook earned six rubles a month.) Tolstoy was overcome with shame on hearing about the punishment. A bitter family scene ensued,** after which the writer recorded in his diary his

---

* Tolstoy's estates, since he had lost interest in them, were poorly run and he did not see much money coming from them. The family's main income came from the sale of Tolstoy's literary work and enabled the Tolstoys to live in style both in Moscow and Yasnaya Polyana on about 15,000 rubles a year at that time.

** The Countess blamed Tolstoy for the incident. According to an entry in her diary (15 Dec., 1890) her husband advised the police to scare the peasants, then let them go. However, once they were brought to trial there was no way to release them and they were punished. The Countess' version of the incident was regarded with scepticism even by members of the

intention to leave his wife. A few months after the peasants were punished he formally renounced all title to his estates, and they were divided among his children and his wife. By July 1892 the distribution had been completed—Yasnaya Polyana itself passed to Tolstoy's wife and their youngest child, Ivan.

To illustrate the magnitude of Tolstoy's renunciation it should be mentioned that eight years after the transaction the children of Tolstoy, to whom his Samara estate had passed, sold it for 450,000 rubles (the writer had paid 20,000 for it in 1871). The prerevolutionary ruble being worth more than five present-day American dollars, the sum Tolstoy's children received for that one estate may therefore be estimated at well over two million dollars.* The Yasnaya Polyana estate without the main building had a price tag in 1911 of one and a half million American dollars.** The value of only two estates of Tolstoy's many holdings can give some idea of the considerable wealth that Tolstoy threw away. Tolstoy's act was unprecedented in Russia, yet it went almost unnoticed since very few outsiders knew the real value of the writer's property. It is doubtful that Tolstoy himself knew it or cared to know.

Now that Tolstoy was totally dissociated from the landowner class and freed from the burden of owning property, he was able to travel and

Tolstoy family who knew that Tolstoy was the last person to suggest that the police "scare the peasants." Besides, in the other two incidents recorded, Tolstoy was firmly on the side of the peasants while his wife insisted on their punishment:

1. In July 1906 several peasants were caught felling oaks on the estate. Tolstoy wanted to forgive them but the Countess sent them to trial and they were sentenced to jail.[17]

2. In September 1907 some peasants were again arrested on the Countess' complaint for stealing oaks. Tolstoy wrote a letter to the Governor of Tula Province asking for their release but they were sentenced to two months imprisonment.[18]

* There was great excitement and rejoicing in Tolstoy's family over the successful business transaction. Tolstoy himself did not share the joy, and remarked to his confidant, the musician Goldenveizer: "I have it always on my conscience that I, with my wish to renounce property, once bought estates. It is funny to think that it seems now as if I had wished to make provision for my children, and in doing so I did them the greatest injury. Look at my Andryushka: he is completely incapable of doing anything, and lives on the people whom I once robbed, and whom my children keep on robbing. How terrible it is to listen to all this talk now, to watch it all going on! It is so opposed to my ideas and desires and to everything I live by."[19]

** After the death of little Ivan in 1895 the Countess and her sons became owners of Yasnaya Polyana. When Tolstoy died the family wanted to turn the house into a national shrine and sell the rest of Yasnaya Polyana to the Americans for one and a half million dollars. A member of the family travelled to New York in January 1911 to conduct sales negotiations with rich businessmen. On learning about the possibility of seeing Tolstoy's birthplace in foreign hands, the Russian public became so indignant that Tolstoy's sons had to issue the following statement in April, 1911: "We in fact conducted negotiations with American billionaires/milliarderami/ but only concerning the sale of land and not the house itself. Our common desire is to see the complete estate sold as national property."[20]

41

help the peasants wherever he was needed most. In 1891 the drought that affected thirty-six Russian provinces was followed by widespread famine. The populations of whole villages in European Russia were starving during the winter of 1891-92, and they pleaded desperately for help. Accompanied by his daughters, Tatyana and Marya, Tolstoy visited the stricken areas late in 1891. On finding the peasants cold and hungry he organized bakeries and with the help of Ivan Raevsky, a landowner friend of his, established a network of kitchens. Since Tolstoy's means were inadequate for what he hoped to achieve, his wife came to his assistance. In a letter which was published in November 1891 in almost every newspaper in Russia she described the horror of the famine and the efforts of her family in trying to prevent large-scale starvation. She made an appeal for help, and her countrymen responded very generously to it.

Tolstoy prepared an appeal of his own for aid to the afflicted peasants, but it was so emasculated by the censors as to be no longer suitable for publication. The tsarist authorities disapproved of Tolstoy's work among the peasants, and resented especially his writing about the famine. Indeed, in the official view no famine really existed, there were simply "crop failures in some localities", as Alexander III declared. Tolstoy sent an uncensored proof of his article to London, where it was published in January 1892 in the *Daily Telegraph* under the title, *Why do the Russian peasants starve?*. In it he blamed Russia's privileged classes for the starvation, asserting that in order to maintain their luxurious way of life they habitually exacted so much from their peasants that they were seldom free from the pangs of hunger. It was high time, Tolstoy informed the world through the article, for the peasants to receive back a modicum of what the landowners had stolen from them.

The article caused great indignation among Russia's governing classes. Tolstoy had not only described in a foreign newspaper with a world-wide circulation a famine whose very existence was being denied by Russian diplomats abroad on instructions from their government, but had even gone on to accuse the country's upper classes of being responsible for it. People in high positions soon caused rumors to circulate to the effect that Tolstoy was mad. Incensed "patriots" organized petitions to have him sent to Siberia or locked up in a monastery.* The voices demanding Tolstoy's incarceration became so strong that they caused his family great anxiety. Fearing that the authorities might act at any moment, Tolstoy's cousin, Alexandra, who was well-known at the imperial court, pleaded for her relative during a private audience with the tsar. To her relief Alexander III assured her that Tolstoy was not in any danger, for the government had

* Tolstoy's contemporary and the author of numerous studies on him, Alexander Prugavin, stated that the idea of imprisoning Tolstoy in a monastery was recommended twice to Alexander III. The dates were allegedly 1886 and 1892 and the recommendations were supposedly made by Konstantin Pobedonostsev, Procurator of the Holy Synod.[21]

no desire to make a martyr of him.

If the article which had been published in London upset Russia's ruling classes, it was very beneficial to the country's peasants. Aid for them poured in from many countries. From the United States, for example, came several shiploads of grain. As a result, Tolstoy was able to increase the number of his kitchens to about two hundred and fifty and feed thirteen thousand people daily. In addition, three thousand children were fed every day in over a hundred kitchens set up specially for them. Tolstoy continued to work among the hungry until May 1893, and it may be stated without exaggeration that without his help there would have been serious social disturbances in the areas affected by famine.*

Famine again occurred in Russia during the period 1897-99. In the three provinces most affected by the calamity (Samara, Kazan, and Simbirsk) a hundred thousand people became ill with scurvy. The seventy-year-old Tolstoy felt it was his duty to join in the relief work. He went to villages in the famine areas, where he saw to the setting up of kitchens and distributed money and provisions to the hungry peasants.

What Tolstoy witnessed during these various missions of mercy served to make it even clearer to him that the emancipation of 1861 had not brought about any fundamental change in the relationship between landowners and peasants. Huge masses of the peasantry continued to spend their lives in hard labor and poverty. It was their labor that supported their landowners' comfortable life-style and kept Russia's state institutions functioning, yet those very toilers were physically abused for the slightest misdemeanor. Tolstoy was incensed during his travels in various provinces upon seeing the peasants beaten everywhere. Although corporal punishment was at that time considered to be an integral part of Russian social life, Tolstoy considered it a barbaric and shameful custom which was long overdue for elimination.

Corporal punishment was indeed an ancient Russian practice. Beatings and maimings were administered a thousand years ago by both secular and ecclesiastical authorities for breaches of the law or acts considered heretical—but only to members of the lower classes. With the arrival of the Tartars in the thirteenth century physical cruelty became more widespread and no one was safe from it. After they regained their independence the Russian rulers themselves asserted the right to discipline

---

* Tolstoy's activities during the famine of 1892 attracted the attention of the whole world but it was not the first time that he devoted time and energy to succoring hungry peasants. While at his estate in the Province of Samara during the summers of 1873 and 1874 Tolstoy had aided with grain and money those suffering from the famine then rampant in that part of Russia. No relief had been sent there by the authorities, and Russia as a whole did not learn about the serious situation prevailing until a letter from Tolstoy was published in a Moscow newspaper. Following Tolstoy's letter, donations of over two million rubles—an enormous sum at that time—had been sent to help those afflicted.

any of their subjects however cruelly* they chose, regardless of title or position.

During the reign of Ivan the Terrible physical punishment and savage torture became rampant in Russia. Knouting, impaling, hanging, flaying alive, cutting perceived foes to pieces and throwing them to hungry bears were commonplace practices under this sadistic and demented ruler, many of whose victims were hereditary nobles. Ivan often participated in such acts of torture after which, according to the historian Nicholas Karamzin, he was "in a much more elevated spirit". This tsar also killed his own son in a fit of anger.

Physical cruelty in Russia abated somewhat after Ivan the Terrible's death, only to become widespread again during the reign of Peter the Great. This tsar may not have been a sadist like Ivan, but his "erratic behavior" cost many lives. Not only did he strike blows with his ever-present club at the slightest provocation, but he personally beat several persons to death. He participated in the mass execution of captured members of rebellious armed units, and he was one of the interrogators in his Secret Chancellery when his son, Alexei, died there. He considered the knout too Asiatic, so as an alternative to it he introduced the practice of "running the gauntlet", which the Russian senate in 1712, bowing to his demands, ordered to be used as the standard punishment for peasants who were unwilling to join the imperial army. A man was tied half-naked to muskets, with the bayonets thereof touching his chest, and was dragged between rows of soldiers each of whom struck a hard blow on his back with a rod about two yards long and nearly an inch in diameter. It took less than a thousand strokes to cause death, but cases are on record of as many as six thousand being ordered. This punishment was reserved for the lower ranks; commissioned officers of the imperial army were demoted or fined when found guilty of wrongdoing.

By the eighteenth century many Russians considered that the knout and other forms of corporal punishment were a national disgrace. During the reign of Catherine the Great they were finally abolished—for the nobility. The beating or maiming of rich merchants, honorary citizens and members of the clergy was proscribed under subsequent laws. The peasants, however, continued to be knouted as before, and they were

---

* The most often used, and the most dreaded, instrument of punishment for several centuries was the knout. It consisted of a strip of leather about a yard long, to one end of which was attached a wooden handle and to the other a "tail"—a wide piece of leather about fourteen inches long—which actually hit the victim. The tail was usually changed after the tenth blow when blood had made it too soft to inflict severe pain. One blow with the instrument was sufficient to crush the skin and the muscles in a person's back and to expose his bones. The average number of strokes was twenty for men and ten for women, but cases are on record of three hundred being administered. Many victims died under the knout from heart seizures, and also from spinal breakages which executioners were sometimes instructed to cause.

executed when they rioted, even though capital punishment had been officially abolished in 1753. By the beginning of the nineteenth century, however, the knout was slowly being replaced by the lash, considered to be less crippling and barbaric, as punishment for peasants found guilty of nonviolent misdemeanors.

Alexander I allowed the knout to be used only in extreme cases, and limited the number of strokes permitted to forty. Women could be punished by the knout only a year and a half after child-birth. Unlimited use of the knout was permitted in the case of peasant and army riots until it was finally outlawed in 1845. Running the gauntlet remained—the punishment most favored by Nicholas I.

In 1863 severe corporal punishment was abolished in Russia, but beating by birch rods went on unabated. Although the maximum number of strokes was set at twenty, local authorities could in practice order any number they saw fit. Since other classes were protected by law against being beaten, it was mostly the peasants who were subjected to this painful and humiliating form of punishment. A whole set of unwritten rules became established concerning the beating of these unfortunates by birch rods. Heads of family were to be beaten less than younger men, and grandfathers less than fathers. Peasants with some formal education were to receive fewer blows for the same offense than complete illiterates. Use of birch rods endured into the twentieth century, and finally ceased upon the collapse of the tsarist regime.*

In Tolstoy's time it was the government which subjected the peasants to the greatest amount of corporal punishment. Because of unresolved land problems and recurrent food shortages the peasants often resorted to riots, which were severely dealt with by army and police units. The violence practiced by the Russian government against the peasants is described in Tolstoy's book, *The Kingdom of God Is Within You*. In this major work, written mainly during the famine and completed in 1893, Tolstoy set out his doctrine of nonresistance to evil. He believed that all governments were evil since they waged wars, imprisoned dissidents and forced people to pay taxes and to carry out criminal acts. Imbued with a spirit of Christian anarchism, Tolstoy rejected revolutions as a cure for social injustice since

---

* Although institutionalized beating was prevalent among the peasants, it affected all other parts of the Russian society. Inflicting physical pain was a commonplace in streets, schools and in most families—in fact, everywhere. Maxim Gorky who probably, apart from Tolstoy, exposed the widespread beating in Russia most vividly, wrote this in January 1918 a few months after the Revolution: "Nowhere is man beaten so often, with such zeal and joy, as in our Russia. "To smack in the teeth", "to punch up the throat", "in the bread basket", "in the kidneys", "to give a drubbing", "to cuff around the ears", "to bloody the nose" all these are our nice Russian pastimes. We brag about it. People have become too accustomed to being "knocked about from the time they were small"; they are knocked about by their parents and masters; they used to be knocked about by the police."[22]

their aim was the violent overthrow of the existing government to be replaced by another one. Mankind would, according to him, liberate itself from violence only if it followed Christ and refused to have anything to do with governments. Only then would the Kingdom of God on earth become a reality with the realization by people that it was to be found within themselves. After its publication in 1894, this statement by Tolstoy of his personal faith was translated into the major European languages. Discussing the use of violence by governments against helpless victims, Tolstoy provided a Russian example:

> ... I happened to travel on a train to a locality in the provinces of Tula and Ryazan, where the peasants had been starving the year before, and were starving still more in the present year. At one of the stations the train in which I was traveling met a special train which, under the leadership of the governor, was transporting troops with guns, cartridges and rods for the torture and killing of those very famine-stricken peasants. The torturing of the peasants with rods for the purpose of enforcing the decision of the authorities ... has of late been applied more and more freely in Russia.[23]

In an article, *Shame!,* published in 1895, Tolstoy returned to the unsavory subject of corporal punishment in Russia. He asserted that the act of beating was both ugly in itself and humiliating to those subjected to it. Some peasants were known to commit suicide after being sentenced to be beaten by birch rods, rather than submit to the great humiliation. With regard to the view, expressed even in his own circle, that the peasants expected to be beaten and that the rod was of benefit to them, Tolstoy contended that they in fact abhorred the rod and that it spiritually crippled even those who administered it. The main target of Tolstoy in his new writing, as in previous articles of his, was the tsarist government:

> The government of the colossal Christian state nineteen centuries after Christ could not come up with anything more useful, intelligent and ethical to prevent breaking the law than to subject the lawbreakers—adults and sometimes old people—to undressing, throwing them on the floor and beating them with rods on their rear ends.[24]

It was during the 1890s and the first decade of the new century that Tolstoy was most active in his campaign to bring justice to the peasants. In innumerable articles and pamphlets he exposed every type of mistreatment of Russia's largest social class. In his essay, *The Slavery of Our Times,* published in 1900, he described the conditions under which peasants who had left the land after the emancipation to become industrial workers were then living. Most were extremely poor, dwelt and worked in unhealthy surroundings and had very long working hours. On the average over eighty percent of their children died in infancy and alcoholism was rife among them. Tolstoy concluded that their lot had not really changed. Before the emancipation they had been slaves of their landowners, and now they were slaves in factories. The means proposed by the writer for ending the new slavery were more radical than those advocated by Marx and the socialists, which he regarded as utopian. He advocated the abolition of governments which, in his view, were responsible for the institutionalized slavery and violence.

In February 1901 Tolstoy was excommunicated from the Orthodox Church. He was not greatly perturbed by this action since he had long since ceased to regard himself as a member of the church, and had indeed inveighed against it in both his artistic works and his pamphlets. Furthermore, he had had plenty of time to become accustomed to the possibility of his excommunication. In 1892 the rector of the Moscow Theological Academy had had a long talk with him about his alienation from the church without causing him to alter his views. In 1897 a priest had come to him from Tula with instructions from his superiors to make a last attempt—also unsuccessful—to bring Tolstoy back into the fold. The writer was also aware that, in 1899, the Archbishop of Kharkov had made a proposal for his excommunication about which no decision had been made. The first stage of excommunication occurred for practical purposes in 1900, after Tolstoy became seriously ill. The authorities of the church forbade the offering of prayers for the repose of his soul in the event of his death.

Although Tolstoy himself shrugged off his excommunication, large numbers of people from many walks of Russian life demonstrated their love and respect for him. He was cheered by crowds in the streets, and thousands of letters reached him from all over Russia. Many letters expressing solidarity came to Tolstoy from abroad. His house in Moscow was filled with gifts and flowers sent as tokens of support for him. Tolstoy had originally intended to make no comment in the event of being excommunicated, but upon noticing the strong reaction to it from so many of his compatriots he issued, in April 1901, a public statement in the form of an open letter to Russia's Holy Synod which was first published in London. A censored version of the statement appeared later in a St. Petersburg theological journal. In it Tolstoy admitted that the Synod had been right in accusing him of rejecting the church. He went on to assert, however, that far from having revolted against God he desired to serve Him "with all the strength" of his soul.

Within a month of his excommunication Tolstoy completed another pamphlet entitled, *To the Tsar and His Assistants.* He sent copies of it to the tsar himself, his ministers, grand dukes and other influential persons, none of whom however saw fit to respond. Only the censors reacted—by banning the pamphlet. Many Russians nevertheless managed to read it, since members of the revolutionary underground made copies of it by hand and distributed them. The pamphlet was Tolstoy's reaction to the wave of terrorism that was sweeping Russia at the time. In it he warned the tsar that violence would not end until the peasants had acquired the same rights as other citizens of the country. He listed all the oppressive measures still imposed on the peasants, including corporal punishment and restrictions on travel, and declared his conviction that until they were eliminated hatred for the government would grow ever more strong and social peace would never be achieved. In his pamphlet Tolstoy also spoke out strongly in favor of freedom for all religious denominations in Russia. He could see that perfectly honest and hard-working people were severely persecuted by the tsarist government just because their religious views differed from those of the official church. Tolstoy was hopeful that changes could be made. His own involvement in securing religious freedom for the Dukhobors taught him that the government could modify its intolerant attitude toward religious dissent if enough pressure was applied internationally.

Tolstoy's activities on behalf of the Dukhobors attracted the attention of the whole world. The Dukhobors were a Russian religious sect which was founded in the Province of Kharkov in the second half of the eighteenth century. They rejected the notion that God was a separate being, affirming instead that He dwelt in the souls of men. Though they believed in the immortality of the soul, they rejected the concept of hell and paradise. According to them the departed would be granted eternal life at some future time on earth, and not in another world. They did not recognize the power of governments and refused to bear arms, considering that authority should be divine in origin and not at all coercive. It was mainly in consequence of these attitudes to temporal authority that the sect was persecuted under several tsars.

Paul I, in his zeal to stamp out any manifestations of disobedience to his authority, went so far as to banish the Dukhobors to the Siberian mines, ordering in particular that their hands and legs should be kept in irons as long as they lived. Under Paul's successor, Alexander I, the Dukhobors were permitted to leave Siberia and form their own colony in the South of Russia. In 1826, however, a year after his accession to the throne, Nicholas I ordered that all able-bodied men among them should serve in the imperial army. The tsar's order resulted in a virtually incessant meting out of corporal punishment to those forcibly enlisted for they would not bear arms. When even the vicious beatings failed to influence the Dukhobor community to give up their beliefs or accede to Nicholas' wishes, the tsar had them deported to the barren areas of the Caucasus. There they lived when Tolstoy commenced his efforts on their behalf.

In 1895 the Dukhobors held a mass meeting during which they burnt every conceivable type of weapon as a demonstration of their opposition to military service. The authorities launched a savage Cossack assault on them. Their property was confiscated and thousands of them were exiled or imprisoned. When numbers of them began to die of starvation Tolstoy made known their sufferings to the whole world through articles of his which were published in England and in Russia. In October 1897, in a letter to the Swedish newspaper *Stockholm Tagblatt,* he even suggested that the Nobel Prize might be awarded to the persecuted sect. The publicity given to the Dukhobors aroused so much international indignation that the tsarist government stopped persecuting them and they were allowed to leave Russia. In late 1898 and early 1899 three ships carrying over six thousand Dukhobors sailed for Canada, a country where they had been assured religious freedom. The money to cover the cost of the migration came from private donations—in the main from Tolstoy who gave the royalties of his novel *Resurrection* to the sect.

Tolstoy was very ill at the beginning of 1902. He believed, as did his doctors, that he would not recover, and he was quite prepared for death. He wished, however, to make it known to the highest authorities how serious he considered the state of affairs in Russia to be. Taking up his pen for what he expected to be the last time, he wrote a letter to Tsar Nicholas II addressing him as "Dear Brother". He expressed a conviction that the tsar could be of great service to his country, but that the policies he was pursuing would lead it to disaster. He went on to assert that the autocratic form of government had become outdated and that, while it "may answer to the demands of people in Central Africa, cut off from the whole world", in Russia it had become an obstacle to social progress. The Russians had outgrown autocracy and their respect for the tsar's authority had, he went on to declare, on the whole disappeared, but it could return if he gave his people the opportunity to express their wishes. As to what the main wish of the people was, Tolstoy left the tsar in no doubt of his own view:

> All hundred million people would say with one voice that they want freedom in the use of land—that is, abolition of the right to landed property . . . landed property is as crying and obvious an injustice as was serfdom fifty years ago.[25]

The idea of abolishing the right to landed property had come to Tolstoy from the writings of the American economist Henry George. This economist had proposed that the system of private ownership and rental of land be replaced by the levying of a single tax on all those who wanted to cultivate it. The idea seemed to Tolstoy simple and just, and he was captivated by it. The adoption of a single-tax system would, in his view, have solved Russia's greatest social problem by giving the land to those who really worked on it. He was extremely disappointed when he failed to arouse any significant interest in the proposal among influential Russians. Most economists dismissed it as a utopian dream, and no attempt was made in Russia to implement it.*

* The idea of the single-tax received support from the Russian liberals during Alexander Kerensky's regime in 1917 when plans were made to include it in the new Russia's constitution.

In February 1904, war broke out between Russia and Japan with a surprise attack by a Japanese force on the Russian fleet lying at Port Arthur. Many Russian sailors died in the attack and great damage was inflicted on seven of their ships. The tsarist government had no problems in mobilizing its manpower to respond to the armed provocation. Patriotic feelings ran high in Russia and thousands, including Tolstoy's own son Andrei, volunteered to fight the enemy. Tolstoy did not share their enthusiasm. He was appalled at the slaughter of thousands of peasants who had been sent to war without having any idea of what had really caused it. As in the Crimean War, it was the lot of peasants to fight with outdated weapons under the command of incompetent officers. Tolstoy refused to accept the notion that the war was solely the fault of the Japanese and protested against the slaughter of peasant masses in an article, *Bethink Yourselves!*, which was banned in Russia but published in England. Tolstoy may well have been the only person of any prominence in Russia to speak out against the war, which, it was hoped, would be brought to a victorious conclusion in a few weeks with the exaction of reparations from the Japanese for their sneak attack. Many Russians who had been able to see Tolstoy's article considered it treasonable, but when news of the huge losses suffered by the tsar's forces reached Russia, people began to take a different attitude. After the destruction of the Baltic fleet in the Tsushima Straits in May 1905, Tolstoy's criticism of the military operations as senseless killing of Russia's poorly-armed peasants became generally accepted.

Frustration over the victory the Japanese had achieved served to intensify the revolutionary situation which already existed in Russia and the government of the country was soon on the verge of collapse. The tsar's authority was at its lowest ebb and Tolstoy, loved and respected as he was, could have become the most powerful person in the country. He refused, however, to lead any political party or group, as he was not interested in power. His life mission was to secure a better deal for Russia's oppressed peasantry, as he quite clearly stated:

> Throughout this revolution I occupy the status, voluntarily assumed by me, of advocate for the hundred million peasants. I rejoice at everything that makes, or might make, for their good, and I do not sympathize with anything which does not have this main goal or which detracts from it.[26]

As the revolutionary events unfolded Tolstoy could see that his philosophy and teachings were totally unsuited to those turbulent times. He cautioned both the government and the revolutionaries to avoid

The Bolshevik rule that followed Kerensky's short-lived government showed no interest in the implementation of the single-tax.

violence—but he was not heeded. His warning that real social justice "can only be attained by the religious and moral perfection of individuals" was disregarded. The antagonism between rulers and ruled went too deep for there to be any peaceful solution to Russia's social problems. The country was headed towards a complete breakdown.

After the bloody suppression of the revolution of 1905, strife in Russia continued. There were numerous strikes, acts of sabotage and armed clashes between rioters and the authorities. The countryside became engulfed in violence, with frustrated peasants venting their anger on landowners in acts of vengeance, which in turn provoked savage retaliation by the police and army. Even the peaceful vicinity of Yasnaya Polyana suffered from violence. The estate of Tolstoy's son, Mikhail, was extensively damaged by arson, and the farm buildings of his daughter, Tatyana, were burnt down. Unknown assailants shot and seriously wounded the coachman and gamekeeper of a neighboring landowner. Happily, Yasnaya Polyana itself was left unharmed.*

Tolstoy's last important, and probably best remembered, reaction to public events in Russia was an appeal he addressed to the tsarist government in 1908, entitled *I Cannot Remain Silent*. In Russia it was banned immediately after appearing in newspapers, but abroad it appeared in translation in hundreds of publications. The event which moved Tolstoy to make his eloquent appeal was the hanging of twelve impoverished peasants who had attacked the estate of a landowner. Since the authorities claimed that such executions served the general welfare of the Russian people, Tolstoy wanted it to be generally known that he was one of those who passionately disagreed. He expressed doubt as to whether the authorities would ever be able to eradicate revolutionary unrest by cold-blooded murder. He thought that if the elementary desire of the Russian peasants for the big estates to be broken up and distributed among them continued to be frustrated, executions would serve only to strengthen that desire. Tolstoy claimed that, by refusing to countenance radical change, the tsarist authorities had completely discredited themselves in the eyes of the Russian people. He vowed that he would publicize his opinions by every means at his disposal until either the executions stopped or he himself was arrested and hanged like one of the victimized peasants.

Tolstoy's last two years were not happy. Much as he loved the peasants he was unable to break away from the splendor of Yasnaya Polyana and

---

* In September 1907, the night watchman at Yasnaya Polyana, fired warning shots to scare away some intruders. After this incident the frightened Countess, much to Tolstoy's annoyance, asked for police protection. The matter was given great publicity and some newspapers pointed out that Tolstoy, the prophet of nonresistance to evil, had asked for help from the authorities to protect his estate. Tolstoy had nothing to do with the whole affair, but it upset him greatly.

really live like one of them. He was painfully aware that the way he lived was inconsistent with the principles he espoused but, having reached the age of eighty, he could hardly adjust himself physically to a much more rigorous way of life. His dissatisfaction at failing to be in accord with his own views was compounded with his frustration that the land at Yasnaya Polyana, contrary to his expressed wishes, had not been distributed among the peasants who worked on it. Whenever he urged that it should be so distributed, he came into conflict with his wife who could never understand why he sought to identify himself with the peasants. Since the land no longer belonged to him, he was powerless to act on his own and realized with great sorrow that he would die without his desire being fulfilled.

On the 10th of November 1910, Tolstoy finally decided to leave Yasnaya Polyana for a place where he planned to live according to his beliefs and principles. To this day no one really knows what his intended destination was, and in any case he never reached it. He left the train he was traveling on at Astapovo station, about two hundred miles south-east of Yasnaya Polyana, suffering from a severe chill. He was taken to the stationmaster's house where he died on the 20th of November.

Since the authorities feared disturbances, Tolstoy's family was asked to have him buried as soon as possible, before large crowds from other parts of the country could assemble. A detachment of police was present at the funeral. Upon observing the policemen the mourners ordered them to their knees. They complied. Otherwise no incidents occurred. According to an eye-witness the funeral was a solemn occasion; it seemed as if the peasants were burying one of their community:

> The imposing simplicity of the funeral made a touching and exalting impression. The chanting of the *De profundis* by the many thousands following the rude coffin, which was borne by peasants, heightened the impression. At the head of the cortege were two peasants, bearing an impoverished banner of coarse linen, attached to two birch poles, with the inscription: "The memory of your good deeds will not die amongst us."[27]

Russia's peasants have kept their word.

Tolstoy's dream came true two years after his death. His daughter, Alexandra, bought the Yasnaya Polyana estate from her brothers and, in deference to her father's wishes, distributed it among the peasants. Her mother, the Countess, kept the house, the park, which she opened to the public as a shrine, and some 180 acres of land.*

---

* In May 1911 the Countess, in a letter to Nicholas II, offered Yasnaya Polyana to the Russian state for sale. There was no reply. In November 1911 the Countess dispatched another letter to the tsar in which she stated that "if the Russian government does not buy Yasnaya Polyana then my sons, some of whom are destitute, will be forced with deep regret (s glubokoi serdechnoi bol'yu) to sell Yasnaya Polyana in pieces or whole to private

After the collapse of the monarchy in March 1917 there was a wave of arson and destruction on estates in the Province of Tula, carried out by peasants who were furious that their hopes of having the land divided among them had been frustrated by the Provisional Government. Although the Countess believed that an attack on Yasnaya Polyana was imminent, the peasants left it unharmed. After the Bolsheviks seized power in October, the estates were distributed among the peasants. Overseeing the distribution in the area of Yasnaya Polyana a peasant committee decided, in April 1918, to take away about a hundred acres from the property of the Countess. Aware of the cruelties that peasants had inflicted on unprotected landowners, the Countess feared for her life and was quite resigned to losing most of her land. She knew that no authority could intervene on her behalf with land-hungry peasants on the rampage. Yet her land was not broken up. In the midst of their orgy of destruction and bloodshed the peasants recalled Tolstoy's efforts to help them and could not bring themselves to deprive his widow of any of her property. The committee annulled its decision and apologized to the Countess for the distress caused to her.[28]

On the 13th of June 1921, Yasnaya Polyana became the property of the Russian Federated Republic. It was to function as a cultural and educational center. The decree for this final act was signed by the chairman of the Soviet government's Executive Committee, Mikhail Kalinin—a peasant's son.

---

individuals." Nicholas II responded on the 20th of December 1911: "I find the idea of Yasnaya Polyana being purchased by the government inadmissible. The council of ministers should discuss only the size of a possible pension to the widow."[29]

In January 1912 the tsarist government awarded an extremely generous pension to the Countess—10,000 rubles a year.

Russia Rediscovers Tolstoy

Tolstoy's name was not unknown among the Marxist revolutionaries of 1917. He had attracted their attention long before they made their successful bid for power, and Lenin himself wrote seven articles on him between 1908 and 1911. He found him profoundly contradictory:

> On the one hand, we have the great artist, the genius who has not only drawn incomparable pen pictures of Russian life, but has made first-class contributions to world literature. On the other hand, we have the crazy landlord obsessed with Christ. On the one hand, we have his remarkably powerful, forthright, and sincere protest against social falsehood and hypocrisy; and on the other hand, we have the "Tolstoyan," i.e., the jaded, hysterical sniveller called the Russian intellectual, who publicly beats his breast and wails: "I am a dreadful, wicked sinner, but I am engaging in moral self-perfection; I don't eat meat any more, I now eat rice pudding."[1]

Lenin considered that passivity in the face of evil, which was embedded in the mentality of the Russian masses and which Tolstoy had made part of his personal philosophy, was in large measure responsible for the defeat of the revolutionary uprising of 1905. However, although he criticized the "utopian" and "reactionary" doctrine of the man, Lenin always acknowledged that Tolstoy was a great literary artist whose works secured a place for him among the foremost writers of the world. Lenin was also careful not to dissociate Tolstoy completely from the revolutionary movement, for he recognized the earnestness with which the author had castigated the ruling classes and the institutions of the tsarist autocracy.

Leon Trotsky, who after Lenin was the most conspicuous, and probably the most powerful, leader of revolutionary Russia, had written two articles on Tolstoy—one, in German,[2] on the occasion of the latter's eightieth birthday in 1908, and the other, in Russian,[3] upon his death two years later. Trotsky detected a deep moral affinity between the convictions of Tolstoy and the tenets of socialism. He differed radically from Lenin in his assessment of the role played by the writer during the revolutionary events of 1905. Recalling his days as Chairman of the St. Petersburg Soviet during the fighting, he acknowledged Tolstoy's significant contribution to the revolutionary situation. Trotsky thought that an "honorable chapter" should be dedicated to Tolstoy in the book to be written about the social upheaval of 1905.

Anatole Lunacharsky, a literary critic who was People's Commissar for Education during the nineteen twenties, also thought highly of Tolstoy. With the control he exercised over the cultural life of the country he could have easily prohibited any reissue of his work had he disapproved of the great writer. Far from doing this, Lunacharsky encouraged the publication of Tolstoy's artistic work. Moreover, he boldly expressed views favorable to Tolstoy as a thinker at a time when other Marxists were totally rejecting his teaching as being "reactionary."* As early as 1911 he had declared that of all the public figures of his time, "Leo Tolstoy was the closest to the hearts of the progressive-minded class of European society."[4]

Several other important personalities of the new Russia were admirers of Tolstoy. Vladimir Bonch-Bruevich, Lenin's private secretary, who became an important party official in the early twenties, had been one of the writer's collaborators. As such he had accompanied the third party of Dukhobors to Canada as an interpreter in 1899.**The influential author, Maxim Gorky, who had known Tolstoy well and visited him on many occasions, once declared: "This man is like God."[5] He was the first Marxist to publish reminiscences about Tolstoy in Soviet Russia.*** Lenin's wife, Nadezhda Krupskaya, had written about Tolstoy, too.[6]

Notwithstanding the presence of such persons in high positions, many militant Bolsheviks thoroughly disapproved of Tolstoy. To be sure, most of them had only a vague idea what sort of person he had been; but the very fact that he had belonged to the aristocracy and once owned a large number of serfs was sufficient for them to attach the "class enemy" label to him. But Tolstoy did not become a subject of open dispute during the early years of the Soviet regime, for the civil war was raging, the militants lacked the administrative power to exclude the man and his writings from the cultural life of the country, and the leaders kept silent about him. A situation of stalemate prevailed, therefore, as far as Tolstoy's place in Soviet Russia was concerned. There can be little doubt, however, that Tolstoy's works in public libraries became the subject of high-handed actions by local officials once the civil war was over. Professor Herman Ermolaev of Princeton University refers to a case which took place in the sixth year of the new regime:

---

* A special mention should be made of Georgi Plekhanov, a prominent Marxist theoretician who died abroad the year after the Revolution. For Plekhanov, Tolstoy was the ideologist of the aristocracy—a poor thinker and a reactionary. He regarded Tolstoy the novelist as a chronicler of the life and mores of the upper classes.

** He published a book based on his experiences, entitled *The Dukhobors on Canadian Prairies* (Petrograd, 1918). Bonch Bruevich' wife, Vera Velichkina, worked with Tolstoy during the winter of 1891-92 among the starving peasants in the famine areas of Central Russia.

*** Gorky's reminiscences of Tolstoy were published in Petrograd in 1919. It should be noted that in spite of his veneration of Tolstoy, Gorky never regarded him as his teacher on ethical or spiritual matters. In his famous play *The Lower Depths (Na dne)* 1902, Gorky created a character, Luka, who was always ready to give moral advice but in reality cared little for people. Luka's attitude and words suggested to the audience that Gorky shaped Luka after Tolstoy.

It is noteworthy that in 1923 Gorky branded as "spiritual vampirism" the withdrawal of certain works by foreign and Russian philosophers, and also the works of Tolstoy and Leskov, from the largest Soviet libraries. He even thought of renouncing his Soviet citizenship as a sign of protest.[7]

During the early years of Soviet power, it was a group of dedicated disciples and former collaborators of Tolstoy, together with members of his family, who continued to disseminate his works. The publishing house *Posrednik* continued to issue cheap editions of Tolstoy's writings—mostly of a religious and ethical character—until the mid nineteen twenties. Among the most active and devoted of those determined to publish the works of Tolstoy and otherwise keep his memory alive in Soviet Russia were: Vladimir Chertkov, Tolstoy's close friend who had published his banned works in England; Nicholas Gusev, his secretary; Paul Biryukov, his biographer; Valentin Bulgakov, secretary during his last year; and Vsevolod Sreznevsky, a highly respected scholar. Two other persons worthy of mention are Alexander Goldenveizer, a musician and devoted admirer of Tolstoy, and Dushan Makovitsky, the writer's physician and personal friend, who left Russia in 1920. Makovitsky's notes proved to be such excellent material for research on Tolstoy that they kept scores of scholars occupied for decades. They were published in four large volumes in 1979 in Moscow.

Various members of the Tolstoy family joined in the efforts to secure a place for the writer in the new Russia. His wife, Countess Tolstoy, turned Yasnaya Polyana into a cultural shrine, and managed it until it came under the protection of the Soviet government in May 1919, six months before she died. Tolstoy's eldest daughter, Tatyana, was in charge of the Tolstoy Museum in Moscow from 1923 until her emigration to France in 1925. The writer's eldest son, Sergei, remained in Russia and was engaged in research on his father until his death in 1945.* It was, however, Alexandra, the youngest of Tolstoy's daughters, who became the most active in promoting his ideas. She had a number of conflicts with the Soviet authorities, was arrested five times and, in 1920, was sentenced to three years in prison. Released after one year, she was appointed director of Yasnaya Polyana. In 1929, she went to Japan on a lecture tour and did not return to Russia. She settled in the United States in 1931. There she became president of the Tolstoy Foundation, which engages in many charitable activities in the spirit of her father, and remained so until her death in 1979. Some of her activities in emigration were sharply disapproved of in her native country. As late as in 1961, she was called a "traitor" in a literary publication

---

* Sergei's greatest contribution, a book on his father, *Ocherki bylogo* (Sketches of the Past), appeared posthumously in Moscow in 1949. The book was well received and its second edition appeared seven years later.

commemorating the fiftieth anniversary of her father's death,[8] after which she has not been mentioned at all. In the Jubilee edition of Tolstoy's works which, according to its editorial board, includes every word written by him, Alexandra's name has been replaced by three dots at every mention.

The efforts of those who loved Tolstoy and wanted to see his writings in print bore fruit. Between 1918 and 1923, of all Russian classical authors Tolstoy was the one most published by private firms in his homeland (nearly half a million copies), while Chekhov and Turgenev were ahead statistically in classical issues by state publishing houses. By 1924, however, Tolstoy had become the most published of all the Russian classical writers; and by 1930, the annual output of his works had reached about five million copies. Soviet publishing houses have issued his collected works in considerable numbers over the years. The largest edition of these, the Jubilee, which appeared between 1928 and 1958, consists of 90 volumes. The driving force behind this major undertaking was Chertkov, until his death in 1936, when Gusev assumed charge of the editorial board for the edition. Besides the Jubilee project, a twelve-volume edition appeared in 1928, a fifteen-volume one in 1928-30, a twelve-volume one in 1948, a fourteen-volume one in 1953, a twelve-volume one in 1959 and a twenty-volume one in 1960-65.

In the process of keeping Tolstoy's works in print and his ideas alive during the early Soviet years, a considerable advantage was the fortuitous circumstance that some people in other countries perceived a link between Tolstoy and the Bolsheviks. For example, in 1919 there appeared an article in a popular New York periodical[9] in which it was stated that Lenin's responsibility for the Revolution was insignificant in comparison with that of Tolstoy. In the same article was reproduced the observation of Aylmer Maude, Tolstoy's English friend and translator, to the effect that more than any other writer, Tolstoy was the greatest spiritual influence in establishing the Soviet government in Russia. With the article appeared a photograph of Tolstoy with the caption: "The great ancestor of the Bolshevik."

In 1925, Charles Sarolea, professor of French at Edinburgh University, wrote an article entitled, *Was Tolstoy the Spiritual Father of Bolshevism?* Sarolea knew Tolstoy well and had visited him at Yasnaya Polyana in 1905. He journeyed to Russia after the Revolution, but must have misinterpreted the politico-literary situation there, for he stated in his article that the Bolsheviks claimed Tolstoy as their patron saint even as the French revolutionaries claimed Rousseau. Sarolea then went on to say that the Soviet government glorified Tolstoy by establishing museums in his memory. He was, of course, wrong. No evidence whatsoever existed in 1925 to support his contention that the Bolsheviks regarded Tolstoy as their "patron saint." The Tolstoy museums which he spoke of as having been established by "the dictators" had in fact been in existence since before the Revolution. Yasnaya Polyana, for example, was opened up to the public by Countess Tolstoy soon after her husband's death in 1910. There were regular visiting hours to view Tolstoy's rooms and his grave. As for the Tolstoy Museum in Moscow, it developed out of the Tolstoy exhibition held in Moscow in 1911, and opened to the public the same year.

After a short analysis of Tolstoy's teachings, Sarolea concluded in his article that Tolstoy had been the greatest cause of the collapse of the tsarist regime,* and declared:

> We are reluctantly but irresistibly driven to the conclusion that Tolstoy has done enormous harm in unnerving and emasculating the Russian soul, in producing an attitude of moral paralysis and acquiescence to tyranny."[10]

Stefan Zweig, the renowned Austrian writer and a devoted disciple of Tolstoy, was another who regarded him as having been instrumental in bringing about the Revolution.** He regarded Tolstoy's role as positive and in the last three lines of the following assessment he closely approaches the present Soviet view of Tolstoy's contribution to the revolutionary movement in Russia:

> None of the nineteenth-century Russian revolutionaries smoothed the path for Lenin and Trotsky so much as this anti-revolutionary Count, who was the first to defy the Tsar and who, pursued by the Holy Synod, had left the Church; who had shattered all existing authority with hammer blows, and who demanded social reconciliation as the necessary condition for a new and better world."[11]

There was no doubt that the Soviet authorities were aware of the inclination of observers abroad to regard Tolstoy as their ally, yet they kept silent about him. Those now in high positions who in the past had written articles to demonstrate the influence of Tolstoy, either in the negative or the positive sense, ignored him as if he had never existed. It is indeed remarkable that analyses of Lenin's prerevolutionary articles on Tolstoy started to appear only after Lenin died, and it was not until 1931 that the statement was made that he had meant to write "a lot more about Tolstoy,"[13] and not until 1935 that the Party's principal newspaper, *Pravda,* declared that Lenin stressed, soon after the Revolution, the necessity of publishing Tolstoy's complete works "including all cuts made

---

* Nicholas Berdyaev, the prominent Russian religious philosopher who was expelled from his country in 1922, also considered Tolstoy to have been a progenitor of the Revolution; but, unlike Sarolea, he absolved him from any responsibility for its consequences. He stated that

both Tolstoy and Dostoyevsky in their different ways rejected the European world, civilized and bourgeois, and they were precursors of the revolution. But the revolution did not recognize them, just as they would not have recognized it.[12]

** The view that Tolstoy, more than any other individual, was responsible for the fall of the tsarist regime still persists. For example, Ronald Hingley of Oxford maintains this opinion in his book, *Russian Writers and Society, 1825-1904,* published in 1973.

by the tsarist censorship."[14]

The only reference to Tolstoy known to have been made by Lenin after the Revolution is recorded in an article of Gorky's, published in 1924. It concerns an episode which allegedly took place in 1918 while Gorky was visiting the Kremlin. Gorky recalled that Lenin pointed at a copy of *War and Peace* lying on his desk and remarked: "'He, brother, is an artist! Do you know what is astonishing? Until this count we had no real muzhik in literature.' Then looking at me with his Asiatic eyes he asked: 'Whom could one put next to him in Europe?' He himself answered: 'No one.'"[15]

The silence of party leaders concerning Tolstoy becomes understandable when one learns that they had been accused of Tolstoyism (meaning in this instance a soft, forgiving attitude to enemies) by radical revolutionaries on a number of occasions. Such charges became especially persistent after the halting in July 1920 of what seemed to be a victorious offensive against Poland. Strong differences of opinion existed among the Soviet leaders as to whether the offensive should be pursued or an armistice sought. While the debate was going on, the Poles managed to regroup and bring up reinforcements; and in August they mounted a vigorous attack against the Red forces, which they routed. The outcome of the war was no longer in doubt and in October the Bolsheviks were obliged to agree to an armistice. Under the Treaty of Riga negotiated the following year, Poland secured substantial territorial gains at the expense of Russia. Historical documents available today indicate that valid arguments existed both for and against the continuation of large scale military operations against Poland. Nevertheless, the interruption of those operations was considered at the time by many rank and file party members to be proof of their government's "Tolstoyan" attitude towards the enemy. Facing criticism from several quarters, Lenin found it necessary to make three speeches[16] during 1920 and 1921, in which he denied any leaning by the Party towards Tolstoyism as perceived by its critics.

Though the Party took strong measures to counter attitudes of nonviolence within its own ranks, it could not prevent the spread of Tolstoy's ethical ideas among the general populace. During the civil war, scores of Tolstoyans refused to bear arms and were shot in consequence. Even after the hostilities ended, the Soviet authorities continued to encounter problems with them over military matters. As late as 1928, Lunacharsky remarked that a certain number of Tolstoyans had adopted attitudes clearly inimical to the effective exercise of Soviet state power, not least in the important sphere of national defense.[17] Agricultural colonies run in accordance with Tolstoy's religious principles managed to survive in spite of the drastic measures taken against them by the authorities. According to one Soviet source some such colonies were still in existence in the country as late as 1935, the largest of them—with some five hundred members—being in the Kuznetsk Basin.[18]

The prevalence of Tolstoyism in Soviet Russia in the nineteen-twenties remains to be investigated but, even without data on the matter, it is quite evident that the movement was a source of much worry to the authorities. Shortly after Lenin's death in 1924, Lunacharsky declared during a public lecture in Moscow:

> At the present time in Russia, and in somewhat different forms in other countries, some of the basic ideologies dividing mankind are Marxism and Tolstoyism..."[19]

While he might appear to have been exaggerating, Lunacharsky must have based his statement on known facts. He pronounced Tolstoyism to be an enemy of Marxism second only to the bourgeoisie. However, his lecture left the audience with a deep sense of ambiguity as far as Tolstoy himself was concerned: Tolstoyism had been declared hostile to the Soviet order, but Tolstoy had not. The question of what relevance, if any, the man himself could have for the people at large in post-revolutionary Russia still remained without an answer. The literary critics eventually provided one, but only after Tolstoy had become the subject of one of the most heated debates ever witnessed in Soviet Russia.

The first critics to rise above the level of reminiscences and approach Tolstoy from a purely literary point of view after the Revolution were the Formalists. They were literary scholars who founded *Opoyaz* (Society for the Study of Poetic Language) and the Moscow Linguistic Circle, and had their heyday between 1914 and the mid nineteen-twenties. The Formalists regarded literature as a form of artistic expression which existed on its own terms, and they concerned themselves in the main with the study of forms and devices. Such an approach was not reconcilable with the Marxist view that ideology and an author's class background were the factors to which paramount importance should be attached in literary analysis, yet the Formalists entirely disregarded demands that they should accommodate themselves to the current orthodoxy. They nevertheless managed to propagate and develop their ideas unhindered until about 1924 when Trotsky, Lunacharsky and the influential party leader, Nicholas Bukharin, severely criticized them. In Trotsky's view the Formalists had "an extremely arrogant and immature" neo-Kantian idealistic philosophy, while Lunacharsky dismissed their writings as a "form of escapism," as did Bukharin, who called their poetic devices "a catalogue, lacking the most important and valuable ingredient—ideology." Whereas Trotsky and Bukharin urged the Formalists to rise above the "cult of the word" and pay more attention to Marxism, Lunacharsky declared Formalism to be "one of the stubborn relics of imperial Russia."

It was in 1919 that the prominent Formalist, Boris Eikhenbaum, wrote his first article on Tolstoy in the form of an introduction to a volume containing *Childhood, Boyhood* and *Youth*. Contrary to the prevailing practice of scholars writing about Tolstoy—many of them former friends of his—of paying great attention to his early life, his spiritual crisis and his insatiable thirst for "truth," Eikhenbaum simply ignored such matters and stated that Tolstoy's lifelong concern—especially after completing *Anna Karenina*—was a search for new forms for his artistic works. He asserted that Tolstoy had a running battle with art all his life, and it was only in his last years, during the writing of *Hadji Murat*, that he managed to rest from this battle. Such a view was, and still is, contrary to that of most Tolstoy scholars, who maintain that after the publication of *Anna Karenina* Tolstoy evinced a decreased interest in artistic matters and focused his attention on religious, ethical and social problems. Eikenbaum's article attracted little attention at a time when the new Russia was struggling to survive, but it had the effect of antagonizing people who had known Tolstoy well and who had attached great significance to his spiritual crises and social preoccupations. These people were seeking to demonstrate to the new rulers of Russia that Tolstoy, besides being a man of letters, had also been an active participant in the struggle against the tsarist regime and should, therefore, be revered and respected. In insisting that Tolstoy was just an artist searching for new forms, Eikhenbaum could only pose a threat to the writer's admirers, and he was soon ostracized by them.

In a work on Tolstoy's early literary years, published in 1922,[20] Eikhenbaum sought to show that Tolstoy modeled himself as a writer on the styles of the eighteenth century. He had come to this opinion through an analysis of Tolstoy's diaries in which, he stated, were revealed all the devices used in the future novels. Eikhenbaum's investigation of Tolstoy's stylistic and compositional devices must have given him some doubts about the author's originality. Although he did not assert this directly, he implied that the time had arrived for a reassessment to be made of the writer who was in danger of being turned into an icon—probably quite consciously risking the ire of the traditionally minded Tolstoy researchers of the time. In the introduction to his work he referred to the fact that a gap existed between himself, "an outsider," and the established Tolstoy scholars; but that gap was undoubtedly the result of his having, in the eyes of many of the latter, perpetrated an insult to Tolstoy's memory by making him the subject of Formalist investigations. Eikhenbaum complained that despite all efforts he had not been able to consult Tolstoy's manuscripts, which remained inaccessible to "outsiders." Although Eikhenbaum did not mention names, people acquainted with the facts knew that the main obstacle to the access he sought was Gusev, one of the most influential custodians of Tolstoy's manuscripts, who maintained until his death a thoroughly hostile attitude towards Eikhenbaum.

An enlarged version of Eikhenbaum's book was published in 1928.[21] It is a scholarly work which, even today, is regarded as an authoritative source of information on Tolstoy. In it Eikhenbaum departs a little from the full rigor of his Formalistic approach, relating Tolstoy to his period through a greater use of biographical and historical material. Although subjected to considerable pressure, Eikhenbaum did not offer any apology for earlier statements of his, and his modified approach represented not so much a change of mind as—in his own words—"the evolution of literary criticism." He was essentially concerned with the first ten years of Tolstoy's literary career, yet he contrived to make known two "discoveries" of his concerning *War and Peace,* a work which belonged to a later period and which he dealt with fully in a subsequent volume.*

His first "discovery" was that Tolstoy had made radical changes in the historical novel he planned to write, as a result of the "enormously important" meeting he had had with Pierre-Joseph Proudhon, the French socialist with strong leanings towards anarchism, in Brussels in 1861. During this meeting Proudhon acquainted Tolstoy with his manuscript, *La Guerre et la Paix,* which was on the point of being published. Eikhenbaum believed that Tolstoy's decision to introduce a large amount of historical and philosophical reflection into his own work was in some measure a consequence of what had transpired in Brussels. The connection between Tolstoy's *War and Peace* and Proudhon's work is, according to Eikhenbaum, made quite evident by the identity of titles. Tolstoy, he went on to assert, did not, for political reasons, wish to mention Proudhon by name, but decided to dedicate his novel to the Frenchman's memory. Eikhenbaum expressed his astonishment that not a single Russian literary critic had perceived the close association between Proudhon's book, which came out in Russian translation in 1864, and Tolstoy's *War and Peace,* which was first fully published in 1869.

Eikhenbaum's "discovery" was not well received in Russia; if anything, it made things more difficult for him. The very idea that the greatest work of Russian literature could have been conceived and given its title in a foreign land was almost insulting to many Russians. Soviet literary scholars of today simply ignore the suggestion. Furthermore, in the most detailed study of the creation of *War and Peace,* which appeared in 1966, Proudhon is not even mentioned.[22] Echoes of Eikhenbaum's "discovery" did, however, continue to be heard in the West. Ernest Simmons of Columbia University, in his voluminous *Leo Tolstoy* published in 1946, remarked that "although Proudhon's book is a work on the principles of international law, Tolstoy was indebted to it for much more than the title. A study of *La Guerre et la Paix* reveals a good deal about the whole theory

---

* The 1928 book, *Leo Tolstoy in the 1850s,* was the first volume of a large monograph dealing with Tolstoy on which Eikhenbaum worked till the end of his life in 1959. The second volume of the monograph, entitled *Leo Tolstoy in the 1860s,* was published in 1931. The third volume, *Leo Tolstoy in the 1870s,* appeared in 1960. The fourth volume was near completion when it was dropped accidentally into Lake Ladoga during World War II.

of war that Tolstoy incorporated in the novel.[23] Henri Troyat, in his widely read book *Tolstoy,* originally published in France in 1965, mentions as a fact that Tolstoy acquired the title of his great novel from Proudhon.[24] On the other hand, R.F. Christian of the University of St. Andrews, who is probably the leading Tolstoy scholar in the West, today regards Eikhenbaum's assessment of Proudhon's influence on Tolstoy as "a not very convincing case."[25]

Eikhenbaum's second "discovery" was that Napoleon, as portrayed in Tolstoy's *War and Peace,* had nothing in common with the French emperor. According to Eikhenbaum, the Napoleon of the novel was a mouthpiece for the expression of ideas which Tolstoy had shared, in his patriotic mood after the fall of Sevastopol in 1855, with certain free-thinking French historians and publicists of the eighteen-fifties who were sceptical about the greatness of the French ruler. Eikhenbaum might have been correct, but his findings have never been accepted by Soviet scholars doing research on Tolstoy. They are inclined to regard Napoleon in the novel as the incarnation of conceit and aggression and it is irrelevant for them whether or not he resembles the real historical figure. In any case, there was great reluctance among literary experts in Russia even in Eikhenbaum's time to dwell on weak points in *War and Peace,* a trend that became significantly stronger as the years went by. It remains a question whether Eikhenbaum's inquisitive mind failed to appreciate that Tolstoy was much more than just a writer to the Russians or whether he perceived clearly that Tolstoy was being gradually transformed into a nationalist symbol and resented the fact.* One wonders why he included in his 1928 book an introduction to *War and Peace* which Tolstoy had written and then discarded:

> The lives of government officials, merchants, theological students, and peasants do not interest me and I hardly understand them. The life of the aristocracy . . . interests me and is dear to me."[26]

This statement, although never included in any edition of *War and Peace,* has been a perennial source of embarrassment to Tolstoy scholars in the Soviet Union ever since Eikhenbaum exhumed it, as it were. It is not something that a Soviet reader is supposed to see, especially if he is of peasant origin, since it might come as a mild shock to him. These words

---

* In the nineteen-thirties, Eikhenbaum was perhaps the only person in Soviet Russia conducting research into foreign influences on Tolstoy's writings. In 1937, he published an article[27] in which he claimed that in writing his *Kreutzer Sonata* Tolstoy "used the whole plot" of the story *Le cocu* of the French writer Paul de Kock. Two years later, he was rebuked— although surprisingly gently—by the Tolstoy scholar Pavel Popov who, though in disagreement with Eikhenbaum's indiscreet claim, nevertheless called his study "fresh" and "original."[28]

which illustrate Tolstoy's great attachment to the aristocracy during the writing of *War and Peace,* were "explained" by the Tolstoy specialist, Tamara Motyleva, in 1978. According to her, Tolstoy's remark was part of a polemical outburst, and it is therefore inappropriate to take literally his assertion that peasant life did not interest him at that time.[29]

Considering Eikhenbaum's uncompromising attitude towards Tolstoy, it is not surprising that in spite of his brilliant intellect he remained, in effect, excluded from participation in officially approved Tolstoy research and was the target of many attacks in Soviet publications. In 1934, he had to defend himself against accusations of withdrawing from Soviet reality.[30] His views were characterized as reactionary and he was taken to task for allegedly investigating Tolstoy's early style entirely through the prism of literary mores and the private life of the writer.[31] In 1947, the Soviet scholar, Konstantin Lomunov, remarked that, as far as Tolstoy research was concerned, "Eikhenbaum was creating artificial problems having no connection with those raised in Lenin's articles on Tolstoy."[32] The most dangerous attack on Eikhenbaum came in 1949, when he was accused of being a "cosmopolite."[33] A purge was under way at the time and people were being executed on that very charge.

It is quite evident that the greater part of the criticism to which Eikhenbaum was subjected concerned his supposed indifference to ideology. Even though he made a surprising disavowal of his Formalism in 1957, when he urged Soviet literary historians to make a profound study of Lenin's articles on Tolstoy,[34] ideologically inspired criticism of him did not cease even after his death. For example, as late as 1975, Lomunov remarked that "in B. Eikhenbaum's well-known book, *Leo Tolstoy in the 1860s,* Lenin's conception of Tolstoy is completely ignored. The author did not once turn to Lenin's articles on Tolstoy—not once!"[35]

While Eikhenbaum aroused the anger of disciples and former collaborators of Tolstoy by subjecting his writings to Formalist analysis instead of treating him as a sacrosanct symbol of Russia, Victor Shklovsky, another Formalist, provoked them even more. In the introduction to his book about *War and Peace* published in 1928[36] Shklovsky warned his readers that he was out to undo some of the legends which had grown up around Tolstoy, and by the undoing of legends he really meant "cutting Tolstoy down to size." He ridiculed the assumption that in setting out to write *War and Peace,* Tolstoy had assembled a whole library of works dealing with the Franco-Russian war of 1812. He dismissed the generally acepted notion of a "people's war" against the French, and he cast doubt on a number of other notions which had already been transformed into inviolable truths in Russia. But his crowning provocation was writing about Tolstoy in irreverent terms. He described the huddling together of the orphaned Tolstoy children on long winter evenings, so touchingly narrated by the adult Tolstoy, as an exercise in eroticism. He dismissed the writer's efforts at self-improvement with the observation that "on his estate Lev Nikolaevich invented a new method of feeding pigs; and all that time, every day, he was inventing his own ethical system."[37] One gains the impression that Shklovsky deliberately sought to annoy the "recognized" Tolstoy experts who, as he hinted, were preventing him from consulting archival material concerning the writer. Like Eikhenbaum, Shklovsky was subjected to harsh words by critics on a number of occasions, not only for his methods but also for ignoring Lenin's articles on Tolstoy. Also, like Eikhenbaum, he disavowed in the nineteen-fifties his earlier views about Tolstoy, describing them as "erroneous."[38]

Another group of critics, usually known as the sociological school, was active at the same time as the Formalists. For them the most significant thing about a writer was his class origin, and from their standpoint they too set out to analyze Tolstoy. A leading member of this group, Ivan Kubikov, published a book in 1928 on Tolstoy[39] in which he regarded him as a typical representative of the Russian aristocracy who loved his class and paid little attention to the peasantry. According to Kubikov, Tolstoy evinced a hatred of Napoleon in *War and Peace* because the latter had disturbed the peaceful idyll of landowners' lives.

An unusual feature of Kubikov's work is his taking to task of Tolstoy for being a Russian nationalist who belittled the courage of Napoleon's soldiers. Referring to Marshal Ney's retreat from Smolensk with an army of six thousand pursued by some eighty thousand Russians, Kubikov quotes from *War and Peace* to show that Tolstoy regarded Ney as a coward who deserted his troops. In fact, Kubikov asserts, the marshal fought in the rear of his army and left only when his soldiers, greatly reduced in number, were out of danger. Napoleon, according to Kubikov, also did not leave his soldiers until they were out of danger, yet Tolstoy described his behaviour as "the last degree of baseness." In contrast to Napoleon, Emperor Alexander I is portrayed, as Kubikov puts it, "with all the colors of the rainbow." Kubikov, like Shklovsky, doubted that the war against Napoleon was patriotic in character. He brought to light documents proving that in cities occupied by the French (including Smolensk and Moscow) friendly relations were established between the local population and the invaders, and whole areas in Smolensk province recognized Napoleon's authority.

It is hardly a matter for surprise that, as a former exile to Siberia, Kubikov liked *Resurrection* best of all Tolstoy's works, as it is permeated with criticism of the prerevolutionary order. Indeed, Kubikov seems to have been so impressed by *Resurrection* that, although he had described Tolstoy earlier in his book as "a typical representative of the Russian aristocracy who loved his class," he proceeded to call him "the unmasker of the ruling nobility and the bourgeois-capitalist system of life." Unlike the Formalists, who never lost sight of the artistic content of

Tolstoy's works, Kubikov in his summary totally ignores Tolstoy the writer:

> As a preacher of the new Christian ethics with non-resistance to evil, and as a supporter of conservative peasant ways of life, Tolstoy could not have been acceptable to the revolutionary-minded proletariat and the progressive peasantry."[40]

Another member of the sociological group who wrote a book on Tolstoy was Lvov-Rogachevsky. In this work, *From Country Mansion to Peasant Hut* (1928), he concerns himself with the way of life and personal outlook of Tolstoy the man in relation to the disintegration of the estates of the Russian nobility, while hardly mentioning Tolstoy the artist. The main subjects of his attention were Tolstoy's spiritual crisis and constant striving for moral improvement, which he explains in simple sociological terms. He observes that Tolstoy was not the only rich landowner who completely changed his pattern of life by throwing himself into a "peasant ocean" for spiritual renewal. According to him, many a person born on an aristocratic estate underwent spiritual crises in the course of his life because of injustices in the social structure of tsarist Russia.[41]

Almost everyone in Russia who was writing a book or an article on Tolstoy in the mid-twenties endeavoured to have it published in 1928 while Russia and the world were celebrating the hundredth anniversary of Tolstoy's birth. In Russia, this year also marked the beginning of the final confrontation between the friends and the foes of Tolstoy, the outcome of which was quite obviously going to be decided not by Formalists, sociologists or any other such group, but by the most influential of the critics—the Marxists. The latter occupied the seats of power and would have the last word as to whether Tolstoy was needed in Soviet Russia or not.

One of the most prominent of the Marxist critics, Vladimir Friche, was also the most articulate opponent of Tolstoy's influence in Soviet Russia. Before and during the centennial year he wrote a number of articles on Tolstoy which were published in one volume in 1929.[42] In these articles Friche conducted a one-man crusade against the tendency to "idealize" Tolstoy as an artist, and especially as an ideologist—a process which, he noted with alarm, was beginning even among his Marxist associates. He considered Tolstoy's mentality to be as religious and authoritarian as that of any feudal lord, and to be totally alien to the Soviet spirit. Tolstoy's God was a landowner elevated from the master of an estate to the master of the whole world, declared Friche. He contended that Tolstoy was in 1928 more harmful than he had been before the Revolution. Referring to Tolstoy's teachings, he demanded:

> How can the masses be recruited into the Red Army if the military is un-Christian?

67

What attitude should they adopt toward the Soviet state if any state is evil?... How can they relate to their own and foreign bourgeoisie if one has to love everybody, including enemies?... Can we rally them to build socialism, when socialism, according to Tolstoy, is a devilish invention, a satanic provocation?[43]

Friche emphasized that Lenin would have repeated the warnings he issued in 1911 that Tolstoy's teachings, and especially any attempt to idealize them, would cause "the most immediate and profound harm."

It was Lunacharsky who endeavoured to redress the balance from the Marxist viewpoint. In an article published in the centennial year— probably the most favorable to Tolstoy since the Revolution—Luna- charsky also referred to Lenin, but to completely opposite effect:

We are going to honor in Tolstoy one of the greatest artists of our literature... We are going to honor in him an honest revolutionary who profoundly shook the pillars which supported the then-existing order of society and of the church of the ruling classes... Lenin had expressed an ardent desire to make Tolstoy accessible to everybody, and foresaw that his beneficial influence would be especially strong in the days to come... Tolstoy was for Lenin above all a typical peasant revolutionary.[44]

Although Lunacharsky stated in the same article that the "negative sides" of Tolstoy should not be overlooked even during the jubilee, his standpoint was that the writer should maintain a place in Soviet Russia as a valuable adjunct to the country's cultural life. He did, however, go to extremes in his promotion of Tolstoy when he wrote that Lenin regarded the writer as a "peasant revolutionary." Lenin never actually did, and angry Marxists who thought that Tolstoy was harmful to the general mass of Soviet people were quick to point out the fact. As did Fedor Raskolnikov, a high-ranking party official, who called Lunacharsky's remark "a monstrous distortion of Lenin."[45]

Other persons then prominent within the Party took strong exception to Lunacharsky's views on Tolstoy. The most influential of them was Mikhail Olminsky, a professional revolutionary and publicist who had been in prison for underground activities before 1917. He took part in the October Revolution and subsequently held high positions in the Party, including membership on *Pravda*'s editorial board. After his death in 1933 his ashes were deposited in the Kremlin wall.* In an article which appeared in 1928 in a literary journal of which he was an editor, Olminsky dismissed

---

* The greatest posthumous honor that can be accorded to a person in the Soviet Union is for his body to rest in the mausoleum on Red Square in Moscow. Only Lenin now has this honor, though he shared it with Stalin from 1953 to 1956. The second highest honor is burial beside the walls of the Kremlin. The third is the deposit of the honored person's ashes in the actual wall of the Kremlin, after the removal of a few bricks. The fourth is burial in the ancient Novodevichy Cemetery in Moscow.

War and Peace and *Anna Karenina* as "counterrevolutionary works" on which he had wasted time reading while in prison. He expressed the view that Tolstoy served the forces of reaction not only in his artistic works but also in his publicistic writings, and remarked that if people did not appreciate that fact it was because "Tolstoy very skillfully camouflages his reactionary character and only an ideologically trained communist can unmask it."[46]

Olminsky's article was afterwards reprinted in the magazine *Ogonek* (Little light) along with a statement by its editorial board which was remarkable, in view of the author's high position in the Party:

> The very interesting article of M. Olminsky published by us, in general expresses correctly our party's point of view on the social movement known in the eighties as Tolstoyism. We, however, categorically disagree with Olminsky's assessment of Tolstoy the artist and with his statement that *War and Peace* and *Anna Karenina* are counterrevolutionary works.[47]

Ogonek went on to quote Lenin in order to demonstrate that Tolstoy was, in his artistic works, on the side of the progressive forces. In fighting back, Olminsky had enough power and influence to use the Party's central newspaper, *Pravda*.[48] In its pages he accused *Ogonek* of having quoted only the beginning of one of Lenin's articles. He produced another statement of Lenin to the effect that "Tolstoy's doctrine is certainly utopian, and in content is reactionary in the most precise and profound sense of the term."[49] Olminsky added that Tolstoy was for many years associated with the most infamous, most militant ultra-conservative journal, *Russkii vestnik* (Russian Herald), serving the reactionary forces of Russia. Olminsky's strong condemnation of Tolstoy's artistic and publicistic works was not unexpected. He had created quite a stir with his earlier article, also published in *Pravda,* which amounted to a call to banish Tolstoy from Soviet Russia. Its title, *Lenin or Tolstoy,* in itself indicated the general tone of the writing which was aimed in particular against the approaching jubilee celebrations:

> The publicity about Tolstoy has assumed a purely "American" character, the kind that one can see everywhere in bourgeois countries when they advertise cosmetics or insecticides. You can ask anyone; all communists are outraged by this unrestrained advertising campaign.[50]

If Olminsky thought that most party members would support his efforts to banish Tolstoy from Soviet Russia, he was mistaken. So also was Peter Kogan, a prominent Marxist literary historian. Concerning the polemics then current in Russia to decide whether Tolstoy was "harmful" or "useful", Kogan expressed the view that those Marxists who considered that the writer should be denied recognition had a stronger case, since

Tolstoy had on the whole, and "perhaps unconsciously", supported the system of exploitation.[51] Kogan believed that a substantial majority of Marxist critics were united in bitter and uncompromising disapproval of Tolstoy's expressed attitudes to revolutionary action. Of those Marxists who did not belong to the "substantial majority" he named Lunacharsky and Trotsky. It seems, however, that both Olminsky and Kogan over-estimated the militancy of Marxist groups toward Tolstoy and did not take into account the fact that the "uncompromising disapproval" that some might have felt had gradually mellowed as the years went by.

Contrary to generally accepted belief, the militant RAPP (Russian Association of Proletarian Writers) was favorably disposed toward Tolstoy. Its leading figure, Leopold Averbakh, in his book on cultural revolution[52] urged that proletarian writers should study Tolstoy. Completely ignoring current contentions that the writer's philosophy was harmful and his artistic works reactionary, Averbakh declared that Tolstoy's creative methods were "the most suitable for us".[53] He immediately added that Lenin himself had said that Tolstoy's realism amounted to "the tearing down of all and sundry masks".[54]

Alexander Fadeev, another influential RAPP leader, later to become head of the Writers' Union, referred to Tolstoy in 1928 as a writer who "by his artistic method tried to achieve maximum truth". Fadeev, a dyed-in-the-wool Bolshevik, approached Tolstoy almost with humility, urging his follow proletarian writers to learn from him and the other great realist authors of prerevolutionary Russia. Fadeev ignored all the points upon which as a communist he might have clashed with Tolstoy, remarking only that "Tolstoy did not understand that man was the product of a given social environment".[55] Fadeev demonstrated his literary inclination in his own works. In his work, *The Rout,* a novel published in 1927 which has become a Soviet classic, Fadeev consciously employed techniques used by Tolstoy in *War and Peace*—especially the psychological portrayal of characters and the vivid description of battle scenes.

A major Marxist critic, Alexander Voronsky, in a collection of essays published in 1928, discussed the importance of classical Russian literature both for ordinary readers and for professional authors. He believed that writers could create valuable works only after mastering the artistic methods of Tolstoy and Dostoevsky.[56] He did not, however, have the chance to become an active participant in the struggle for the acceptance of Tolstoy, since he was expelled from the Party the year after his essays appeared. Readmitted in 1931 after a brief exile in Siberia, he was again arrested in 1937 during the Purges and presumably died in a prison camp. Voronsky could have been the first Marxist critic to argue after the Revolution that to learn from the classics of Russian literature—including those of Tolstoy—was not reactionary but vital for the development of Soviet literature. He voiced this opinion as early as 1923, when he was editor of the influential journal *Krasnaya nov'* (Red virgin soil).

By the fall of 1928 almost everyone who had any strong views as to whether Tolstoy could have a place in the new order had had a chance to state his opinion. Only one last thing remained: for the Party itself, as the ultimate authority, to deliver its verdict on the matter. This it did in September, on the eve of the hundredth anniversary of Tolstoy's birth, in the form of an unsigned article in *Pravda*. This ran:

> Tolstoy did not understand the proletarian movement. The revolution was alien to him. For several decades he used all his artistic talent and enormous influence to demonstrate the harm and fruitlessness of revolutionary action, and to suggest to the masses that they should give up the class struggle and not fight violence with violence . . .
>
> Is it right then that the Bolsheviks, who have chosen revolutionary violence, should honor Tolstoy in connection with the hundredth anniversary of his birth? . . . Is it right then that the party, which regards religion as the opium of the people, should publish the complete works of Tolstoy, in which the most reactionary teaching of religion has a very prominent place? . . .
>
> We do not refuse, and we do not think of refusing, Tolstoy's artistic heritage . . . One has to take Tolstoy as he is. We must truly, and without fear, show him to the masses as he is—with all his merits and faults. Tolstoy deserves this".[57]

The style of the writing, with repetitions of "is it right" (pravil'no li), is very close to that of Stalin, who had by this time become the undisputed ruler of Soviet Russia with the eclipse of his principal rival, Trotsky.* Stalin undoubtedly had the ultimate responsibility** for the article and its quite unambiguous conclusion, for only a party member with supreme power could have overruled Olminsky, the "outraged communists" and the "substantial majority" of Marxist critics, and decided the jubilee debate in Tolstoy's favor.

It would be a mistake to think that the decision to accommodate Tolstoy in Soviet Russia was simply a whim of Stalin. It arose out of the realities faced by the country at that time. Hopes for world revolution had been dashed with the departure of Trotsky. Foundations were being laid for a less militant attitude to the outside world in the form of the establishment of diplomatic relations and the conclusion of non-aggression treaties with a number of countries. At the same time, the Stalinist strategy of eliminating Russia's industrial backwardness by "building socialism in one country" was being translated into reality in the form of

---

* Trotsky was in exile at that time and was deported to Constantinople in February 1929 aboard a Soviet steamer.

** That Stalin clearly saw the necessity of Tolstoy's acceptance in Soviet Russia is mentioned in the memoirs of Tolstoy's daughter, Alexandra. She wrote that as early as 1926 when the idea of Tolstoy's jubilee was conceived, it was Stalin who promised money to cover the expenses. (The jubilee committee requested one million rubles.) Alexandra thought that Stalin was indifferent to Tolstoy and looked at the jubilee solely as an opportunity to make propaganda for the Soviet regime abroad.[58]

the first five-year plan. It was in the process of being launched, and was so ambitious that it was going to demand all the physical and spiritual strength of which the country was capable.

In such a situation Russia could hardly afford to expel Tolstoy from its cultural life, for it needed him. This fact could be clearly discerned from the instructions supplied by Lunacharsky's commissariat to cultural workers on how to prepare the Russian people for Tolstoy's jubilee:

> In spite of the fact that Tolstoy was by his class origin alien, and in some respects even hostile, to us, the coming jubilee will have enormous social importance. First, it will allow us to distribute Tolstoy's works among the working masses and thus give them real artistic classical literature . . . and so not only raise their cultural standards but also fight for the purity of our language. Secondly, Tolstoy's works are of great historical value . . . a whole cycle of Russian history . . . is reflected in the writings of our genius."[59]

After these lines, in which Tolstoy was for the first time called "ours" officially in Soviet Russia, the instructions became more businesslike, itemizing twenty works of Tolstoy which were to be recommended reading for the "working masses".

Childhood
Boyhood
Youth
The Cossacks
The Snowstorm
Sevastopol in May
Sevastopol in August
Strider
A Morning of a Landlord
Lucerne
Three Deaths
Polikushka
War and Peace
Anna Karenina
The Power of Darkness
The Fruits of Enlightenment
The Kreutzer Sonata
Master and Servant
Resurrection
Hadji Murat[60]

Not surprisingly, Tolstoy's writings concerning religion and ethics were not included. It is, however, interesting to note that in 1928 Tolstoy's outpourings of patriotic sentiment for the tsarist empire were still somewhat embarrassing, and so his story, *Sevastopol in December,* was excluded from the list. Also excluded was *A Prisoner in the Caucasus,* in which Russian army officers engaged in a war of conquest make derogatory remarks about the natives. The popular story *After the Ball,* in which a Tartar soldier is beaten to death for an attempt to run away from the imperial army, was likewise excluded. Another notable omission was *The Death of Ivan Ilyich,* which might have been regarded as a portrayal of an empty life, hardly of relevance to a people about to embark upon a great plan of industrialization.

Alexander Werth, a keen British observer of the Russian scene, who in 1928 closely followed the events surrounding the centenary of Tolstoy's birth, thought that the Soviet government's attitude toward the writer was "one of the strange paradoxes of present-day Russian life".[61] Werth referred to an article in a weekly bulletin issued by Russia's largest state publishing house in which Tolstoy was described as a great craftsman, at the same time as his ideology, class position and doctrine were demonstrated at great length to be incompatible with communist ideology. Yet, Werth went on to say a few pages further on in the same bulletin, plans were announced for publication of five or six different new editions of Tolstoy's writings, including one which was allegedly to contain practically every word he had ever put on paper.

There is no doubt that this paradox existed, but not for long. References to Tolstoy's spiritual and ideological incompatibility with the Soviet regime were radically reduced after the jubilee year. It should be added that Tolstoy's works themselves were not much in evidence for a few years as far as publication or debates were concerned. When interest in Tolstoy was renewed in the second half of the thirties, allusions to the fact that the writer could have been alien to the existing system were as absent as if they had never existed.

Russia's Giant

It is a matter of speculation today as to what behind-the-scenes activities may have occurred after the debate over Tolstoy's acceptability in Soviet Russia was cut short with the appearance of the article in *Pravda* in the fall of 1928. It is unlikely that persons interested in Tolstoy were actually ordered to cease writing on him with publication in mind. Yet after the harvest of the jubilee year a sharp decrease occurred in the amount of published work on the writer. The largest annotated Soviet bibliography,[1] a three-volume study compiled by Nina Shelyapina and her colleagues, lists only one work on Tolstoy in 1929, two in 1930, two in 1931, and then not a single one for the next four years. It is necessary to mention that, although large, Shelyapina's bibliography is not reliable. Either by oversight or by intent she has omitted important works by authors who have been purged or otherwise removed from the Soviet literary scene, or have expressed views unacceptable to those in control of official research on Tolstoy. For example, in the first volume of her biography, which allegedly lists every work, including newspaper articles, published in Russia between 1917-1958, Shelyapina has "overlooked" the existence of a book that appeared in 1930. That book, written by a trained psychiatrist, Alexander Evlakhov,[2] was potentially more dangerous to Tolstoy's reputation in Soviet Russia than any essay characterizing him as a reactionary aristocrat.

In this work Evlakhov presents information serving, he alleges, to indicate that Tolstoy was a person deeply disturbed mentally and an epileptic from 1867 onward. After undertaking a detailed investigation of the medical history of Tolstoy's parents and grandparents, Evlakhov concluded that they were all abnormal. After a similar examination of Tolstoy's brothers he found Nicholas to be an alcoholic, Sergei a schizophrenic, and Dmitry a mystic who habitually went about dressed in rags.

Evlakhov dismisses Tolstoy's entire ethical system as a reflection of his epilepsy, asserting that he never really cared for anyone and never believed in himself or others, and that his lifetime weakness of bursting out crying without apparent cause was proof of his unbalanced psyche. He considers that even Tolstoy's final departure from his home occurred after an epileptic seizure,* and alleges that the other attempts he made to run away from his family, in 1884, 1895, and 1897, were also consequences of his sickness. Tolstoy's witnessing of an execution by the guillotine during a visit he made to Paris in 1857 is cited as proof of the morbid curiosity he

---

* "Psychomotor epilepsy" would probably be the term used in modern medicine.

had about killing. Evlakhov presents further examples of this curiosity after scrutinizing passages in letters and diaries written by Tolstoy during his army service in the Caucasus and the Crimea. He even supplies gory details of Tolstoy's treatment of wild animals during his hunting trips.

Evlakhov saw the greatest manifestation of the writer's sickness in his contradictory attitudes towards sex and women. Tolstoy's diaries and letters contain many disparaging remarks about the sex act, which he regarded as a dirty display of animal instinct, and about women, whom he was inclined to view as the source of all evils.* Yet, observes Evlakhov, Tolstoy had numerous affairs and even when he suggested to others, including married couples, that they should abstain completely from sexual activity, he continued to demand his own conjugal rights. Most of the support Evlakhov obtained for his diagnosis came from Countess Tolstoy's private diary where the writer's behavior is described, in a number of cases, as heartless and hypocritical. The longest entry to that effect is that for the 20th of November, 1890.

Evlakhov's book must have attracted the attention of the most highly placed figures in Soviet Russia, since no less a person than Lunacharsky wrote a lengthy introduction to it. He warned readers of the book that Evlakhov had a negative attitude toward Tolstoy which served to diminish its value. He nevertheless added that it might not do any harm to pay attention to the analysis of a doctor who opened the public's eyes to some truth about Tolstoy, who had "for long been the subject of much incense burning."[3] Lunacharsky did not attempt to refute Evlakhov's diagnosis of Tolstoy's epilepsy. He did, however, point out that epilepsy and genius often go hand in hand, for which reason the malady had since ancient times been called a "divine sickness". He suggested that somewhere in Evlakhov's book there should be a study of the special relationship between epilepsy and genius. Having gone so far as to call the work "extremely useful," Lunacharsky emphasized that he did not find its conclusions satisfactory. After all, he observed, the study had been written from a narrow, professional point of view, and was in consequence "a half-finished product for Marxist literary historians."

Lunacharsky obviously wrote his introduction to Evlakhov's book with the approval of the Party's leadership; and his remark about Tolstoy having been the subject of incense burning (in which he himself had participated in no small way) suggests that the same leadership thought that praises were being bestowed on the writer a bit too lavishly. The

---

* There had been numerous observations made on Tolstoy's negative atittude towards women by people who knew the writer personally. Even as great an admirer of Tolstoy as Gorky once remarked: "His attitude to women, as far as I can see, is one of irreconcilable hostility. He likes to punish them... Is it the hostility of a man who had not obtained as much happiness as he is capable of, or an enmity of the spirit towards "the humilitating impulses of the flesh"? Whatever it is, it is hostility, and very bitter, as in *Anna Karenina.*"[4]

publication of Evlakhov's book, inevitably disagreeable to anyone feeling reverence for Tolstoy, could have been prevented by a single telephone call from the Kremlin. The fact that it was not made indicates that the study must have fulfilled some specific purpose; to serve, perhaps, as a sop to militant Bolsheviks of Olminsky's type who were outraged at the outcome of the jubilee debates concerning Tolstoy's place in Soviet Russia. It was certainly ideally suited to this purpose, for in dismissing Tolstoy's entire philosophy as the product of a diseased mind, it was bound to strike a chord of agreement in the militants. Furthermore, it was entirely free of political polemics, and therefore could not trigger off any debates in which one Marxist critic would have been pitted against another.

The strange spectacle of a supposedly ardent admirer of Tolstoy suddenly recommending as "useful" a book designed to harm the writer's reputation had a parallel in the action of the well-known literary scholar of the time, Mstislav Tsyavlovsky. A member of the editorial board of the 90-volume jubilee edition of Tolstoy's works, he contributed an introduction to a book of pseudo-reminiscences about the writer by Lev Zilov, published in 1934 and reissued in 1937.[5] This work, which like Evlakhov's, was omitted from Shelyapina's biography, contains forty-one stories, some based on actual events but most purely products of Zilov's imagination. The book could have been an inspired caricature of a genre of mawkish reminiscences about Tolstoy—as its author doubtless intended it to be— had not the man who emerges from the stories been so moronic, hypocritical, and clownish as merely to cause some bewilderment. After all, Tolstoy had written literary masterpieces, and quite a number of highly respected people had known him personally and been impressed by his dignity and intellectual power.

In one of Zilov's stories the elderly Tolstoy was in his Moscow home reading his essay on money to three guests. The essay was embarrassingly senseless and one of the guests, an economist, politely told his host so. Tolstoy at once exploded with anger and stormed out of the room. After some minutes of embarrassing silence, another guest made a remark to the effect that their host was the author of literary gems, whereupon the door opened and Tolstoy, who had been eavesdropping, re-entered and thanked the guest for his remark. Then all three were dismissed. As they walked along the street outside, they were overtaken by a cheerful Tolstoy, clad in a rough sheepskin coat and pulling a hand sledge with a green slop bucket rattling on it as he ran along.[6]

It is remarkable that Tsyavlovsky not only agreed to write an introduction to Zilov's book but in doing so expressed the view that the purpose of the rather earthy stories was to create a "sober view" of their subject and thereby counteract the "icon-like idealization so widespread in the literature about Tolstoy".[7] One is led to wonder about the real reason for Tsyavlovsky's being appointed a member of the editorial board of the

77

jubilee edition of Tolstoy's works.

After Tolstoy had become acceptable in Soviet Russia his influence on proletarian writers was no longer considered to be harmful. It was not only the Bolshevik Fadeev who regarded Tolstoy as a great master; this view was held by a number of other Soviet authors. Among these the most distinguished was Mikhail Sholokhov. In fact, Tolstoy's impact on Sholokhov was seemingly so evident that Soviet critics reproached him for mechanically imitating the great writer in his major work, *Quiet Flows the Don*.* In portraying his characters Sholokhov manifestly sought to achieve the same degree of psychological penetration as Tolstoy did in *War and Peace,* and with considerable success. Sholokhov's hero Gregory is drawn as impressively as Prince Andrei, and his female protagonist, Aksinya, is as remarkable as Natasha. Furthermore, both narratives are structured along family lines. And again, in the epic sections of the two novels, scenes and locations are constantly changing and the military operations, unfolding in vast panoramas, vitally affect Russia's future.

In spite of the general similarities, it is very unlikely that Sholokhov conceived his great novel in imitation of *War and Peace.* The presence of detectable artistic devices of Tolstoy could be explained by the sheer force of the influence the great writer had on subsequent generations of authors. It is interesting that Sholokhov, unlike Fadeev, sought to disclaim any significant influence by Tolstoy on his writing. Whenever the subject of literary impact on his work arose, he would mention several writers in addition to Tolstoy. Asked point-blank in 1937 whether he had been under Tolstoy's influence when he was writing *Quiet Flows the Don,* he gave the answer: "Tolstoy is unattainable . . . all good writers have influenced me."[8] Suggestions made by the critics in the nineteen-twenties that Sholokhov had "borrowed" from Tolstoy never developed into a debate since the young author found himself accused of the more serious misdemeanor of plagiarism or, to be more precise, of having published somebody else's manuscript. To many it seemed incredible that the twenty-one year old author of some rather mediocre stories could have created a masterpiece.

After the publication of the first volume of *Quiet Flows the Don* in 1928, rumors relating to Sholokhov's alleged plagiarism became so persistent that he had to be defended publicly. In March of 1929 a number of influential Marxist critics and writers, including Fadeev and Averbakh, repudiated the charges in *Pravda* with the assertion that Sholokhov was definitely the author of the new work. The rumors nevertheless continued to circulate, and the accusations of plagiarism became more numerous after the publication of Sholokhov's second novel, *Virgin Soil Upturned,* in

---

* There are numerous studies published outside Russia which perceive a link between *War and Peace* and *Quiet Flows the Don.* Many critics obviously share the opinion of the American scholar, Helen Muchnic, that *"Quiet Flows the Don* is full of stylistic and structural echoes of *War and Peace."*[9]

1932. The artistic qualities of this work—especially its second part, which appeared in 1960—were markedly inferior to those of the first novel, yet the author received the country's highest literary award, the Lenin Prize, for it. After the Swedish Academy decided to honor Sholokhov with the Nobel Prize for *Quiet Flows the Don* in 1956, in spite of the novel's having first appeared a quarter of a century earlier, its author's alleged plagiarism was discussed in two books.

The first of these books, published in the West in 1974,[10] was written by a Soviet literary historian who preferred to be known as "D." According to "D," the principal author of *Quiet Flows the Don* was Fedor Kryukov, a Russian writer who had been an officer in the White Cossack army during the civil war and who died of typhus in 1920. Sholokhov is dismissed by "D" as an untalented "co-author," without any resemblance to Tolstoy, who wrote all the weak parts of the novel. This opinion is fully shared by Alexander Solzhenitsyn, who contributed an introduction to "D"'s book.

The other book on the subject of Sholokhov's alleged plagiarism came from the pen of the dissident author, Roy Medvedev. The manuscript of it had been well-known and widely circulated in Russia before it was published in Paris in 1975 under the title *Qui a écrit "Le Don paisible"?* (Two years later it appeared in English entitled *Problems in the literary biography of Mikhail Sholokhov.*) Even though he admits the possibility of another author's existence, Medvedev evinces respect for the talent of Sholokhov, whose contribution to the creation of the epic novel was, in his view, "far more considerable than "D" or Solzhenitsyn believes."[11] Medvedev observed that *The Iliad* and *The Odyssey* had been subjected to textual analysis by computer which proved that both were written by the same author. He went on to suggest that the text of *Quiet Flows the Don* could be similarly analyzed.*

Today, in spite of the sceptical remarks published abroad regarding Sholokhov's authorship of *Quiet Flows the Don,* Soviet critics and literary historians continue to regard him as the writer who comes closest to Tolstoy in contemporary Russian literature. *Quiet Flows the Don* is often mentioned in the same breath with *War and Peace,* and Sholokhov's debt

---

* In 1975, a project to determine the authorship of Sholokhov's novel was initiated by a joint Swedish-Norwegian research group of scholars and computer experts. An article providing a detailed plan of the undertaking came to the attention of Sholokhov himself who invited its author, Geir Kjetsaa, to his house in Russia where the two met in December 1977. Sholokhov denied on that occasion having ever read Kryukov, and expressed the view that the rumors to the effect that he had committed plagiarism were inspired by envy.[12] In 1978 Kjetsaa published a preliminary report (intended to be followed by a detailed one) setting out the results of the computer analysis of selected passages by both Sholokhov and Kryukov. His conclusion was: "Kryukov, as far as language and style are concerned, is much further from the text of the novel than Sholokhov. Furthermore, in a number of cases mathematical statistics can even exclude Kryukov as the author of *Quiet Flows the Don* whereas there is no proof for Sholokhov's exclusion."[13]

to Tolstoy in creating his major novel is an acknowledged fact. As the years have gone by, Russian scholars have managed to find more evidence suggesting the closeness between Sholokhov's and Tolstoy's creative processes. For example, the similarities between the heroine of Sholokhov's novel, Aksinya, and Anna Karenina have been pointed out on a number of occasions. Needless to say, the possibility of any irregularity in the appearance of *Quiet Flows the Don* on the literary scene has not been discussed since the late 'twenties.

Any investigation into the matter of Sholokhov's alleged plagiarism is embarrassing to the Soviet literary establishment, which holds Sholokhov in very high esteem. Indeed, he is widely regarded as the personification of that establishment, being a member of the Soviet Academy, a several-times elected member of the Supreme Soviet, and a personal friend of high-ranking party officials. In 1959 he accompanied the late Nikita Khrushchev on a visit to the United States. *Quiet Flows the Don* is still regarded as the greatest Soviet classic* and has been published in millions of copies and translated into a number of languages. Yet, as Medvedev has observed, Sholokhov is sharing the fate of other Russian winners of Nobel Prizes:

> Every Russian winner of the Nobel Prize has been treated unkindly by fate. The first of our compatriots to win the Nobel Prize was Ivan Bunin, who had emigrated to France following the revolution. The second was Boris Pasternak who was subjected, after the award, to torment and persecution sufficient to make him officially renounce the Prize and the citation. A later winner, Alexander Solzhenitsyn, has been forcibly expelled from his country, in which all his principal works have yet to be published. Finally, Mikhail Sholokhov has had to spend all his life defending himself against charges of plagiarism.[14]

Soviet literary historians occasionally refer to two other writers who openly dared to emulate Tolstoy in the twenties. One is Leonid Leonov, who was in fact far more influenced by Dostoevsky than by Tolstoy; the other, Konstantin Fedin. However, these two writers stood for many years far from the mainstream of Soviet literature, and they had minimal influence on policy concerning it. Their personal attitudes towards Tolstoy were therefore of little consequence for, being outsiders, they were not able to participate in the debate regarding his acceptability in Soviet Russia. Decades later, however, when both had achieved recognition and respect as writers, they played a very important role in "promoting" Tolstoy.

Leonov, regarded as a "fellow traveler" (a non-communist who accommodated himself to the Soviet regime) during the twenties, was sharply criticized for his novel, *The Thief* (1927), in which a former political commissar with the Red forces in the civil war loses faith in the revolution and becomes a criminal. Leonov's subsequent novels and plays, which

---

* It has undergone two drastic revisions—in 1953 and 1956.

dealt with industrial development in the thirties and the war years, were well received and have served to establish his reputation as one of the most talented Soviet writers. In 1957 he was awarded the Lenin Prize for his novel, *Russian Forest.* Three years later he was chosen to deliver the main speech at the Tolstoy memorial meeting, held in the Bolshoi Theater in Moscow. Leonov's speech, from which excerpts are quoted in the introduction of the present study, has become an important indicator of the official view of Tolstoy's importance to the Russians today.

Fedin, like Leonov, was for many years considered alien to the spirit of proletarian literature. He was severely rebuked by Marxist critics for his stories *The Shepherd* and *Transvaal,* both published in 1926, in which he emphasized the positive qualities of individual well-to-do peasants in postrevolutionary Russia. Averbakh called him "the apologist of rich peasantry"[15] and Friche stigmatized him as "a member of the new bourgeoisie."[16] However, in the thirties Fedin established himself as an accomplished writer and he achieved considerable success after the war. In his postwar writings references to Tolstoy occupy a prominent place. Fedin was elected to the Soviet Academy, and headed the Writers' Union from 1971 until his death in 1979.

Tolstoy's name figured briefly in the early thirties in the debates concerning the acceptance of socialist realism by Soviet writers. Socialist realism is a literary doctrine which, in its essentials, requires of writers an ideological commitment. Isaak Nusinov, an eminent Marxist critic who in 1928 put Tolstoy next to Lenin ("Tolstoy and Lenin are the two greatest Russian geniuses, the two greatest geniuses of mankind in centuries"[17]), argued that Tolstoy's psychological methods were alien to socialist realism. Tolstoy's approach, according to Nusinov, served to suggest that man was good as long as he remained an individual, and that when he began to function as a social being deterioration set in immediately. Nusinov advised Russian writers to turn to Balzac and Stendhal who, he considered, had a social approach to the characters in their works.[18] Unfortunately, he paid dearly for his advice to learn from Western writers. In 1947 he was sharply rebuked by Fadeev, the secretary of the Writers' Union, for his observation that Russia's greatest poet, Pushkin, owed much to European literature. He was arrested shortly afterwards and died during a purge of Jewish intellectuals.

At the first congress of the newly created Writers' Union, which took place in 1934, socialist realism was adopted as binding for all members. In the large number of speeches delivered to the congress Tolstoy's name was mentioned only three times. Karl Radek, an internationally known revolutionary who was to be sentenced to imprisonment at a show trial four years later, referred to Tolstoy twice. Dismissing James Joyce's writings as "a heap of dung teeming with worms," Radek told the delegates that "as teachers, Balzac and Tolstoy are enough for us," and that if he were to write novels he "would learn how to write them from Tolstoy and Balzac, not from Joyce."[19] The other mention of Tolstoy to the congress, which was made by Gorky during a speech on Soviet literature, was even more informal than that of Radek. Gorky said simply that Leo Tolstoy's influence on René Bazin, Estaunié, Thomas Hardy (in his *Tess of the D'Urbervilles*) and various other European writers is commonly acknowledged.[20]

Quite evidently, there were no generally accepted attitudes to Tolstoy which could have served as guidance for those carrying out research on him in the early 'thirties. It appeared, furthermore, from the support prominent party members had given to the recently published books of Evlakhov and Zilov that Tolstoy's place in the new Russia was not yet secure. Some of the influential persons who had campaigned vigorously against Tolstoy's acceptance in 1928 were still to be reckoned with. The majority of articles published in the Soviet press in the thirties on Tolstoy reflect the caution and restraint with which the writer was presented to Russian readers. There appeared repetitious interpretations of Lenin's views on Tolstoy in various Soviet periodicals, nearly thirty of them by the end of the decade. One zealot even contrived to describe an occasion when Tolstoy was reading Lenin with great interest,[21] notwithstanding the fact that none of the reputable Russian scholars who painstakingly collect every bit of information on Lenin has ever referred to an instance of Tolstoy reading anything of his. Apart from analyses of Lenin's articles there appeared at that time a number of short studies in which practically all known interests of Tolstoy—music, chess, cycling, vegetarianism, etc.—were referred to without any attempt to relate them to the man as a great writer and thinker.

Putting aside the second part of Eikhenbaum's major work on Tolstoy,[22] it may be said that serious research on Tolstoy in Russia began again in 1936 with the publication of a monograph by Nicholas Gudzy[23]—a scholar who had already established a reputation in the field of old Russian literature. Gudzy became interested in Tolstoy's later works in 1928, with particular reference to *Resurrection*. His monograph represented a great step forward, since, being replete with references to archival material, its approach was truly literary. The good reception it received served to indicate that conditions were ripe for scholars to pay serious attention to Tolstoy again. Gudzy followed up the work with numerous other studies, most of them concerning Tolstoy's manuscripts.

In 1936, there also appeared the fourth and final volume of the Soviet edition of the diary of Countess Tolstoy, which dealt with the last year of her husband's life.* It is common knowledge that the Tolstoys did not have an entirely harmonious partnership. After their marriage in 1862 they enjoyed a happy relationship for many years. However, the Countess began

---

* The first volume had been published in 1928.

to have serious differences with her husband towards the end of the eighteen-seventies when he was undergoing a deep spiritual crisis and contemplating radical changes in the family's way of life. The Countess, fearing that their numerous children might be deprived of a privileged aristocratic upbringing, violently opposed her husband's plans. As the years went by the clashes between them became more frequent and more intense. Tolstoy's children, relatives, friends, and disciples all became involved in the conflict and quite understandably took sides.

Numerous books have been written over the years, and published both in and out of Russia, by witnesses to the stormy scenes between Tolstoy and his wife as well as by persons who only knew of them at second hand. The judgments made in these books invariably fall into one of three categories: that it was Tolstoy's egoism, idiosyncratic behavior or even genius that poisoned his married life and led eventually to his forsaking his home; that it was the Countess who was insensitive to Tolstoy's spiritual needs and, being mentally unbalanced, made Tolstoy's life unbearable in Yasnaya Polyana; or that there were no guilty parties, the marital misery of the Tolstoys having been caused by destiny, in the hands of which both were but puppets.

For some reason, the Countess felt compelled to make public intimate details of her relationship with her husband. Immediately after his death she embarked upon a compilation of the letters Tolstoy wrote to her during their married life, which she published in 1913.[24] The letters document the years of happiness and also enable the reader to obtain more than just a glimpse of the burden of "being married to a genius and a great man."[25] The diary of the Countess was an entirely different sort of record. In it she explicitly represented herself as Tolstoy's victim during his later years. It may be presumed that she would have modified certain entries in the diary had she been alive when it was eventually published, since some of the observations entered in it are so uncomplimentary to Tolstoy as to necessarily cause embarrassment to many who were devoted to him. When the diary was reviewed in 1939 in *Literaturnoe nasledstvo* (Literary heritage), a publication of the Soviet Academy, it was characterized as "the writings of a hysterical woman." It is interesting to note that it was Tolstoy himself whom the Russians tended to blame for his wife's hysteria: "it is known that Tolstoy's mistrustful and unbalanced temperament, the result of numerous ordeals he had gone through, caused Sophie Andreevna to become mentally ill."[26]

This opinion radically changed, however, when the diary of the Countess was reissued in 1978. In the lengthy introduction to it, which expressed the official view on the writer, Tolstoy was absolved of any responsibility for the unbalance of his wife's mind. There were allegedly two reasons for that unbalance, the first being a death in the family:

Among the many factors making the writer's family life unhappy there was one tragic one, the death of his seven-year-old son, Vanechka, who was loved by all. This stunning blow crushed Sophie Andreevna, pushed her to the limits of despair, robbed her of any interest in life, and increased her nervous tension and hysteria.[27]

The second reason for the mental state of the Countess which was put forward was the influence of Vladimir Chertkov who, towards the end of Tolstoy's life, was not only the writer's closest collaborator but was also privy to many of his intimate thoughts and plans, which even the Countess did not know. Chertkov, according to the current view, always pitted Tolstoy against the members of his family circle, and disapproved of any display of patience and gentleness by him towards the Countess as definite symptoms of mental disorder developed in her. The introduction states that:

Chertkov's aggressive actions and his interference in Tolstoy's family affairs greatly complicated the writer's life and were burdensome to him, even though the spiritual communication he had with the friend who shared his ideas meant a lot to him. Knowing the existence of Tolstoy's intimate world yet being excluded from it caused Sophie Andreevna's morbid jealousy, suspicion and mistrust to increase to extremes.[28]

Chertkov was a respected figure in postrevolutionary Russia, even though he was a descendant of one of Russia's most ancient and aristocratic families, and he remained a convinced Tolstoyan until the end of his life. In September 1920, he was received in the Kremlin by Lenin himself, who allegedly asked him to make an inventory of all available Tolstoy manuscripts. In 1928 he was appointed editor-in-chief of the 90-volume jubilee edition of the writer's works, of which seventy-two volumes had been published under his supervision before he died in 1936. It was known in Russia that Tolstoy and Chertkov had been close friends for twenty-seven years. The 928 letters that Tolstoy sent to Chertkov fill five volumes of the writer's complete works. Because of the intimate relationship which existed between the two men, those engaged in research on Tolstoy in Soviet Russia have always been at pains to be respectful to Chertkov's memory. Therefore, even if a scholar came to the conclusion that Chertkov's influence had been negative in some respect, he always weighed his words carefully. One is led to speculate upon what could have induced the literary authorities, in 1978, to represent Chertkov as the evil spirit of the Tolstoy household and apply the words "despot" and "fanatic" to him. After all, the Countess was quite blunt in her diary about the main source of her unhappiness: it was the change in the behavior and attitude of her husband towards her. Chertkov's interference in her life was but a byproduct of that change, so it is hardly fair to represent him as the destroyer of the Tolstoys' family peace.

The first major Soviet contribution to research on Tolstoy was a study entitled *Leo Tolstoy*, which appeared in 1939 in the form of two successive issues of *Literaturnoe nasledstvo*. The opening remarks of the introduction provided by the publication's editorial board reflected the fact that research on Tolstoy was no longer characterized by the aimlessness and hesitation evident in the decade after 1928. They indicated that the writer was now regarded as an unassailable giant of Russian and world literature, and as such not to be made the subject of carping remarks about his "utopian" or "reactionary" doctrine. The editors stated that:

> Tolstoy occupied a special place in the history of world literature. A genius of the artistic word, the greatest realist who gave a historical portrayal of Russian life, the mighty unmasker of the autocracy and the church—Tolstoy raised the world importance of Russian culture to lofty heights. Thanks to Tolstoy's activities, Russian culture, in Lenin's words, represented a step forward in the artistic development of the whole of mankind.[29]

A change in the Soviet attitude to Tolstoy is evident in this statement. In 1928, the debate concerned Tolstoy's acceptability in Soviet Russia itself. Now, some ten years later, that acceptability was plainly no longer in question, and Tolstoy's special place in world literature was being emphasized. However, it was not until later that the assessment of Tolstoy's influence in the world developed into a major trend. In 1939, the two main objectives of research on Tolstoy, as perceived by the scholars of the Soviet Academy, were still to be pursued in Russia itself. They were the analysis of Tolstoy's works with reference to articles by Lenin, and the publication of all archival material connected with Tolstoy.

The first of the two special issues of *Literaturnoe nasledstvo* contained penetrating studies by recognized literary experts, including one by Eikhenbaum. The second volume was taken up by variants of draft copies of Tolstoy's works, his letters, and reminiscences by Tolstoy's contemporaries. The scholarly superiority of the first volume over the second is quite evident, yet the former is not listed in Soviet bibliographical compendia. Shelyapina includes the second volume in her bibliography without a hint of the existence of the first.

The reason for the "disappearance" of the first of the two volumes was the presence in it of an article by the internationally renowned Hungarian Marxist philosopher-critic, Georg Lukacs, who was at that time living and working in Moscow. The article constituted a very illuminating study of Tolstoy, yet it evoked a storm of indignation. Lukacs regarded Tolstoy's artistic development as having taken place under the influence of writers of the European literary mainstream—in particular, the great realists of the eighteenth and nineteenth centuries such as Fielding, Defoe, Balzac and Stendhal.[30] He obviously had not realized that such a view would be vigorously opposed by those firmly convinced that Tolstoy grew out of the Russian soil. In several of his statements Lukacs sounded very much like

Eikhenbaum in the twenties. However, the former eminent Formalist refrained, in his own article in the ill-fated issue, from pointing out any foreign influences in Tolstoy's work, and treated him entirely as a Russian writer in his own native environment. Lukacs for his part looked upon *War and Peace* with its free-flowing style and calm and measured development of action as having something in common with the village idylls to be found in the great English novels of the eighteenth century.[31] He also regarded Tolstoy as the last of the great writers of the bourgeois-realist school with its line of descent from Cervantes to Balzac.

Such attitudes to Tolstoy were manifestly at odds with those then acceptable in Russia. Lukacs nevertheless went on to indicate, in words which must have had a pre-1928 ring to his Russian readers, that Tolstoy's philosophy could in no way be reconciled with socialist ideology:

> Tolstoy's world outlook is deeply permeated with reactionary prejudices...Tolstoy understood very poorly the historical essence of capitalism and did not understand the proletarian revolutionary movement at all.[32]

Lukacs had been living in Austria at the time of the great debate on Tolstoy, and so must have failed to realize that the attitudes of Russian scholars doing research on Tolstoy had changed to such a degree that statements such as those he made, whatever their ultimate validity, were no longer acceptable. The most vociferous of the opponents of Lukacs were the critics, Mark Serebryansky and Valery Kirpotin, who contended that the Hungarian was trying to demonstrate that reactionary views went hand in hand with Tolstoy's literary talent, and such a notion amounted to a distortion of Marxism-Leninism. The implication was quite clear: Tolstoy's views were not reactionary, since he had created masterpieces.

Lukacs was a Marxist of impeccable scholarship and so it was quite out of the question for anyone in Russia at that time to seek to prove that he was mistaken in his pronouncements about the "reactionary" nature of Tolstoy's views. He had, furthermore, been alluding to Lenin in the offending statement, whose repudiation was therefore almost impossible. To apply the term "reactionary" to the great national writer caused much offense in Russia but, nevertheless, eighteen years had to pass before Lukacs was challenged in his assessment of Tolstoy's views. In 1957 Mikhail Khrapchenko questioned the validity of Lukacs' statement that Tolstoy's outlook was deeply reactionary. He declared that "without separating Tolstoy the artist from Tolstoy the thinker, Lenin by no means regarded Tolstoy's views as reactionary on the whole—he found them many-sided."[33] What Lukacs might have made of this statement is hard to tell. He was in prison at the time for his participation in the Hungarian uprising of 1956, and so was in no position to make any comment.

Khrapchenko's article was followed by a stream of studies by other Soviet critics who singled out Lukacs for attack on the grounds of his alleged distortions of Lenin's views and his promotion of "revisionism in esthetics." After his release from prison, Lukacs simply ignored his Soviet critics, even though he continued with his interest in Russian literature. He wrote two essays on Alexander Solzhenitsyn,whom he called "heir not only to the best tendencies in early socialist realism, but also to the great literary tradition—above all of Tolstoy and Dostoevsky."[34] That judgment he based on Solzhenitsyn's longer novels, publication of which has never been permitted in the Soviet Union; in consequence, he fell into even more official disfavor in that country.

After Lukacs died, in 1971, the attacks on him became less numerous, and would appear to have ceased altogether in 1975 after the publication of an article by Konstantin Lomunov, in which Lukacs was taken to task for what he had written in 1939 in *Literaturnoe nasledstvo*. Even on this occasion, however, the criticism was not made at a scholarly level or, apparently, with any close reference to what Lukacs had actually written:

> In his article on Tolstoy and the development of realism, Lukacs compared the great Russian writer to French novelists and came to the conclusion that Tolstoy as an artist was much lower than Balzac or Stendhal. Why? Because, Lukacs indicated, Tolstoy looked at reality with the eyes of the ignorant, exploited peasantry.[35]

Lukacs, who held Tolstoy's artistic talent in very high regard, never said this. Moreover, any student of Lukacs knows that it was never his practice to assign writers to "lower" or "higher" categories of importance.

Indignation over Lukacs' 1939 article about Tolstoy was in reality indicative of the existence of a compelling reason to disagree publicly with one of the greatest intellects of the international communist movement. The article, as submitted for publication by Lukacs a year earlier, had been accepted by an editorial board consisting of several ideologically tested Tolstoy experts, and so it may be inferred that the views Lukacs expressed in it had then been officially acceptable, and certainly not considered to constitute "a distortion of Marxism-Leninism." Had the article indeed been objectionable, it certainly would not have been printed in such a distinguished publication, or anywhere else in the USSR. Implicit in the situation is the fact that there occurred a fundamental change in official Soviet attitudes to Tolstoy in 1939 or shortly thereafter. There is little doubt that the change had to do with the anticipated outbreak of war with Germany.

Several countries had already been ravaged, and the Soviet leaders must have realized that it was only a matter of time before the USSR became involved in a terrible struggle. It was accordingly of vital importance to raise the patriotic spirit of the population and Tolstoy was the ideal agent for doing so. He had not only described Russia's earlier fights against its enemies with superb mastery, but had risked his own life in the course of five years' service in the Russian army. The Soviet establishment proceeded, therefore, to extol the patriotism that Tolstoy had demonstrated by his own conduct and with his own pen. If, however, the great writer was to become the embodiment of Russia's power to withstand a foreign invasion, it was by implication imperative that all suggestions—no matter how intelligently they might be made—that he had been indebted to the West, or could not be associated ideologically with the existing system of government, should be suppressed forthwith.

One of the first indications of Tolstoy's new role was made through a revised official attitude to his story *Sevastopol in December*. This writing provides an outpouring of patriotic sentiment unmatched even in *War and Peace*. In it Tolstoy went so far as to describe the masses of serfs in uniform who stuck doggedly to military duty while being mown down by enemy fire, and made them respond to their aristocrat general, who asked them to sacrifice themselves, with a joyful cry of "we will die, hurrah!" This high-pitched patriotic exaltation of tsarist Russia by Tolstoy had always been a source of mild embarrassment to the Soviets during the earlier prewar period. It was almost apologetically that Russian scholars would quote passages from a letter that Tolstoy sent to his brother Sergei from the battle zone and explain that the writer had been carried away by the powerful wave of patriotic enthusiasm which swept through Russia during the Crimean War. *Pravda*'s critic, David Zaslavsky, observed in 1933 that Tolstoy's soldiers and sailors, the "heroic defenders" of Sevastopol, had been well-drilled depersonalized slaves, and that his artistic truth was in reality a glaring historical lie.[36] Viktor Shklovsky, writing in 1936, considered that though the story *Sevastopol in December* glorified Russian arms in lavish terms, Tolstoy did not present a true picture of the Crimean War, lacking as he did both respect for the soldiers who had fought in it and the ability to speak out frankly.[37]

By the end of the decade, remarks critical of *Sevastopol in December* were not permitted to appear in print. The distinction between tsarist and Soviet Russia and the unbridgeable gap which had existed between officers and ordinary soldiers in the imperial army—both previously so much emphasized by Soviet historians—were either being glossed over or simply ignored, and they have been disregarded ever since. Thus was *Sevastopol in December* given a firm new lease as a moving, unperishable evocation of Russian patriotism transcending political systems. In this process Tolstoy's own participation in the Crimean War was "rediscovered" and he became "the great patriot" of innumerable articles. Even his part in punitive actions against the mountain tribes of the Caucasus during the conquest of that region, which he himself considered in his later years to have been shameful, came to be regarded by Soviet historians as a period of distinction in Tolstoy's military career.

Tolstoy's other two stories relating to the siege of Sevastopol offer little to stir up patriotic fervor, for the writer's exaltation over Russian military prowess in the Crimea had already run its course by the time he wrote them. He had quickly come to understand the ugly reality of the war, and the tone of his writing changed accordingly. He felt it was out of place to talk about patriotism in relation to "hundreds of mutilated, freshly bleeding bodies," and his main concern had become to express the "truth" about the slaughter. Since Tolstoy had great trouble with the tsarist censors* in regard to the publication of his "truth," his second Sevastopol story, *Sevastopol in May,* came to be regarded as a condemnation of war in general, stripped as it was of all its romantic and heroic embellishments. Tolstoy further showed in this story that many Russian officers at Sevastopol were motivated to fight not by patriotism, but by vanity and hopes of quick promotion.

In some Western studies of Tolstoy the opinion has been expressed that after witnessing the slaughter the writer consoled himself with the thought that the Russians were acting in self-defence.[38] This view is based on the following sentence from *Sevastopol in May:*

> We must at least take consolation in the thought that we did not begin the war, that we are defending our country—our native land.[39]

These words were never written by Tolstoy. They were added to the story by Ivan Panaev, the editor of *Sovremennik,* to placate the censors. Tolstoy recognized the necessity of Panaev's insertion but he detested it. He professed that each time he read the story he would have preferred "a hundred strokes by the rod than to see those lines."[40] He instructed his translators to exclude Panaev's phrase; nevertheless, it appeared in the first English translation of the story, which was published in New York in 1887 with an enthusiastic introduction by William Howells, an admirer of Tolstoy. The phrase has also appeared in subsequent English and other Western translations, but it is absent in Russian editions published after 1880. In that year Tolstoy finally managed to eliminate the hateful words since they were obviously not reconcilable with the philosophy he had by then adopted of not countering evil with evil. Panaev's insertion was never included in any post-revolutionary edition of the work—even the jubilee. A discrepancy therefore continues to exist between the texts read in Russia and the English translation of the story.

In November 1855, Tolstoy was posted from the war theater to St. Petersburg, where he completed the final installment of his Sevastopol stories. It concerns the withdrawal of the Russian army from Sevastopol

* It is estimated that over one-third of the full text of *Sevastopol in May* was eliminated by the censors.

The story appeared unsigned in the September of 1855 issue of *Sovremennik* under the title *A spring night* (Vesennyaya noch'). The editors were embarrassed to add Tolstoy's name or initials to a story so extensively maimed by censorship.

and the capture of the fortifications of the city by the Anglo-French forces.*
Tolstoy's contemporaries felt embarrassment and anger (in the first of the
three stories the soldiers had sworn to die rather than surrender the city)
upon reading his account of the end of the siege. Soviet critics, commenting
on the story on the eve of the German invasion, did not dwell on these
sentiments, but singled out the incompetence of the tsarist military
command, as alluded to by Tolstoy, as the principal cause of the retreat in
the Crimea. They affirmed, though, that the action of defending Sevastopol caused so much loss and damage to the other side that the outcome
could not really be regarded as a disaster. Today this view is firmly
established in Soviet writings about the Crimean War.[41]

After Germany invaded the Soviet Union in June 1941, Tolstoy's
descriptions of the defense of Russia against its enemies in earlier conflicts
began to come off the presses in a veritable cascade.

> Within three weeks after the outbreak of hostilities *Book Annals* reported the
> publication of four reissues of Tolstoy. The first of these was 150,000 copies of *Tales of
> Sevastopol,* the story of the heroic defence of that fortress during the Crimean War—a
> collection of tales destined in 1941 to give new hope to the badly shattered Soviet
> divisions, some of them perhaps defending the very same city of Sevastopol. Almost
> overnight the *Pravda* plant printed 150,000 copies of the portion of *War and
> Peace* ... where Tolstoy describes the courage and effectiveness of the peasant guerillas
> fighting Napoleon's troops in 1812. The Children's Publishing House produced 50,000
> copies of the same chapter... Finally, the State Publishing House printed 100,000
> copies of the description in the same novel of the battle of Borodino, the one that
> marked the turning point in the Franco-Russian war.[42]

Strangely, not a single recognized Soviet writer was considered to
have produced works as important for the country's defense as those of the
aristocrat who had died in 1910. No passionate descriptions of Red
victories in the civil war, so abundant in the literature of the post-
revolutionary period, were permitted to compete with Tolstoy's masterfully drawn war scenes in instilling love for the homeland. The great
writer's artistic talent reigned supreme, and his patriotic stories, detached
from any political ideology, became more popular than ever among the
Russians. Not only was Tolstoy the most published author in Russia in
1941, but his name began to be used with the epithet "the great" (velikii),
which had been reserved for Stalin for some time. Other great figures of
Russian history such as Admiral Nakhimov, Field-Marshal Suvorov and
Saint Alexander Nevsky were glorified again, but never to such a degree as
to eclipse Tolstoy. Not a single dissenting voice was heard against his newly
acquired status. Even Kubikov, who in 1928 had ridiculed him for his
Russian nationalism and criticized his portrayal of Russia's enemies as
unfair, deemed it necessary to speak out in positive terms about the

---

* Entitled *Sevastopol in August 1855,* it was the first of Tolstoy's works that appeared under
his full name, Count Leo Tolstoy, rather than under his initials, L.N.T.

patriotic content of Tolstoy's works.[43]

Besides the appearance of mass editions of Tolstoy's works, other signs pointed to the writer's full return to the national scene. In March 1942 the country's most prestigious theatre, the Maly, staged the play *The Patriotic War of 1812* based on *War and Peace*. Prokofiev completed his opera *War and Peace* in 1943* and it was given its first performance the following year. It has remained popular in Russia since. Tolstoy's presence was felt even in the battle areas. Messages were received from beseiged Leningrad, where several hundred lives were being lost daily to cold, hunger and enemy shells, that 100,000 copies of *War and Peace* had been published and *Anna Karenina* given a stage performance. There were reports of copies of Tolstoy's works having been found on the bodies of Red Army men, especially during the new siege of Sevastopol. There were accounts that army commissars read passages from Tolstoy to their men in the front lines, and continued at the soldiers' insistence to do so even when enemy guns began to fire. Also serving to bolster national determination were newspaper photographs of the ruins of newly-liberated Yasnaya Polyana.**

The episodes of war in which Tolstoy's name was invoked were numerous, and they had a tremendous emotional impact on the Russians. Tolstoy became very close to the Russians, since he was their mighty ally in the war in which Russia's very existence was at stake. As the fighting went on, Tolstoy's name became synonymous with Russia, and in the bloody battles of Russia's conflict with Germany the process of Tolstoy's acceptance in his homeland was completed by history.

The emotional associations of Tolstoy with Russia's war-time experiences had a profound effect on the official evaluation of the writer. Studies depicting him as the greatest Russian author were gradually superseded by writings in which he was seen as the world's greatest and the inspirer of many authors in other countries. Since Russia's influence was vastly expanded as a result of her victory in the war, the assertions of Soviet literary experts that Tolstoy had a uniquely high position in the cultural

---

* Two other operas have been inspired by works of Tolstoy: Nicholas Strelnikov's *The Fugitive,* based on the story *What For?* and first performed in Leningrad in 1933 (it has not proved successful); and an opera by V. Rubin, based on *Sevastopol Stories,* which was performed in Novosibirsk in 1970 and in Moscow the following year. In addition to the operas two ballets have also been composed: one of them—based on the story *After the Ball*—was coldly met by the critics when performed in Minsk in 1971, but the other—Rodion Shchedrin's *Anna Karenina*—was so well received when performed at the Bolshoi Theater in 1972 that it was included in the repertoire of that theater when it toured Italy two years later.

** Although Yasnaya Polyana was seriously damaged when it was fought over and occupied, its library escaped damage, in no small measure because of the solicitude of the German military authorities, according to a recent statement by a Russian Tolstoy scholar.[44] Of 15,000 volumes, some extremely rare and valuable, only four were found to be missing when an inventory was taken after the Germans left.

history of mankind went hand in hand with the country's newly found role in international affairs.

One of the most prolific literary historians investigating Tolstoy's contribution to the literature of a number of countries is Tamara Motyleva. In a study published in 1943, she claimed that Tolstoy had significantly influenced literary trends in the West. In the following year she provided a list of Western authors whose works were inspired to a great extent by the writer,[45] and a further statement of her views on the world importance of Tolstoy appeared in 1946.[46] A specialist on Romain Rolland, Motyleva received a crushing blow in 1948 when she was accused of being a "cosmopolite" ally of the bourgeois West and dismissed from all her positions, including a senior post at Moscow University and one at the Gorky Institute of World Literature. She must have had an inkling of what was about to befall her, since the articles she wrote in 1947 and 1948 were frenzied attacks on American, British, Swiss* and French critics of Tolstoy. In 1948 she even publicly rebuked three of her countrymen, the authors of a school textbook, for "misinterpretation of *War and Peace.*"[47] Motyleva was spared and merely had to remain in professional limbo for two years. As soon as she was out of danger she renewed her earlier efforts to work on Tolstoy's international reputation with even greater vigor.

Motyleva's principal published work, a comprehensive study of Tolstoy's world significance, appeared in 1957. Although a landmark in Soviet research on Tolstoy, it is not a scholarly work, as it contains many unsupported statements and drags Tolstoy's name into the sterile debates of the cold war. On the first page of the chapter of this work which deals with America, one reads that "the roots of American literature are to be found not only in English literature but in Russian as well. The traditions of American literature are defined by Tolstoy, Turgenev and Chekhov."[48] In support of this rather dogmatic statement, Motyleva cites an article in *Literaturnaya gazeta* (The Literary Gazette), the newspaper of the Writers' Union, whose author claimed to have heard it from the American playwright, Lilian Hellman. On the following page Motyleva states that:

> Tolstoy began to attract the attention of American men of literature from the mid-1880s onwards. This attention became especially strong at the turn of the century when articles of Tolstoy critical of imperialism, and in particular, of the aggression of the United States against Cuba and the Phillipines appeared in the foreign press.[49]

According to Motyleva, the source of this declaration was a study by the

---

* For example, Motyleva dismissed the book *Tolstoi vivant* (Genève, 1945) by Maurice Kuez, the former Swiss tutor of one of Tolstoy's grandsons, as "bourgeois slander on Russian literature."[50] Kuez' "slander" was writing in reverential terms about Tolstoy's doctrine of non-resistance and his placement of the moral perfection of an individual person higher than participation in social struggle.

Soviet critic Alexander Shifman, published in 1954, in which Tolstoy's alleged principal function was to be "the unmasker of world imperialism."[51] Shifman's writing is a typical example of the worst literary excesses of the cold war period in the Soviet Union, and no Russian scholar with a serious interest in Tolstoy would use it as source material.* Motyleva's poorly selected sources of information, taken together with a large number of quite unsupported statements that she made in the process of intemperately attacking the so-called enemies of Tolstoy abroad, did much to harm the reputation of her 1957 study. She appeared unable to grasp—or else considered it inexpedient to exhibit any awareness of—the simple truth that in Western countries statements about Tolstoy, whether favorable or unfavorable, are not controlled by political establishments.

An unprecedented number of writings on Tolstoy appeared in Russia in 1960 to mark the fiftieth anniversary of his death. In this year the annual "harvest" of items on Tolstoy, from important research works to newspaper articles, which was 400 to 500 in the nineteen-fifties, jumped to 1,500, a numerical record likely to remain unsurpassed for years to come. Such a mass of writings reflected both domestic adulation of Tolstoy carried to the point of excess and the trend to represent him as the most popular writer in the world.

However, a delay occurred in the production of the most important of the contributions due to appear in 1960, and it was not published until a year later. This was another two-part issue of *Literaturnoe nasledstvo* devoted entirely to Tolstoy. The first two entries in it took the form of reproductions of addresses which had been delivered at public meetings and concerned, respectively, the writer's importance at home and abroad. The first address had been given by the author Leonid Leonov in the Bolshoi Theater. Highly emotional, it was intended to demonstrate how dear Tolstoy was to the Russians. The second address, dealing with Tolstoy the artist, had been delivered in Venice in 1960 by the critic Vladimir Ermilov before an international gathering convened in honor of the writer. The theme of Ermilov's address was that Tolstoy was, more than ever before, an invaluable asset to the whole of mankind. Like many of his colleagues in similar circumstances, Ermilov carried his message to extremes, and his address contained a few statements which were so dramatic in nature as to necessarily be questioned even by those with the greatest respect for Tolstoy, as the following examples indicate:

---

* That times change even in Russia has been demonstrated by the fact that a book Shifman wrote six years later, in which he investigated Tolstoy's role as "unmasker of bourgeois culture," was not deemed suitable for publication in Moscow or Leningrad. It was issued by the Tula state publishing house of which Shifman was an editorial board member. Only one review appeared of what was in effect a political attack on the U.S.A.—in a Tula newspaper.

Tolstoy was the only writer in world literature who could create a novel portraying human happiness.[52]

Anna Karenina is the only tragedy in world literature which by its significance and artistic strength can be compared to Shakespeare's *Hamlet*.[53]

No one raised man and human personality to such heights as Tolstoy.[54]

Such declarations apart, Ermilov's address was a remarkable a-chievement, being completely free of attacks against the imagined enemies of Tolstoy abroad, and emphasizing the role the writer could possibly play in uniting mankind for the preservation of peace.

Over thirty Soviet scholars contributed to the same issue of *Literaturnoe nasledstvo*. Their articles represented Tolstoy research of a very high academic order. Even Motyleva struck a note of restraint. Her article, which was concerned with Tolstoy in relation to contemporary Western literature, could have been published by any university press in the world. Taken as a whole, this collective study is hardly marred by political cliché, and constitutes one of the most objective publications about Tolstoy ever to have appeared in the U.S.S.R. It should not be forgotten that 1961 was a year in which the so-called "thaw," which followed Stalin's death, was very palpable. Politico-literary controls were then so relaxed that even Alexander Solzhenitsyn decided to submit his explosive manuscript, *One Day in the Life of Ivan Denisovich,* for publication. The overall easing of tensions was definitely reflected in the field of research on Tolstoy.*

It is useful to mention at this point that a significant distinction exists in the field of Tolstoy research in the U.S.S.R. between those specialists who concern themselves with the writer in relation to Russia itself and those who study his influence abroad. The former group includes some highly respected and influential scholars, some of them members of the Soviet Academy, whose approach to Tolstoy is perhaps conservative, but very thorough. However, out of the thousands who write on Tolstoy in his own land only a few can hope to achieve eminence. This is because works of domestic origin about the writer are so abundant that only a scholar with a brilliant intellect who is prepared to labor painstakingly for years in libraries and archives can hope to produce a study of some aspect of his

---

* The easing of political controls over literary life in Russia in 1961 is likely to have contributed to the appearance in print of an unusual doctoral dissertation, concerning the contacts Tolstoy had with English realist writers. It was written by E. Zinner, a member of staff at a teachers' college in Irkutsk in Siberia. The unusual characteristic of the work is its consistently friendly and relaxed attitude towards England where "Tolstoy is known and his talent appreciated."[55] Zinner of course endeavors to demonstrate Tolstoy's influence at every opportunity, but he does so in a dispassionate manner, without regarding those whose views he disagrees with as enemies of the Soviet state. Zinner's presentation is very impressive, and it is difficult to imagine that anyone in Russia could have more knowledge of Tolstoy's contacts with English authors than he evinces.

The fact that parts of Zinner's dissertation appeared in 1940 indicates that his work was completed a long time ago, and was published when it was least likely to create controversy.

work which has a ring of originality.

The other group, the scholars who write about Tolstoy's status abroad, are still not very numerous. This fact should, on the face of it, facilitate the establishment of a scholarly reputation in the field, but in reality the activity is highly susceptible to fluctuations in the climate of international politics. Since the carrying out of literary research involving Western countries is a highly coveted activity in the Soviet Union, it is scarcely a matter for surprise that some of the people involved in it seek zealously to match their findings to current political attitudes. Soviet literary experts specializing in Western studies on Tolstoy have another handicap. When they see fit to criticize Western scholars, as is often the case, they discover that they have phantom opponents. Except for a few passing remarks they may make, Western scholars generally ignore the Soviet experts and even those who have been singled out as targets for attack do not deign to react in kind. The absence of reaction, which would seemingly be of advantage to the Soviet experts, is in practice very harmful to them. They never know whether a Western scholar they have subjected to criticism agrees with their remarks, considers them brilliant, or dismisses them as foolish. In consequence, the intellectual satisfaction that comes from a discussion with another scholar who offers new arguments to reinforce his case does not come to them. In the absence of any exchanges of this type a Soviet expert may lose his sense of proportion to the point where he is no longer regarded as a useful member of the world's academic community.

Whatever the pitfalls may be for those Russians who investigate Tolstoy's influence abroad, it is a result of their activities that research on Tolstoy is becoming more and more part of the international academic scene. This development should be welcomed in any country since Tolstoy still remains a giant figure in the world's culture. According to data collected by UNESCO in both 1957 and 1965, Tolstoy is the world's foremost author on the basis of the number of translations of his works and the number of languages into which his writings are translated.[56]

In 1962 only one monograph was published on Tolstoy in Russia.[57] In the following year, however, interest in the writer increased again with the release of Sergei Bondarchuk's film *War and Peace,* which was highly praised not only in the U.S.S.R. but abroad as well. Important contributions to Tolstoy research were made by Boris Bursov, Vladimir Lakshin, and Viktor Shklovsky, all investigating the writer's importance in his homeland.[58]

It was Tolstoy's influence in other countries which again received attention in the mid-sixties, a fact which was made evident by the appearance in 1965 of a two-volume issue of *Literaturnoe nasledstvo* devoted to this subject. The material published in the two volumes embraces the period between 1856 and 1960, and the contributors—who were from sixty countries—included thirty-seven from the West. The first of the volumes opened with an article by Lomunov, who has become a leading Soviet expert on Tolstoy's prestige abroad, entitled *World Authority* (Vsemirnyi avtoritet). In it Lomunov listed, more or less in chronological order, the distinguished men of culture, science and politics who thought very highly of Tolstoy. He also mentioned a few who did not, including one president of the United States—Theodore Roosevelt.*

Lomunov's article was followed by an introduction to a collection of observations about Tolstoy made by writers of various countries, written by Motyleva. She was her old self again, bluntly stating that "we are interested here above all in the literary aspect of the international ideological struggle connected with Tolstoy's heritage."[59] She then proceeded to divide the literary world into writers who approached Tolstoy "with deep respect and love" and those who "did not understand Tolstoy and did not love him." Motyleva appears unable to abandon—or else constrained to foster—the idea that in Western countries the established authorities conduct a bitter struggle against Tolstoy's acceptance, and that only in countries which are "building socialism" is the writer truly loved and read. By way of proof of this notion she revealed that Tolstoy is the favorite writer "of Bulgarian peasants and Mongolian cattle breeders."[60]

The remainder of the articles making up the two volumes, mostly contributed by foreign writers, are marked by a constant use of superlatives and contain little which is memorable.

One of the most noteworthy studies of Tolstoy published in Russia in 1966 was a book by a Leningrad scholar, Elizabeth Kupreyanova, concerned with the writer's esthetic principles.[61] This work not only constituted a refreshing break from the monotony of extolling Tolstoy's greatness at home and abroad but also provided testimony that persons of independent mind were still able to get their writings published in the U.S.S.R. Kupreyanova is known for her integrity and courage, and she adopts a surprisingly objective approach to Tolstoy. The word "surprisingly" is entirely appropriate, since no Russian scholar writing about Tolstoy after the war had previously dared to refer to him as having been "wrong," as Kupreyanova does in several places in her book. Yet her Tolstoy emerges great—perhaps even greater than from a study in which superlatives are used with reference to everything he said or wrote. She is not afraid to sound a bit like Lukacs:

---

* Roosevelt took exception to Tolstoy's view that the United States had an expansionist policy and that the military was too powerful in America. The President also considered that Tolstoy's ethical teaching had some "foolish and immoral" parts. He attributed even the collapse of the Duma to the alleged fact that the Russian liberals were saturated with just such "folly" as that taught by Tolstoy.

In the political sense Tolstoy's world outlook was in many respects reactionary. Chernyshevsky's outlook was the pinnacle of the progressive politico-revolutionary thought of his epoch. If Tolstoy had always reasoned like Chernyshevsky we would have had a second Chernyshevsky, not Tolstoy. History arranged things differently. In Chernyshevsky's person it provided the greatest political thinker of his time and his nation, and in Tolstoy's person it provided the greatest artist.[62]

Tolstoy's "genetic links" with members of West European philosophical and esthetic schools are analysed in great detail by Kupreyanova. She pays special attention to the influences exerted on Tolstoy by Rousseau and Kant, at the same time giving a warning that it would be erroneous to associate the ideas of these philosophers directly with those of Tolstoy. The writer's esthetic principles were formed, Kupreyanova asserts, as a result of interaction between Western and Russian philosophical ideas. Kupreyanova also made a thorough investigation of Tolstoy's attitude toward Western art, particularly music, and disagreed with the writer's position in a number of instances.

Tolstoy's assertive judgments about European art at the end of the nineteenth century are absolutely wrong and unjust. Wagner, Berlioz, Brahms and Richard Strauss, allowance being made for the complex and peculiar nature of their works at that time, were not decadent in the sense that they seemed to be to Tolstoy, who categorically rejected them. Tolstoy was inclined to consider even the later Beethoven decadent.[63]

Kupreyanova's book was sold out immediately upon publication, and has since become a highly prized item. Its popularity derives from the refreshingly straightforward approach of its author, who comments upon issues that other scholars usually deem it safer to gloss over or avoid, and perhaps even more for the way she directed her mischievous wit towards her fellow Tolstoy scholar, Lomunov. It was the general belief in Russia that Lomunov had in large measure built his academic career upon interpreting Lenin's articles on Tolstoy and pointing out the distortions or neglect of those articles in the writings of domestic and foreign authors. Obviously sharing this view of Lomunov, Kupreyanova went so far as to criticize him for vulgarizing Lenin.[64] It seemed that the ideological pundit had been beaten at his own game.

Lomunov was, however, misjudged by many. He took six years to respond to Kupreyanova's sallies, but the means he adopted to do so earned him great respect. In 1972 he published a book[65] under the same title, and dealing with the same subject, as Kupreyanova's in 1966. By choosing the same title he implied that he could write as good a book on Tolstoy's esthetics as she had—and he did so. Although not characterized by the same forthrightness of approach as Kupreyanova's, the new work of Lomunov was one of quality, by Soviet standards. It is doubtful, however, whether its purport is likely to be appreciated in the West, where the Soviet utilitarian approach to esthetics is not generally approved of. Lomunov affirms that real art has to fulfill important social functions, and any reader of his book must know this if he wishes to follow his arguments.

Lomunov achieved two objectives with his book. He proved that he was more than an interpreter of Lenin's articles on Tolstoy—he was a Tolstoy scholar in his own right. He also proved himself a gentleman—by not attacking Kupreyanova in his book, but by simply ignoring her. Lomunov's "revenge" was nevertheless very conspicuous since, in listing practically everybody in Russia who had ever expressed any view about Tolstoy's esthetics, he neglected to mention Kupreyanova's major contribution to the subject, let alone discuss it.

Lomunov's creative energy in the 1970s was truly phenomenal. Soon after completing five hundred pages on Tolstoy's esthetics, he started working on another major project. It concerned Tolstoy in relation to the whole world, and was published in 1975 in 50,000 copies (as compared to the 10,000 copies of his earlier work) for a general readership.[66] The book is very fragmented in character, since Lomunov had to deal with an enormous amount of material for the compilation of his work. It is remarkable that the book appeared at all; it was considered to be impossible to deal with the subject of the reaction of the whole world to Tolstoy's writing and teaching in a single book. As if the publication of two comprehensive studies within three years was not sufficient proof of scholarly industry and devotion, Lomunov produced in 1979 a major work on the subject of Tolstoy's *Resurrection*.[67] With his incredible energy, Lomunov is perhaps the only Russian scholar to have produced major studies of Tolstoy both in his Russian dimension and as a world figure.

During the nineteen-seventies two Russian scholars, both women, also produced major studies of Tolstoy's standing abroad. They were Victoria Gornaya and Dilyara Zhantieva.

Gornaya concerned herself with how the writer figures in the literary criticism of the West. Her extremely detailed study is an account of writings that appeared in Belgium, France, Great Britain, Italy and the United States, and is in the main free from personal attacks on individual critics. She does, however, take Sir Isaiah Berlin to task for allegedly insulting Tolstoy's memory by comparing him to Joseph de Maistre. But this criticism stems from Gornaya's earlier work[68] in which she closely examined Berlin's well-known study of Tolstoy's views on history, *The Hedgehog and the Fox*. She regarded as unsound his view of the way thinkers and writers are separated into foxes (who know many things) and hedgehogs (who know but one important thing). In Berlin's assessment of Russian writers, Pushkin was a fox and Dostoevsky a hedgehog, while Tolstoy lived in a state of conflict between what he was (a fox) and what he thought he was (a hedgehog). According to Berlin, such a conflict was clearly evident in Tolstoy's views on history. Gornaya considered that if there was any conflict at all—which she doubted—it was the result of contradictory trends in Tolstoy's world view, which left their mark not only on his philosophical writings, but on his artistic works as well. Gornaya strongly disagreed with Berlin's contention that Tolstoy's philosophy of history was close to that of Joseph de Maistre. In her opinion, since Berlin must have known that de Maistre was a reactionary ("the apostle of darkness") and a defender of slavery, his attempt to liken Tolstoy to the Frenchman inevitably led to a distortion of the true views of the Russian writer.[69]

In her 1974 study, which is the outcome of her reading of an enormous quantity of source material, Gornaya conducts a personal investigation to detect and refute the "distortions" of Tolstoy's outlook by Western critics and literary historians. Her tone, though sometimes heated, is never objectionable, and her arguments are scholarly. She even, on occasion, praises Western authors who have expressed views about Tolstoy which she is prepared to accept. For example, she commends the American critics, Louis Auchincloss, Ralph Matlaw, Logan Speirs, and Edward Wasiolek for their expressed disagreement with Henry James' Formalist approach to Tolstoy's great novels. Gornaya strongly supports the contention of the French writer Armand Lanoux that Tolstoy's historical fatalism—a denial of the role of the individual in history—as expressed in *War and Peace* is no longer acceptable. ("The heroic fight of the Russian people headed by Lenin more than anything else refutes these conceptions" is one of Lanoux's observations). Gornaya, a highly trained specialist, knows full well that those conceptions had been refuted long before Lanoux's time, even by some of Tolstoy's own contemporaries, and the patronizing praise she accords him is quite plainly in recognition of his expressed political views. In general, Gornaya does not find it possible to be optimistic about the possibility of the Marxist view of Tolstoy gaining acceptance in the West. As she remarks, "some Western critics even today do not know, ignore, or wrongly interpret Lenin's articles on Tolstoy."[70]

Zhantieva deals in the manner of Motyleva with recent British literary criticism of Turgenev, Tolstoy and Dostoevsky.[71] She criticizes almost everyone in Britain who has written about Tolstoy. One person has not understood the inner life of Tolstoy's heroes (she refers to Janko Lavrin), and another has been remiss in not expounding the social and political problems in *Resurrection* (Theodore Redpath). Yet another has erroneously examined Tolstoy through the prism of Freud's teachings (Frank O'Connor). Such views are only to be expected after Zhantieva's prefatory observation that the majority of studies by British scholars do not satisfy "the demands of objectivity." (It becomes abundantly clear later that by "majority" she means "all," and that "the demands of objectivity" are her own demands—or those she represents). Typical of the level of objectivity at which she writes is her summary of Gordon Spence's book *Tolstoy the Ascetics* and George Steiner's *Tolstoy or Dostoevsky:*

Spence, Steiner and many others united together in their ideological struggle against the Soviet Union accuse, without any support, Soviet literary experts of not understanding or valuing the heritage of Russian classics.[72]

In 1978, Russia and the world celebrated the 150th anniversary of Tolstoy's birth. A survey of the numerous publications issued in Russia to commemorate the event does not form part of the present study. However, the general remark could be made that in 1978 Russian research on Tolstoy was showing definite signs of fatigue. Few original contributions were produced, and most of the items published were commemorative writings reissued for the occasion: The Countess' diary, the reminiscences of Tolstoy's contemporaries, recollections of peasants, etc. Some of these items were published without reference being made to the fact that they had appeared before. For example, a book by Susanna Zhislina[73] devoted to recollections of Tolstoy provided by Russian peasants, which had been published in 1941 and again in 1968, was reissued in 1978 without any indication being given that it was not written for the anniversary.

Special issues of Russian literary journals appeared in 1978 to mark the jubilee. In the scholarly Leningrad publication, *Russkaya literatura* (Russian Literature), there appeared an article in which the literary historian Nikita Prutskov made observations concerning Tolstoy's attitude to religion. This would seem to suggest that the last frontier of Russian research on Tolstoy—the presentation of Tolstoy's religious teachings to the Soviet public in an officially acceptable manner—may be on the point of being crossed. It is hard to say whether Prutskov was planning a major work on Tolstoy's religious beliefs, or simply endeavoring to find out whether the time was ripe for one. In either case, he did his best to point out that Tolstoy's convictions had little in common with accepted notions of religion. He maintained that "Tolstoy's religious teaching reflects muzhik logic ... in Tolstoy's religious ideas we sense muzhik rationalism, the wish to interpret everything in an earthy manner ... life itself was God for Tolstoy."[74]

The interpretation of Tolstoy's religious ideas in an atheist state may turn out to be the most formidable undertaking that Soviet scholars can ever face. Tolstoy's religious and ethical views took shape during the course of many years and were often subjected to the scrutiny of the writer's critical mind. Apart from being a firm believer in God, Tolstoy had an impressive knowledge of theology. Whenever he happened to discover a contradiction in the teachings of the established church, he would go back to the ancient scriptures for guidance. He could read the Greek and Latin texts in the originals, and when he was approaching seventy he acquired a working knowledge of Hebrew.

Prutskov, like many others before him, has fallen into a trap in taking Tolstoy's simple descriptions of his religious beliefs at face value. It was not muzhik logic that shaped Tolstoy's religious outlook; it was one of the greatest minds that Russia has ever produced that did so—his own. Tolstoy's path to simple religious and ethical truths was long and tortuous. Only a believer in God who is in conflict with generally accepted dogmas can fully comprehend that path. For this reason it is difficult to name anyone among the known Soviet Tolstoy scholars who would be capable of undertaking an analysis of Tolstoy's religious ideas, let alone interpreting them from a Marxist point of view.

The number of publications issued during Tolstoy's last jubilee reflected only one aspect of the writer's recognition in his native land. There exist other aspects as well which demonstrate Tolstoy's special place among the Russians. The writer has the unique distinction of having five museums devoted to him. Two in Moscow, one in Leningrad, one in Yasnaya Polyana, and one at the railroad station which used to be called Astapovo—the place where Tolstoy died. These museums contain, apart from Tolstoy's personal belongings, a great many works by Russia's finest artists, such as Nicholas Gay, Ivan Kramskoi, Ilya Repin, Paolo Trubetskoi and others, who considered it a great privilege to paint or sculpt the writer. Tolstoy's likenesses, as created by these artists, have been reproduced in very large numbers and are to be seen everywhere—in private homes, schools, clubs, military academies, etc.

Tolstoy's popularity in his country has also been strengthened by the mass reproduction of illustrations to his novels. To the Russians, the heroes of Tolstoy's books are not simply literary characters—they have become real people.* Even a Russian with only a rudimentary interest in literature can describe Prince Andrei or Natasha from *War and Peace* in great detail. The excellent illustrations of Leonid Pasternak (the father of Boris Pasternak, the author of *Doctor Zhivago*) for *Resurrection,*** which were very much appreciated by Tolstoy himself, have made the novel's heroine, Katyusha Maslova, a popular figure even though she never lived.

Soviet school curricula are organized in such a way that Russian school children have read and studied at least twenty-five stories before they reach the age of ten. By the time they are sixteen they have all read *War and Peace,* and very likely *Anna Karenina* and *Resurrection.* In universities whole courses are devoted to Tolstoy, and he is very prominent as

---

* Tolstoy himself thought that his characters lived their lives independently of him. There were said to have been tears in his eyes when he came to write of the suicide of Anna Karenina, whom he regarded as a fine woman. In vain would it have been suggested to him that, as he had created Anna, he could have ended the novel about her on a happy note had he so wished; for he believed he had no control over her ultimate fate.

** Pasternak probably created the largest number of paintings and drawings featuring Tolstoy. Disregarding those in private hands and abroad, and considering only the ones on public display in Russia, the Tolstoy State Museum in Moscow alone houses twenty-eight of Pasternak's portraits of the writer, eight portraits of members of his family and friends, five illustrations to *War and Peace,* forty-four to *Resurrection* and six to the story *What Men Live By.*

a topic for dissertations. One can, of course, always ask: is it the real Tolstoy that Russian students become acquainted with? It seems that most people in the West acquainted with the degree of ideological controls in in present-day Russia would give a negative answer to this question. A qualified observer of the Russian educational scene states that:

> The Soviet student does become acquainted with the most important artistic works by Tolstoy. However, he learns much less about Tolstoy the man, and about the positive ideas which permeate all the author's creative work. The emphasis in the interpretation of Tolstoy's literary heritage is on the writer's criticism of the tsarist regime, of the church, and of the corrupt society. Tolstoy's suggested solutions to the problems encountered in his works receive little mention in Soviet textbooks. The selection of material for study in school, and the interpretation it receives, help to create in the student's mind an image of Tolstoy which will serve the general purpose of Soviet education, but which must be regarded as one-sided and incomplete.[75]

This is very true and well put, yet it does not give the full picture. The Russians might have access only to a one-sided and incomplete Tolstoy in school during their formative years, and they might read distorted accounts of him in the form of assessments by ideologically-tested literary experts. They might even hear it asserted that he would have wanted his compatriots to live under the Soviet political system. Yet the most important fact is that Tolstoy is still in Russia, because the ideas emanating from his writings transcend the official ideology. It is obvious that Tolstoy is a greater component of the Russian national consciousness than any political system. The Russians have an everlasting ethical yardstick in Tolstoy which no ruling group can ignore. They can immediately spot parasites in powerful positions, heartless bureaucrats, and unjust penal systems, because Tolstoy described them all. To the Russians Tolstoy represents a pure, unpolluted stream of wisdom and truth, a fact which explains why their present politically controlled literature, with some of its very talented writers, is cast aside by tacit consent whenever Tolstoy's works come up for discussion.

This concludes the condensed investigation into the process of Tolstoy's acceptance in postrevolutionary Russia, a process which has resulted in the largest body of writings on a single author in that country. It would, of course, be preposterous to assume that the large amount of literature on Tolstoy issued by state publishing houses in Russia is a real indicator of the nation's affection for him. There could be hundreds of books published for each jubilee of the writer by literary experts and the average Russian could still be indifferent to him. The conclusions reached by Russian scholars regarding Tolstoy's views and artistic accomplishments might influence a number of people with a cultivated interest in literature, but as far as the Russian masses are concerned their effects are minimal. The question then arises: if the average Russian is not familiar with the experts' opinions in praise of Tolstoy's writings, what makes him read the works of this author? An attempt will be made in the following chapters to answer this question.

Tolstoy's New Readers

There prevails a fairly general belief that Tolstoy's renown among his compatriots was established with, or soon after, the publication of *War and Peace* and *Anna Karenina*. The fact is that these two masterpieces of Tolstoy's were, for many years after they first appeared, read only by a very small proportion of Russia's population. As far as the vast majority of the Russian nation was concerned, Tolstoy as a novelist was virtually unknown. He became well known among the Russian masses as the years went by as a fighter for social justice, since his pamphlets and parables, distributed legally or by the revolutionary underground at very low prices or free, reached every hamlet.

The first parts of *War and Peace* began to appear in March 1865 in serial form, under the title *1805,* in the journal *Russkii vestnik* (Russian Herald), which had some three thousand subscribers. The separate publication of the novel was issued in five thousand copies in 1867. All six volumes of *War and Peace* had been completed and were on sale before the end of 1869. In the country, where over 80 per cent of the 120 million inhabitants were illiterate,* only a privileged few could read the novel due to its profusion of French expressions. The price of the work was prohibitive, well beyond the means of ordinary working people.**

As for the part played by the critics, recognition of Tolstoy's great novels as masterpieces was neither immediate nor unanimous. Many of them found serious faults in both *War and Peace* and *Anna Karenina,* and fiery polemics concerning those works continued into the post-revolutionary period. But approval by the critics, even if it had been unanimous, could not itself have secured for Tolstoy the position of great eminence he eventually achieved in Russia. Other nineteenth-century authors such as Nestor Kukolnik, Vladislav Ozerov and Alexei Timofeev "had been issued certificates of immortality"[1] by Russian critics but are virtually unknown to their countrymen today.

In any case it is difficult to imagine that a nation would revere a writer after a hundred years and still publish him in large editions just because some clever critics wrote a few favorable articles about him. The process of Tolstoy's acceptance by the Russian people can be likened to the formation

---

* Illiteracy was reduced to 74 per cent in 1897, according to the census taken that year.
** The cost of *War and Peace* as published in 1869 was ten rubles. A village teacher at the time earned about twenty-five rubles a month, and a manual worker half a ruble a day. There is no data available on the annual average wage in Russia at the time of the appearance of Tolstoy's novel but in the 1880s it was still below 200 rubles.[2]

of a mighty river. Scarcely visible rivulets feed streams which in their turn feed and produce the river. The rivulets appeared when Tolstoy fought for Russia at Sevastopol and when he set up his first school for peasant children. The rivulets had become a stream when his pamphlets demanding social justice were available in cheap editions. The mighty river eventually formed when Tolstoy's greatness as a patriot, writer and thinker became evident to the Russian nation as a whole. This occurred only many years after the Revolution when the standard of education of the masses had been improved.*

That Tolstoy is still an immensely popular writer among the Russians is indisputable. It would, however, be erroneous to infer from this fact that his exalted position today is derived from the artistic reputation he acquired before 1917. The Revolution itself, the civil war and mass emigration which followed it, and the policies pursued by the emerging Soviet regime served to change radically the cultural orientation of the Russian people. In this process millions of workers in factories and farms, a high proportion of them newly literate, played the key part in determining which prerevolutionary writers would continue to be published and read in Russia.

As for Tolstoy himself, the acceptance of his literary heritage by the masses—the regime's developing attitudes have been described in an earlier chapter—had to occur in two stages. A substantial proportion of the Russian population had to become able to read and understand works by Tolstoy. Afterwards, they had to develop a capacity for personal identification with situations described in some of these works. The first signs of such identification came in due course as countless Russians discovered, in reading Tolstoy, circumstances which they could relate to those that they were familiar with. They came to realize that the writer, though a man of the nineteenth century, in fact concerned himself with problems that still existed. For example, it was the parallel perceivable between the situation when the Germans invaded Russia in 1941 and the events described in *War and Peace* which secured for that novel an enormous popularity among all Russians which still shows no sign of abating.

Some of Tolstoy's writings are so broad in scope that the parallels with personal experience which readers are able to perceive in them transcend limitations of country and nationality. *Anna Karenina* and *The Death of*

---

* Although it had been planned to eliminate illiteracy by the tenth anniversary of the Revolution, there were in 1927-28 still about twenty million illiterates and Soviet Russia was still a backward country as regards public education. In 1920-23 there were 206 students of higher education in the U.S.A. per thousand population, in England 187, in Germany 149, in France 107, and in Soviet Russia 63. In Europe only Romania and Portugal were behind Russia in public education. The 1925-26 Russian budget for elementary education was 67 percent of the 1913 budget, and teachers were earning less than half the amount that they did before the Revolution.[3]

Ivan Ilich, for example, can, in satisfactory translation, be easily read and appreciated by non-Russians. *The Death of Ivan Ilich* is, as a matter of fact, more popular in France than it is in Russia. In general, however, most of Tolstoy's works have more appeal for Russians than for foreigners, and it is the reaction of the Russians to some of them which will now be investigated. The selection of these works for closer examination has been made with reference to the available statistical and bibliographical compendia in which the Russians' affection for them is indicated.

The simplicity of the literary tastes of the Russian masses in the 1920s is reflected in the fact that the most popular works of Tolstoy were his fables and fairy tales (virtually unknown in the West), and his stories *Polikushka* and *After the Ball.*

Tolstoy started writing these fables and fairy tales after he had completed *War and Peace,* and he continued to produce them until the end of his life. He himself enjoyed reading fairy stories, having a love of them which went back to his own childhood. The orphaned Tolstoy children had often passed long winter evenings letting their imaginations run wild in the invention of stories and then telling them to one another. The impressions some of these stories made on the future writer remained with him throughout his life. He was especially fascinated by a story his brother Nicholas had told about a green stick buried at Yasnaya Polyana which, allegedly, had a message on it that would destroy evil in people's hearts and make them happy for ever. Tolstoy believed so strongly in this story that he directed that he should be buried near the supposed location of the green stick—a wish which was duly complied with by his family.

Most of the fables and fairy tales which Tolstoy wrote appeared originally in the *Azbuka* (ABC) which he compiled for schools in the 1870s. He was also active in writing these stories during the last decade of his life. In 1903, at the request of Sholom Aleichem, the popular Yiddish writer, Tolstoy contributed three tales—*Three Questions, Esarhaddon, King of Assyria,* * and *Toil, Death and Sickness*—to a volume intended to benefit the victims of the great pogrom against the Jewish population of Kishinev which occurred in that year. They were published first in Yiddish and later in Russian.

The majority of Tolstoy's fables and fairy tales also appeared in the cheap mass editions of the *Posrednik* publishing house, which has been mentioned in earlier chapters. In many Russian villages these small volumes were the only literature available apart from religious texts, which were also distributed in very large numbers. With the establishment of the Soviet regime the dissemination of religious literature was stopped and a

---

* Tolstoy told Sholom Aleichem that he took the idea of the tale *Esarhaddon, King of Assyria* from the story *Das bist du* (This is you), published in the German journal, *Theosophischer Wegweiser,* in the 5th issue for 1903.

substantial part of what remained was either destroyed or hidden. When the new authorities commenced their campaign to eliminate illiteracy in rural areas, often the only materials to hand for instruction in reading were Tolstoy's fables and fairy tales. As already mentioned, *Posrednik* was permitted to stay in operation, and so works of Tolstoy remained on sale in Russia, even during the civil war when publishing by the government came nearly to a halt because of shortage of paper.

Tolstoy's story *Polikushka* was very popular in Soviet Russia during the 1920s even though when originally published in 1863 it had been completely ignored by the critics. Polikushka was a gentle serf who had a tarnished reputation, having been caught stealing several times. His proprietor, a woman of limited intelligence, wishing to reform him through an indication of trust, sent him to fetch a large sum of money from a nearby town. Polikushka lost the money on his way home and, knowing that no one would believe him, hanged himself. His wife was bathing her baby boy when a neighbor brought tidings of the unhappy occurrence. She rushed to see her dead husband, and the baby drowned in the tub. Confronted with two deaths she became insane. The money was eventually recovered, but the mistress refused to take it back, considering it to be "unlucky". She gave it to the rich greedy peasant who had found it. He had wanted to keep it all, but after a nocturnal visit by Polikushka's ghost decided to use part of it for the ransom of his nephew who was about to be drafted into the army.

The story is based on a real event that was narrated to Tolstoy by a friend during his second trip abroad. It is the first of the writer's stories in which a peasant is the central figure, and he had some difficulty in writing it. The first draft, completed in 1861, was very likely inspired by the emancipation of that year. Tolstoy then kept rewriting it until it was published in its final form two years later. He portrayed in it some of his own peasants, including Aksinya Anikanova, with whom he had become romantically entangled in the late 1850s.*

Tolstoy did not directly attack serfdom in *Polikushka*, yet the descriptions in it of the peasants' living conditions and of the heartbreaking scenes which marked the departure of those recruited for twenty-five years of military service amounted to a definite indictment of the whole order of things. In actual fact, Polikushka's suicide and the horrors which follow it

---

* As a result of the liaison, which lasted about three years, Aksinya gave birth to a boy, Timothy, who later became a coachman to one of Tolstoy's sons. Tolstoy harbored feelings of guilt about this affair throughout his life, and a year before he died he thought he should have apologized to Timothy. Tolstoy recorded his love affair with Aksinya in his diary which he gave to his fiancée to read after their engagement. It took Sophie some time to recover from the effect of the intimate details in the diary and she retained a mixture of jealousy and hatred for Aksinya. Both the Countess and Aksinya died in 1919.

Tolstoy also portrayed Aksinya in the stories *Idyll, Tikhon and Malanya,* and most vividly in *The Devil.*

serve to shift the reader's attention away from the institution of serfdom and towards spectacular personal tragedies, and the story is weakened as a consequence.* As Turgenev remarked in a private letter to a friend: "There was no need for Tolstoy to have drowned the son. It is terrible without that."[4] There is no respite from the horrors for the reader since Tolstoy made no attempts at psychological portrayal in the story. The inner worlds of his characters lay outside the range of the writer's interest. These figures are described solely by their actions—a literary device which has been called "the dialectics of behavior"** in Russian research on Tolstoy.

Tolstoy himself did not like Polikushka, calling it "twaddle on the first subject that comes into a man's head,"[5] and he never dreamt that it would be one day so well liked by his countrymen. Even during the tsarist regime the story attracted more attention than Tolstoy had anticipated, and in Soviet Russia it appeared in a number of separate editions during the 1920s. As late as 1939 it was still one of the works used in the teaching of basic reading to adults.

The popularity of *Polikushka* among Tolstoy's new readers was in large measure the result of the fact that one of the earliest Soviet films—and the first based on a work of Tolstoy***—was made from it in 1919 and became enormously successful. The title role was played by Ivan Moskvin, a talented and popular actor. The film's tragic moments of suicide, drowning and insanity lent themselves easily to the screen and blended well into the reality of the civil war then raging. After being praised by Lunacharsky, then Commissar of Education, the film was shown all over Russia. Tens of thousands of peasants who had never watched a film before saw on the screen persons just like themselves, wearing garments like their own and living in the same squalid conditions as they did. The emotional impact on such unsophisticated audiences, as the tragedy of the gentle Polikushka unfolded before their eyes, was beyond description. It is therefore not surprising that the demand for the actual story became insatiable and abated only in the mid 1940s.

<hr />

* The poet, Alexander Fet, a friend of Tolstoy's, remarked that "everything in *Polikushka* is crumbling, putrid, poverty-stricken, painful . . . it is all accurate and truthful, but so much the worse for that."[6]
** This term was created by Pavel Gromov, whose works on Russian literary figures, particularly on Alexander Blok, are well-known in the U.S.S.R. In the 1970s he wrote two books[7] on Tolstoy's style. In the first of these Gromov speaks of three levels of dialectics in Tolstoy's style and creative ideas: "dialectics of the soul" (a term actually coined by the nineteenth-century Russian critic, Chernyshevsky) which is basically the device of internal monologue; "dialectics of behavior," is the description of the characters' actions and deeds; and, finally, the "dialectics of the author's attitude" when the narrator himself becomes involved in the story.
*** Although a film based on Tolstoy's story *Father Sergius* was shown in 1917, it cannot be considered a truly Soviet film since it was made before the October Revolution.

Due to the film's success and the subsequent demand for the story. Polikushka, more than any of Tolstoy's characters, was firmly imprinted in the consciousness of the Russians for many years. As late as 1960 Soviet cultural authorities considered that there was still enough interest among the Russians to justify the making of a new film on Polikushka. Though of good quality the new film was just one among many made that year in Soviet studios. It was politely received but its success did not come anywhere near that of the old *Polikushka* since the audiences had changed. Although some emotional effect was still felt, any identification of the new viewers with Polikushka, as in 1919, was out of the question.

The story *After the Ball* was, like three other tales already mentioned, intended for inclusion in a volume sponsored by Sholom Aleichem to benefit the victims of the Kishinev pogrom. However, after completing the new story in 1903, Tolstoy decided not to publish it. *After the Ball* did not appear until a year after the writer's death, in 1911. The central idea of the work is contained in an article entitled *Nikolai Palkin* (Nicholas the Stick) which Tolstoy started writing in 1886 but did not finish. This article constituted a passionate condemnation of the savage corporal punishment which was rife in the Russian army in the time of Nicholas I. In it Tolstoy recalled that he knew an army officer who "danced a mazurka with his beautiful daughter at a ball and left early to command his soldiers to beat a Tartar soldier to death with rods for attempted desertion."[8]

For many years it was believed that Tolstoy himself witnessed the execution when, as a student in Kazan, he was courting the daughter of the garrison commander there. In 1948, however, some further information was published [9] on the subject, from which it appeared that it was not Tolstoy himself but his brother, Sergei, who had been infatuated with the daughter of the garrison commander at Kazan. Then, after another twenty-three years, the Tolstoy scholar, Vladimir Zhdanov,* demonstrated on the basis of additional documentary evidence that, although the particular area of Kazan is indeed described correctly in the story, *After the Ball* definitely cannot be regarded as autobiographical.[10] While considering the hero of the story a purely fictitious character, Zhdanov suggested that Tolstoy must have known someone who was the prototype for the Kazan commander.**

---

* Zhdanov's first major work on the writer was a two-volume study, *Love in the Life of Leo Tolstoy,* published in 1928. He also authored a book on *Anna Karenina* and two on *Resurrection,* and edited many volumes of Tolstoy's correspondence with various people. He died in 1971, the year in which his study, *The Last Books of Leo Tolstoy,* in which he deals with the story, *After the Ball,* was published.

** It could be mentioned that Tolstoy in his notes describing his Kazan years refers to the military commander as a Pole. In the story itself the colonel's patronymic is Vladislavich, which also suggests Polish origin. Yet the officer bears a great resemblance to Nicholas I, who crushed the Polish rebellion of 1831 with great brutality.

Ivan Vasilevich, the protagonist of *After the Ball,* falls in love with the beautiful daughter of an army colonel. Ivan is invited to a ball where, after spending the happiest moments of his life dancing with the girl, he is introduced to her father. The colonel is a very distinguished looking elderly man with impeccable manners and a kind smile. At about three o'clock in the morning, after dancing with his daughter, the colonel excuses himself by saying that he has a busy day ahead and leaves. Ivan goes home about two hours later. Being too happy to sleep he decides to take a walk, in the course of which he chances upon the ugliest spectacle he has ever witnessed. Under the command of the colonel, soldiers, formed in two parallel lines, are beating with rods a man who is being dragged, tied to rifle stocks, by two other soldiers. An onlooker remarks that the man is a Tartar who has attempted to desert. Behind the bleeding man walks the colonel, urging the soldiers to strike the victim harder and threatening to punish those who do not use their full strength while delivering their blows. Ivan is shocked to see the colonel directing such a barbarous procedure with evident relish. After the incident, whenever he sees the smile of his beloved he always thinks of what lies behind her father's urbane social exterior and feels very uncomfortable. Soon he stops seeing the girl, and there the story ends.

The topic of cruel corporal punishment being carried out in front of someone unable to bear the sight of it was not new in Russian literature. In 1861, the author Alexander Afanasev-Chuzhbinsky published in the Russian journal, *Sovremennik,* a story, *From an Army Officer's Life* (Iz kornetskoi zhizni), which bears many resemblances to *After the Ball.* The action of the story takes place during the 1840s and the narrator is a junior officer who is infatuated with a beautiful young lady at a ball. While on duty the next day, he was to witness the savage beating of a soldier with birch rods. The plot is so similar to that of Tolstoy that the Soviet critic, Nicholas Lerner, in 1928, saw fit to write an article in which he dismissed the possibility of plagiarism.[11] In 1894 Alexander Kuprin, later a prominent novelist, published a story, *Inquiry* (Doznanie), which also bears very close resemblances to *After the Ball.* In it the victim is also a Tartar, and he is punished for theft in a manner almost identical to that described in Tolstoy's work. The protagonist of the story is, however, not infatuated with a girl. He is simply a junior officer who has compassion for the Tartar and goes to pieces upon witnessing his punishment.

Although Lunacharsky did not include *After the Ball* among the twenty works of literature he recommended "for the working masses" in 1928, the story was one of the most widely read works in Russia at that time. Indeed, it had by the early 1930s become the most sought after and published story of Tolstoy in Russia. The Russians were clearly fascinated by the contrast which was the essence of the story. The brightly lit ballroom, pleasant chatter and powdered ladies' shoulders was masterfully juxtaposed with the gloomy drill field, the moans of the victim and his savagely beaten body. But the oft-employed literary device of contrast, no matter how skillfully pressed into service, cannot alone secure popularity for a story over decades. The Russians of that early Soviet period were obviously reminded more of their own society than of what they knew, or had heard, about the prerevolutionary past.

It is likely that Lunacharsky had a more compelling reason for not recommending *After the Ball* to the readers than the description of a Tartar* being beaten to death in the Russian army. The lack of official endorsement of the story could have been caused by the fact that the savage punishment administered to the victim could not at that time have been attributed solely to the conduct of the tsarist army as easily as is done today.

It seems that Tolstoy was above all appalled by the violence committed upon a person who wanted only to escape from an army into which he had been drafted against his will. This violence did not end with the tsarist regime in Russia; if anything it assumed a much greater intensity after the Revolution. Millions of veterans of the civil war could recall countless cases of cruel reprisals being taken against men who had tried to run away after being forcibly recruited into one or another of the contending armies.** Scores of these veterans had been obliged to take part in the execution of compatriots with whose conduct they were in deep sympathy. When the war was at last over many Russians had to live with guilty consciences for deeds committed during the hostilities. Tolstoy's story constituted a vindication of their belief that it was "they"—those who were in charge—who caused brutality at all times, rather than the ordinary people.

The Red Army, which had a strength of 300,000 men in May 1918 at the outset of the civil war, became a force of five and a half million by the end of 1920. This enormous mass of recruits included a substantial number of people who were forced into the army or found themselves there without really understanding the ultimate goals of the Bolshevik leadership. Resignation was out of the question and the penalty for desertion was death. Moreover, Trotsky, appointed Commissar for War in March 1918,

---

* Tolstoy himself considered the nationality of the victim to be unimportant. In the first drafts of the story he made the Tartar cry out in ungrammatical Russian with a Tartar accent during his punishment. In the final version the Tartar uses correct Russian without an accent. His nationality had become irrelevant; "he was a man staggering and writhing under the blows which were raining on him from both sides." The mention of his being a Tartar was left in the story in its final version only because the action took place in the city of Kazan where the overwhelming majority of the inhabitants were Tartars.

** Desertions were already numerous in Russia in World War I. The total number of deserters from the tsarist army is estimated to have been over two million. Since the Russian Empire was falling apart, the military authorities were unable to cope with such a mass of deserters, let alone execute them. Execution of deserters was to become the accepted procedure in the civil war that ensued.

instituted a system of using hostages. He gave orders that the entire families of former tsarist officers who had joined the Bolsheviks but subsequently defected should be executed.* Human life was held in such small regard at the time that Trotsky even ordered the indiscriminate shooting of Red Army soldiers, including political commissars and Bolshevik party members, near Kazan in August 1918. They were shot for retreating from their front-line positions in face of what appeared to be the overwhelming strength of their opponents.

The White armies likewise absorbed huge numbers of forced recruits, and punished with the utmost cruelty all those who were caught trying to desert. It is a well-documented fact that the White general, Peter Wrangel, used massacre as a means of intimidating Red prisoners into joining his army in 1918 near Stavropol. From a body of about three thousand prisoners he selected nearly four hundred commanders and had them executed publicly. The remainder were then called upon to join Wrangel or share the fate of their superiors. All those who later attempted to desert were slaughtered too. A British officer, who was an adviser to White units during the civil war and witnessed many atrocities observed in his memoirs that if a man was caught after deserting he was shot, and that rewards were offered for bringing in deserters, alive or dead.[13]

It has been demonstrated by historians of the period that the civil war, even though it became such a large-scale conflict, was essentially a struggle between groups of "Reds" and "Whites".** The majority of the Russians, especially the peasants in remote areas, neither understood the true nature of the fighting nor wanted to become involved in it. Yet they paid for it by being forced to exterminate one another in great numbers. Tolstoy's *After the Ball* must inevitably have been seen by readers of the early Soviet period as a condemnation of the violence which had accompanied their social upheavals. Indeed, it was not until the mustached, deceptively avuncular features of Stalin ceased to look down on the Russians from posters in the early nineteen fifties that their physical well-being, and even their lives, ceased to depend entirely on the whims of despotic individuals. Some three years after he died, Stalin was exposed by his erstwhile party colleagues as the reincarnation of the Kazan colonel, which he had long been to countless

---

* There is no data available as to the number of actual executions but quite a number of desertions, in spite of the Draconian measures, did occur. At the beginning of the civil war nearly seventy-five per cent of Red Army commanders were former officers of the tsarist army. Towards the end of 1919 this figure was down to 34 per cent.[12] It should be noted that the lower percentage was due not only to desertions but also to the appointment of trained Red military personnel.

** Gregory Melekhov, the hero of Sholokhov's novel, *Quiet Flows the Don,* is loved by the Russians even though he changed sides in the civil war several times. They fully sympathize with his search for a third, more humane, side in the war which,unfortunately for Gregory and countless others, did not exist.

ordinary Russians, the man who had personally ordered the beating, torture and execution of large numbers of people.

Once the threat of savage physical punishment was removed, *After the Ball* gradually lost its relevance for the Russians. Today it is in the main a text for high-school reading which serves to show the cruelty of the regime of the tsar Nicholas I.* In recently published Soviet books on Tolstoy's career as a writer only very short sections are devoted to *After the Ball.* So far, no attempts have been made to establish the reason for the story's great popularity during the early years of Soviet Russia.

While the interest of the Russians in *Polikushka* and *After the Ball* has gradually decreased, the popularity of Tolstoy's novel, *Hadji Murat,* widely manifested in the 1930s, is still great. *Hadji Murat* is generally regarded as one of the most artistic of Tolstoy's works. It takes place in the Caucasus during the early 1850s. Tolstoy himself was convalescing in the capital of Georgia, Tiflis (now Tbilisi) when Hadji Murat visited the Russian military headquarters there. The writer knew of the fame Murat had achieved in the armed resistance of the Moslem peoples of the Caucasus to Russian penetration under the leadership of Shamil.** He also knew that, after a disagreement with Shamil, Murat had defected with some of his followers to the Russians. Tolstoy disapproved of this action of Murat's, describing it as a "base deed"*** in a letter he wrote to his brother, Sergei, in December 1851. He nevertheless described Murat in that letter as the most daring horseman among the natives of the Caucasus.

Murat was hoping as a result of the great harm his defection had caused to Shamil to gain the confidence of the Russian government and eventually rule the Caucasus as its trusted ally. After being well received by the Russians, Murat at once started to plan a rescue of his large family who

---

* There is, of course, also room for symbolic interpretation of this story. For example, the Russian philosopher, Leo Shestov, believed that Tolstoy referred to his own life in *After the Ball.* Tolstoy allegedly thought that life was a fascinating ball when he was young and when he became old it was like running the gauntlet.[14]

** Shamil was believed by these peoples to be the second great prophet of Allah and to receive his guidance directly from Him. His resistance movement spread from his native Daghestan to include more than a dozen mountain peoples, most of whom were inspired by a form of militant Islam called Muridism.

*** In the English version of Henri Troyat's popular book on Tolstoy the Russian word "podlost'", meaning a base, despicable act or deed, is translated as "cowardice". Thus the key sentence in Tolstoy's letter to his brother describing Hadji Murat's defection is read:

> "... The boldest (a dzhigit) and bravest man in all Chechenya has committed an act of cowardice".[15]

"Cowardice" is an unfortunate choice of words since Tolstoy throughout his novel put a great stress on emphasizing Hadji Murat's bravery. Tolstoy knew well that Hadji Murat was many things—cruel, power-hungry, untrustworthy, etc.—but not a coward.

Troyat's French original, published in 1965, gives the true rendition of Tolstoy's remark:

> "... Le plus vaillant (un djiguite), le plus brave de toute la Tchetchénie, et il a commis une lâcheté."[16]

were hostages in Shamil's hands. The Russians were opposed to such a rescue attempt, fearing that Murat could be recaptured by Shamil in the course of it. To make sure that Murat would not undertake any action on his own, the Russians assigned to him a Cossack escort which accompanied him wherever he went. He soon began to feel like a prisoner and to fret about being kept inactive. One day he killed the Cossacks and escaped into the mountains. He was soon spotted and surrounded by the Russians and some of his Caucasian foes. An unequal battle ensued in which Murat was wounded, killed and decapitated.

Tolstoy must have been touched by the tragedy of Murat, since he described it in great detail to peasant children in his Yasnaya Polyana school some ten years after it occurred. There is however no evidence that he was planning to write a novel on the subject at that time, and it was not until nearly forty years later that he began to entertain the idea. Visiting his brother, Sergei, in July 1896 he took a walk around the estate during which he saw a mutilated clump of thistles, called "Tartar"* by the local population. The word "Tartar" and the tenacity of the thistle plant in clinging defiantly to life brought back memories of the Caucasian episode, and he was soon working on the first draft of a story about it which he entitled *Repei* (The Thistle). In this first version he portrayed Murat as a "savage" who found himself in a "civilized" society and who, being close to nature, was spiritually richer than any member of a society built on artificial values.

The very fact that Tolstoy began writing such a work on Hadji Murat at that time was remarkable, since he had firmly resolved not to undertake any more purely artistic work. Yet it turned out to be one of Tolstoy's greatest works of fiction. It seemed as if the artist in Tolstoy overpowered the stern moralist who disapproved of art for art's sake. In 1898 he produced, under the title *Kharavat* (Holy War), a revised draft of the work, in which he placed emphasis on Murat's role in the struggle of his people against the invaders in the name of Allah. In 1903 he decided to make the tsar, Nicholas I, one of the characters in the novel. Tolstoy was much

---

* Ernest J. Simmons, in his major work on Tolstoy published in 1946, quotes lines from the writer's diary relating to that walk:

"... and there on the edge of the dusty gray road grew a bush of burdock. Of three shoots, one was broken, and its white soiled flower hung down; another was broken, bespattered with black dirt, but still alive and red in the center. It reminded me of Hadji Murat."[17]

The word which is omitted from Simmons' translation is "Tartar". What Tolstoy wrote was: "... on the edge of the dusty gray road grew a bush of Tartar (thistle)"/I vot na krayu pyl'noi dorogi kust tatarina (rep'ya)/. "Tartar" was the word that was often used by the Russians to describe the Moslem insurgents of the Caucasus. In the novel it is even mentioned that two Russian officers had managed to gain Hadji Murat's confidence mainly because they spoke "Tartar". This word is essential as a clue to why Tolstoy remembered Hadji Murat.

intrigued by this autocrat's personality and reign, which he had carefully researched. He dictated the last chapter of the work to his wife in January 1905. From then on he kept the manuscript close at hand, making alterations to it from time to time with a view to its eventual publication. It was among the papers on his desk at Yasnaya Polyana when he departed in November 1910, never to return. The work was published posthumously, in 1912.

The published version, written in beautiful Russian, is a remarkable achievement for a man of seventy-seven.* It contains descriptions of the Caucasus in all its beauty, and of the local peoples in their struggles against colonizers. The life of the Russian military is also portrayed and the reader is taken into the Winter Palace in St. Petersburg and the private office of Nicholas I, who is shown in a very critical light. He appears as a conceited, lustful hypocrite who obtains perverse delight from the infliction of cruel punishment on his subjects and is proud of the fact that they feel terrified in his presence. He also appears as a huge snake, since it is his habit to look at people with "fixed, lifeless eyes". Whenever he has to make a decision, he closes them and bows his head, whereupon, after a few moments, an inner voice tells him what he should do. Tolstoy deliberately portrays Nicholas I in a manner similar to that in which he represents Shamil, in order to emphasize that both men were drunk with power. When a member of Shamil's war council asks what is to be done with the family of the renegade Hadji Murat, the despot closes his eyes and sits silently. Those present know that their leader is listening to the voice of the Prophet which is telling him how to proceed. The "inner voice" of Nicholas and the "Prophet's voice" both, it appears, counsel cruel punishment. The tsar orders a Polish student to be flogged to death, and Shamil resolves to have Murat's favorite son killed or blinded if his father fails to return.

The most dignified character of the novel is clearly Hadji Murat himself. He is desperately lonely because, though the Russians have proved to be no friends of his, he cannot return to his people as long as Shamil is in power. He is a tragic hero whose character has been interpreted in various ways by literary critics, including parallels with the author himself.** One can indeed make comparisons between the hero of the novel and the author. Moreover, the popularity of the book among Russian readers

---

* *Hadji Murat*'s artistic qualities served as the inspiration for two films. One was a highly romanticized, distorted version of Tolstoy's novel made in 1929 by Russian emigrés in Germany, entitled *The White Devil* (Belyi d'yavol). The other film, *Hadji Murat,* was made in the mid 1960s in the Tbilisi film studio.
** The British scholar, John Bayley, for example, is of the opinion that Tolstoy identified himself with Hadji Murat, since the writer also "had cut himself off from his own class and his own life, yet had not been able to find any real peace or solidarity in his new life and among his new disciples."[18]

indicates that they might have perceived a link between themselves and Hadji Murat.

The Caucasus, with its majestic, mountainous landscape and its many peoples with their strange and exotic customs, entered the consciousness of the Russian people as early as the eighteenth century. It was in 1783 that Georgia became the first country of the Caucasus to conclude a treaty with Russia, under which the Christian Georgians were assured of protection against any power which might seek to invade their territory. The assurance was an empty one. When the Persians invaded Georgia in 1795 the Russian government left it in the lurch—whether deliberately or due to confusion is an open question, even today.* The Russians moved in only when the Persians had already left Georgia, after killing thousands of its inhabitants and carrying off a large number of prisoners. After these events, Georgia was so weak that it was not only in dire need of protection, but also ripe for annexation by Russia.

The annexation—or, to use the milder term favored by Russian historians, "incorporation"—took place in 1801. The event had far-reaching consequences not only for Georgia but also for the whole Caucasus. With it the attrition of Georgia's population in endless conflicts with the powerful Moslem states of Turkey and Persia was arrested, while Russia was able to press forward with its conquest of the rest of the Caucasus. In order to achieve that conquest, and at the same time consolidate its hold over Georgia, the Russians had first to subjugate Daghestan. That country, with its fierce Moslem tribes, lay between Russia and Georgia. A long and bloody struggle ensued, and half a century after Georgia became part of the Russian empire Daghestan was still resisting its might under the command of Shamil. This little nation caused more damage to Russia's military prestige than has any small country which has ever stood up to its power—with the exception, perhaps, of Finland.

In 1837, Nicholas I attempted to arrange a personal meeting with Shamil in Tiflis at which he expected that the Moslem leader would seek forgiveness for his past conduct and offer guarantees for his good behavior in the future. But Shamil, who himself demanded absolute submission, was a fanatic. He considered that any contact with the Russians, except in the course of combat, would damage the cause of liberating the Caucasus from them. Shamil was also proud and he was unwilling to appear as a suppliant—and least of all in the presence of the emperor of the "unbelievers"—because he considered himself superior to any Russian. Moreover, he did not believe that he had done any wrong, and so it seemed illogical and absurd for him to make excuses for his operations which were

---

* The order to begin military operations against the Persians transmitted from St. Petersburg to the commander of the troops assigned to protect Georgia was delayed by almost a month.

at the time attracting world-wide attention and sympathy. Shamil accordingly refused to meet the tsar, and the hostilities continued.

Curiously enough, the Crimean War, a disaster from Russia's point of view, caused the mountain peoples to gain respect for Russian arms. In their view, an empire which had been able to fight against Turkey and the mighty Western powers without being destroyed was one against which it was hopeless to continue fighting. One by one the insurgent groups abandoned Shamil and went over to the Russians. Shamil was captured by the Russians in 1859,* and within the next five years the remaining fanatical resisters had laid down their arms. In 1864 Russia's conquest of the Caucasus was complete.

The Caucasus came to occupy a unique place in Russian literature in the nineteenth century.** It inspired not only Tolstoy but also Pushkin and Lermontov. Lermontov and Tolstoy actually participated in battles against the mountaineers but, in spite of this, they felt great sympathy for those tribesmen who were fighting so desperately to defend their homeland. However, while their attitudes towards the natives were strongly affected by romanticism, they could see clearly that complete conquest of the Caucasus by Russia was only a matter of time.

Shamil was held in high regard by liberal Russian thinkers of the time. The gifted Nicholas Dobrolyubov declared after the capture of Shamil: "The best sons of Russia will continue his fight for the liberation of the Caucasus."[19] This statement has, of course, remained purely symbolic, but public sympathy for the defeated warriors was strongly felt for many years in Russia. Even today, many Russians know that the peoples of the Caucasus have never really accepted Russian rule and that, although they no longer resist it openly, they remain as fiercely independent in spirit as ever.

Hadji Murat, as portrayed by Tolstoy, is the embodiment of that free spirit, *volya*,*** of which the Russians have an immense appreciation, and which they still desire to possess: that wild, sometimes even violent, abandon which enables them to be really free. Tolstoy admired Murat so

---

* After his capture Shamil lived comfortably for twelve years under "protective surveillance" in Russia, and eventually died on a pilgrimage in Medina.

** The best-known writings in classical Russian literature dealing with this area are *A Prisoner in the Caucasus* by Pushkin and *A Hero of Our Times* by Lermontov. It should be mentioned that Tolstoy himself published a story entitled *A Prisoner in the Caucasus,* in 1872. The plot of the story is based on an incident that occurred during Tolstoy's military service in the Caucasus when he was nearly captured by the mountaineers. Other Tolstoy writings, *The Raid, The Woodfelling,* and *The Cossacks,* also describe the Caucasus.

*** There are two words that mean freedom in Russian: *svoboda* and *volya,* but they convey different ideas. *Svoboda* denotes mostly institutionalized, orderly freedom, whereas *volya* tends to signify personal freedom or will, the liberation of the self. *Volya* rings archaic in modern Russia usage but it is so rich in meanings as to be virtually untranslatable.

much not because he clung to life like a thistle plant but because he lived the way he wanted to—that is, he had true *volya*. He left everything behind him at the prime of life: a beloved family, a respected position and many possessions. Murat knew that a great possibility existed of his being killed by the Russians the moment he gave himself up to them, yet he was not afraid. In his passionate striving for *volya*, he was prepared to risk his life.

Admiration of such courage is likely what most inspired Tolstoy to write *Hadji Murat*. It can hardly be an accident that the manuscript of the work was lying on his desk on the day of his final departure from Yasnaya Polyana.* Perhaps Murat was his *alter ego* who inspired him to make his daring bid to escape from guilt-ridden comfort. The aged Tolstoy knew that he had failed to assert himself on numerous occasions when he had had the chance to do so. Unlike Murat he had not had true *volya*.** He had once told a fellow author, Vladimir Korolenko, how much he envied him for having been exiled to Siberia for political activities. "How many times I have prayed for the opportunity to suffer too for my convictions, but God does not see fit to give me that happiness",[23] he had declared, but in his heart he must have felt that the outburst had not been sincere. If Tolstoy had really wanted to be banished to Siberia there were surely countless courses of action he could have taken. Simply setting up an illegal press in his house for the purpose of printing pamphlets for smuggling abroad would have been one of them. If he had indeed been more daring in the course of his life he might have been less burdened in his old age with feelings of guilt about having failed to match his way of life to his convictions. On a number of occasions, Tolstoy congratulated poor people on their lack of means, at the same time expressing regret for not having the "privilege" of living in squalor. Such behavior quite naturally led to his

---

* There are different views regarding the postponement of *Hadji Murat*'s publication. It has been suggested that Tolstoy was certain that censorship would ban or seriously mutilate the novel. There is an opinion that Tolstoy knew that the novel's publication would have led to stormy arguments with his wife over the royalties and wanted to avoid those scenes.[20] However, the real reason could have been that *Hadji Murat* "so decisively violates the main tenets of Tolstoyan Christianity that its publication would have bewildered and offended the faithful Tolstoyans."[21] As the British scholar, Theodore Redpath, observed: "The full weight of Tolstoy's sympathy seems to be with the resistant mountaineer. Not a trace of the long-cherished philosophy of non-resistance of Christian forebearance, or even of self-perfection, is present."[22]

** Tolstoy's portrayal of Hadji Murat can be compared to Isaak Babel's character, Benya Krik, the legendary leader of Jewish gangsters in prerevolutionary Odessa. Brik was a strong, brave, colorful personality, constantly challenging authority—everything that Babel wanted to be but was not. Benya Krik was for Babel what Hadji Murat might have been for Tolstoy: the embodiment of uncompromising self-assertion. Babel failed to live up to the figure he had created at the beginning of his literary career—he did not have the strength to liberate himself. The price that he paid for his failure was great. After a number of compromises with his environment Babel was executed on false charges.

being ridiculed by his foes in private conversations and in the press, yet until the very end he remained unable to detach himself from the comforts of Yasnaya Polyana. Finally, when already over eighty-two, he took the decisive step to achieve *volya,* and died a few days afterwards.*

Literary critics in the West continue to find it puzzling that Tolstoy, an avowed pacifist, could have written a novel in which he indicated great sympathy for a man of violence. The Russians do not seem to be perturbed by the contradiction. Indeed, Tolstoy would not be so popular among them if he had been no more than a meek man constantly advising others to avoid conflict at all costs. Russian readers of Tolstoy are far more aware than those in other countries that the great writer was engaged in a desperate struggle to attain *volya,* but that this struggle was heavily counterbalanced by religious scruples. If one reads some of the comments made about Tolstoy by his contemporaries, it becomes apparent that his last frustrated attempt to live according to his own free will was not unexpected. The author, Nicholas Timkovsky, who met Tolstoy in the late 1880s thought that everything in him—eyes, ways of expression, manners—conveyed the idea that the basic trait of his personality was not meekness or obedience but struggle to the end. Maxim Gorky thought that in Tolstoy lived "the inquisitive audacity of Vaska Buslaev", a rebellious legendary folk hero of medieval Novgorod. Dmitry Merezhkovsky compared Tolstoy to Stepan Razin and Emelyan Pugachev, the leaders of two bloody and destructive peasant uprisings. The philosopher, Nicholas Lossky, who was expelled from Soviet Russia for non-conformist views, made the following observations about Tolstoy and Russians in general in 1911:

> Tolstoy's whole life is a typically Russian expression of the organic demand for the inner freedom of the soul. This demand is deeply felt by many Russians. Greatly mistaken are those who, on observing the backwardness of Russia in the sense of civil and political liberties combined with the despotic character of the Russian government, consider the Russians a slave people... The Russians satisfy the demand for freedom in

---

* George Orwell pointed out that Tolstoy did try to live according to his free will but by giving up his former life style the writer ended up resembling Shakespeare's character, King Lear, whom he had ridiculed in an essay written in 1904. Orwell wrote: "In his old age Tolstoy renounced his estate, his title and his copyrights, and made an attempt—a sincere attempt, though it was not successful—to escape from his privileged position and live the life of a peasant... And though Tolstoy could not foresee it when he wrote his essay on Shakespeare, even the ending of his life—the sudden unplanned flight across the country accompanied only by a faithful daughter, the death in a cottage in a strange village—seems to have in it a sort of phantom reminiscence of Lear."[24]

Orwell's observations are interesting, but they include an inaccuracy: it was Dushan Makovitsky, Tolstoy's physician, who accompanied him in his flight and not the "faithful daughter". Alexandra joined her father two days after he left Yasnaya Polyana in the Optina Monastery, some eighty miles from there.

completely different forms than, for example, the English... They develop their inner freedom... Thus the paradox becomes clear—our state is the most despotic in Europe and at the same time, our society is perhaps the freest in the world."[25]

Lossky's words ring true even today. Many Westerners who have visited Russia have described encounters in which the broadmindedness of the Russians and the originality of their reasoning made them completely overlook the fact that their government does not encourage unorthodox thinking or behavior. Some visitors have been so astonished by the prevalence of outspoken remarks about political and social issues that they have declared that the ideology of the Soviet state is "dead". There is no doubt that the inner freedom of the Russians is still great and is being constantly nourished by the best traditions of their spiritual heritage,* particularly as manifested in the writings of Tolstoy.

In *Hadji Murat,* the Russians are able to discover a Tolstoy they can identify themselves with far more easily than in his other works. *Hadji Murat* also enables them to escape from the greyness of their lives into a romantic period when there still existed larger-than-life men who took fate into their own hands and calmly faced the consequences. But the basic function of *Hadji Murat* in Russia today is to keep alive a striving for *volya* which is still a component of the Russian national character.

In 1968 the talented Russian writer, Vasily Shukshin, published a screenplay, *I Have Come to Give You Freedom* (Ya prishel dat' vam volyu), about the peasant rebel Stepan Razin. (This work was published as a 400 page novel six years later, shortly before Shukshin's death.) Although Razin's activities lead to appalling atrocities, he is drawn sympathetically, since he tried to bring the precious *volya* to Russia's oppressed masses. The fact that Shukshin became an immensely popular writer indicates that he touched the right chord in the hearts of his compatriots. The bulk of Shukshin's writings deal with contemporary Russia, where his heroes conduct a frantic search for *volya.* Since most of them do not have the opportunity or possess the stamina to attain it, they resort to drink, violence and crime, and even commit suicide.

For Tolstoy the question of self-assertion was a very profound personal matter. For Shukshin it is a serious social problem affecting millions of Russians. The magnitude of the problem causes *Hadji Murat* to be a much appreciated book in Russia today. It serves not so much as an inspiration, but rather as a token of hope that a person can reassert himself no matter how heavy the odds are against him. The expression of the need

---

* The most influential advocate of inner freedom in Soviet literature was the popular and highly-respected author, Konstantin Paustovsky. After 1954, when he was denied the floor at the Second Congress of the Writers' Union, Paustovsky became a prominent figure in the liberalization of Russian literature.

for freedom and self-assertion links Shukshin with Tolstoy, and Soviet scholars are beginning to take note of certain resemblance between the two writers. In a study published in 1978, L. Kiseleva gives examples of similarities in the styles of Shukshin and Tolstoy.[26] Stylistic analysis is the traditional, cautious first step taken by Soviet scholars in establishing thematic and philosophical kinships between writers.

It is hard to predict what scholars will come up with, apart from investigating in detail the longing for *volya* in Tolstoy's and Shukshin's works. It would be intriguing if Tolstoy's influence on Shukshin could be documented. Shukshin, at the beginning of his creative career, openly declared that he was not interested in Tolstoy. He preferred the American writer, Jack London.

Novels Revived by History

The first of Tolstoy's major works to be widely read and discussed in post-revolutionary Russia was *Resurrection*. This is not surprising since almost every institution of the collapsed tsarist regime is represented in a critical light. While articles on *War and Peace* and *Anna Karenina* did not begin to appear in the Soviet press until eight years after the Revolution, *Resurrection* was discussed there as early as April 1918.[1]

The story upon which *Resurrection* is based was not conceived by Tolstoy. Rather, it was a tragic series of events which a notable Russian jurist, Anatole Koni, learned of during his court practice and related to the writer in 1887. A girl from the lower classes was seduced by a young man of the nobility and afterwards abandoned by him. A child was born of the short-lived affair which the girl was unable to support and had to give away. Having the reputation of a "fallen woman", she gradually sank into a life of prostitution in St. Petersburg. One day she was arrested for an alleged theft from a drunken client, and she was sentenced to four months in prison. Her seducer happened to be a member of the jury. Realizing his responsibility for everything that had befallen the girl, the young man resolved to marry her while she was in prison. In spite of all attempts to dissuade him—including those of Koni, who knew him to be the scion of an illustrious family—he remained firm in his decision, and he was making the necessary arrangements for implementing it when the girl contracted typhoid fever and died.

Tolstoy was very impressed by the story and, after several months reflection, wrote a letter to Koni in May 1888 in which he requested permission to base a new novel on it. Koni granted it with alacrity, and begged Tolstoy not to change his mind but to proceed with the project. Tolstoy began writing *Resurrection* in 1889. In his first draft of the novel—he rewrote it six times before he had a version which satisfied him—his portrayal of the male protagonist was recognizably autobiographical, which explains why Tolstoy was so moved by Koni's narrative. Tolstoy, in his youth, had seduced an innocent servant girl, Gasha, at his aunt's estate. He believed that the seduction had led to some very unpleasant consequences for the girl.[2]

In the first draft the psyche of the seducer is central to the plot of *Resurrection*. He is quite pure in his feelings and sincerely wants to redeem his deed when he sees the girl he once loved being accused of participation in a murder. In this version Tolstoy ignored the subject of prevailing conditions in prison and exile. He wrote in a calm and restrained manner and the story, unlike the tale Koni had related, ended happily with the young man marrying the convicted girl and living with her during her exile to Siberia. The two eventually managed to escape from Russia and settle down in London where, since no one knew anything about the young lady's past, they led a peaceful life. In the final pages of the draft, the hero works out the principles of a sweeping tax reform for Russia.

The version of *Resurrection* which was eventually published in 1899 differs radically from the first draft. During the ten years he was working on the novel, Tolstoy became increasingly disillusioned about Russian society, and arrived at the conclusion that it was divided into two groups: a small class of corrupt persecutors and an enormous mass of suffering victims. This development of his social outlook was matched by a constant widening of his conception of *Resurrection* or, perhaps more correctly, of its male protagonist, Prince Nekhlyudov, who is obviously made to see the world through the eyes of Tolstoy. However, the conversion of the young man from a spoiled, aristocratic playboy into an ardent critic of his society and a crusader for better conditions for convicts comes about too suddenly to be convincing. For example, the sort of affair which made Nekhlyudov feel guilty and undergo spiritual change was such a frequent occurrence in the lives of young men of his class that it was regarded as trivial.

Frustration and anger over the social conditions which Tolstoy knew prevailed in Russia obtrude to a much greater degree in *Resurrection* than in any other of his artistic works. Nothing is sacred to him; even religious services become objects of ridicule. As a matter of fact, the description of the Orthodox mass in the prison chapel caused a veritable storm in prerevolutionary Russia.* Even Tolstoy's wife was offended by the crudity of the passage in *Resurrection* where the priest, after Holy Communion, "carried the goblet behind the partition where he drank up God's blood and ate up all the little pieces of His body. Then he carefully sucked his mustache, wiped his mouth and the goblet and reappeared from behind the partition very satisfied, making the thin soles of his calfskin boots creak."[3]

Because of its ever-present, relentless social criticism and Tolstoy's undisguised efforts to pass his "message" on to his readers, Western scholars generally consider *Resurrection* to be the weakest of the writer's major novels. George Steiner remarked that "when Tolstoy came to write *Resurrection* the teacher and prophet in him did violence to the artist."[4] The Canadian scholar, Edmund Heier, thought that the novel "lacks the artistry of *War and Peace* and *Anna Karenina.*"[5] R. F. Christian called it "a

---

* Most of the controversial passages became known to the Russians from editions of *Resurrection* published abroad. Tolstoy's compatriots could not read the novel as it was written by the author. The tsarist censors took care of that when they mutilated over a hundred chapters of it (out of 129), making about 500 deletions and alterations in the text. The deletions were restored in 1918, but it was not until 1936 that the complete and unaltered text was published in Russia in the jubilee edition of Tolstoy's works. All subsequent Soviet issues of *Resurrection* are based on this edition.

vastly inferior work of art to the two great novels which preceded it."[6] Ernest J. Simmons found that at times it became "a blatant purpose novel".[7] Isaak Singer, a winner of the Nobel Prize for literature, remarked in 1980 that "the real Tolstoy is the earlier writer, not the one who wrote *Resurrection.* "[8]

Such seemingly unanimous disapproval of *Resurrection* is, however, a recent phenomenon. When the novel reached England at the beginning of the century, the views expressed were on the whole favorable. The first review in *The Athenaeum,* for example, affirmed that "in this latest production Tolstoy shows the vigour of his early days. There is the same pungency of diction, the same picturesque power."[9] Constance and Edward Garnett—the former a pioneer translator of Russian works into English—who knew Tolstoy and his work intimately were greatly impressed by *Resurrection.* They were quick to grasp that the novel's real worth lay not so much in the literary craftsmanship it evinced as in its whole conception. In their view, "the amazing triumph of *Resurrection* is that it demonstrates that official Russia, and the European upper classes generally, have elaborated a complex structure of state-regulated morality, equally false in relation to the facts of the people's life and to the needs of their soul."[10] G. K. Chesterton evidently agreed with the Garnetts, for he observed in 1903 that "to submit a work like *Resurrection* to the summary treatment which the ordinary novel receives and merits is absurd."[11]

Modern Western critics are quite right when they point out that *Resurrection* has artistic shortcomings and that the work is a "purpose novel". Unlike the Garnetts and Chesterton, however, they might have overlooked the fact that at the time he wrote it Tolstoy was bent on exposing institutionalized violence in Russian society, and was more interested in the social backgrounds of his characters than in representing them artistically. (With *War and Peace* his approach had, of course, been the very opposite.) In order to make *Resurrection* socially realistic Tolstoy painstakingly collected data concerning the judicial bureaucracy, class differences, sexual morality and everything else which had a bearing on the lives of convicts in Russia.

It was, strangely enough, an American, George Kennan, great uncle of the distinguished diplomat-historian, George F. Kennan, who supplied Tolstoy with much of the information about Siberia that he required for *Resurrection.* Tolstoy read the first edition of Kennan's well-documented, two-volume study of Siberia and the exile system in Russia[12], the Russian translation of which did not appear until fifteen years later in St. Petersburg.* Never having been to Siberia, Tolstoy relied heavily on this

---

* Tolstoy had a perfect reading knowledge of English and could speak it well. His French and German were excellent in all respects, and he had a fairly good working knowledge of Arabic, Italian, Spanish, Polish, Czech, and Bulgarian.

work when describing such features of Siberian life as exile convoys, prison buildings and the daily routine of prison inmates, as may be seen from the following comparisons:

In Kennan's work a convoy of prisoners is on the point of setting off: "... When the sick and infirm had all taken the places assigned them in the invalid carts, Captain Gugim took off his cap, crossed himself and bowed in the direction of the prison church and then, turning to the convicts, cried: 'Well, boys, go ahead... '"[13] In *Resurrection* the same episode is described thus: "... When the carts were filled with the sacks on which those who were allowed to ride were seated, the officer of the convoy took off his cap and having wiped his forehead, his bald head and his fat red neck, made the sign of the cross. 'Forward march!', he commanded."[14]

In Kennan's work a halting place for prisoners is described thus: "... A Siberian polu-étape, or half-way station, is a stockaded inclosure about 100 feet long by 50 or 70 feet wide, containing two or three low, one-storey log buildings. One of these buildings is occupied by the convoy officer, another by the soldiers, and the third and largest by the convicts."[15] These lines are clearly recognizable in *Resurrection:* "... This halting place was disposed like all the others along the Siberian highway. In the middle of a yard which was fenced in by a high palisade of pointed logs there were three houses. In the largest one, with barred windows, were placed the convicts, in the second the convoy, and in the third the officers and the office."[16]

Kennan was appalled by the overcrowded Siberian halting places and remarked that "they were built from thirty to fifty years ago, when exile parties did not number more than 150 men, and they now have to accommodate from 350 to 450. The result, as stated by the inspector of exile transportation, is that 'in pleasant weather half the prisoners sleep on the ground in the courtyards, while in bad weather they fill all the kameras, lie on the floors in the corridors.'"[17] In *Resurrection* Tolstoy also refers to the lack of space for convicts: "The quarters of the halting place, originally intended to hold one hundred and fifty people, housed four hundred and fifty. They were so crowded that the convicts unable to find room in the cells had filled the corridor."[18]

These excerpts clearly suggest that Tolstoy, who was strictly attentive to the smallest details in his novels, considered Kennan's book to be authoritative enough to be used as a sort of textbook on matters concerning the treatment of prisoners in Siberia in the late nineteenth century. There is also a possibility that the engaging Englishman in *Resurrection,* who during his wide travels in Siberia had collected data on places of exile and prisons there and preached salvation through faith and redemption, is in fact a representation of Kennan himself.* This person,

---

* The Russian scholar, Nicholas Gudzy, was inclined to think that the Englishman in *Resurrection* was modeled on a certain Dr. Baedeker, a German preacher who, after moving

however, distributed bound copies of the New Testament to the convicts, which Kennan never did for the practical reason that he had to travel as light as possible because of the appalling state of the Siberian roads.

Kennan based his book on the exile system in Russia on his experiences during a visit he made to that country—his fourth—for the purpose of gathering information concerning the revolutionary movement. He had hoped that through talks with exiled revolutionaries he might acquire a better understanding of political events and social conditions in Russia. At the outset of the visit Kennan emphasized to the deputy minister of foreign affairs in St. Petersburg that the system of exile to Siberia had been portrayed very unfavorably by prejudiced writers. A truthful description of the prisons and mines there would be advantageous, rather than detrimental, to the interests of the imperial government. He further assured the minister that he had already committed himself publicly to a defense of the government, and so could hardly be suspected of any intention to seek facts in Siberia which could undermine this position. Impartial representation of observed facts proved to be dearer to Kennan than the maintenance of friendly ties with the imperial government. The report he eventually produced on how the exiles fared in Siberia constituted a shocking account of human suffering. It so upset the Russian authorities that in July 1901, during his next trip to Russia, Kennan was arrested and expelled from the country under armed escort as an "untrustworthy" foreigner.

The popularity of *Resurrection* in Russia after 1917 was also the result of its portrayal of political prisoners, who had assumed positions of supreme authority under the new regime. Yet for a number of years while Tolstoy was working on the novel there was no mention of the revolutionaries. They appeared only in the fourth draft, and it was in the fifth that they became important characters, whose devotion to the cause they stood for was almost idealized. In the sixth and final version of the novel Tolstoy was more restrained in the admiration he evinced for the revolutionaries' activities, and he portrayed them as individuals more realistically. The exact reason for Tolstoy's change of attitude is not known, but it is believed that some of the writer's friends—especially Vladimir Chertkov and his wife, Galya—cautioned him not to be carried away by enthusiasm for the revolutionaries. They allegedly suggested that the praise of persons who resorted to violence to achieve their political aims would be seen to be in total contradiction with his philosophy of not resisting evil with evil.

---

to England in 1858, visited Russia several times before the end of the century. Gudzy did acknowledge that with his keen interest in Siberian prisons the Englishman of the novel bore a closer resemblance to Kennan than to Baedeker. This character underwent a metamorphosis after being first conceived of by Tolstoy as a friend of the regime who was visiting Siberia in order to write a book designed to challenge Kennan's findings.

Tolstoy knew many of the members of the Russian revolutionary underground, (including Alexei Bibikov, who managed Tolstoy's estate in the Province of Samara) and had long talks with them about their activities. He could never share common ground with them, since they always sought to justify the use of violence in their struggle against the tsarist regime, whereas he himself considered violence "immoral and stupid".* Yet in *Resurrection* Tolstoy, whose personal opinions are quite plainly voiced by Prince Nekhlyudov, shows himself to be sympathetic to the revolutionaries who have been convicted of crimes of violence. He emphasized that the savage injustice they had been subjected to in the past absolved them to some degree from blame. He was clearly impressed by the revolutionaries' "high moral standards", their "truthfulness and unselfishness" and their readiness to sacrifice their lives for "the cause".

Though this study will not describe the revolutionaries who appear in the pages of *Resurrection,* one by the name of Simonson merits special mention. The heroine of the novel, Katyusha, falls in love with him because he is "such a special person". He brings about Katyusha's complete spiritual separation from Nekhlyudov and guides her towards resurrection. Simonson is much closer to being a Tolstoyan than a revolutionary. Before his arrest he had broken away from his rich family and worked as a village school teacher among peasants. He abhors violence, and in jail he is constantly concerned about his self-perfection. He refuses to own anything and he is a vegetarian, being against the killing of animals, as well as men.

Tolstoy found it much less difficult to portray Simonson than any of the other convicts, and this character had fully emerged by the time the writer had completed the fourth draft of *Resurrection.* This was not only because Simonson was almost the embodiment of the ethical teachings of Tolstoy, but also because the writer, it is believed, modeled him on a person he had known. According to one Russian authority,[19] that person was a certain Bervi-Flerovsky, a sociologist who had written studies of the working class in Russia. It has been established that Bervi-Flerovsky had studied with Tolstoy at the University of Kazan. The fact that Simonson

---

* George Kennan visited Tolstoy five years before he started working on *Resurrection* and recorded in his book that the writer had at that time a deep dislike for the revolutionaries:

> Tolstoy manifested a disinclination to listen to accounts of sufferings among the political convicts in Eastern Siberia; would not read manuscripts that I bought expressly to show him; and said distinctly that while he felt sorry for many of the politicals he could not help them, and was not at all in sympathy with their methods. They had resorted, he said, to violence, and they must expect to suffer from violence... The Count was not willing, apparently, to show even a benevolent and charitable sympathy with men and women of whose actions he wholly disapproved."[20]

It is quite evident that Tolstoy's attitude toward political prisoners later underwent great changes.

was called Wilhelmson in the earlier drafts of the novel and that Wilhelm was the first name of Bervi-Flerovsky support the theory that he was indeed the person the Tolstoyan revolutionary was modeled on.

It is of interest to mention in this connection that Joshua Kunitz, an American authority on Russian literature, asserted in a book of his, published in 1929, that the prototype of Simonson was a Jew.[21] Though no circumstantial support for this exists in the published version of the novel, Kunitz referred to the "startling evidence in the recently published draft of two chapters of *Resurrection*", the location and date of publication of which he unfortunately failed to supply. Kunitz claimed that Tolstoy attempted, in 1900, to depict an exiled Jewish revolutionary named Wilhelmson, who had appeared as Simonson in the novel. The fact that there is no indication in *Resurrection* that Simonson was first conceived as a Jew suggested to Kunitz that Tolstoy "felt impelled to deprive Wilhelmson of his Jewishness before he could sincerely draw a satisfactory and sympathetic portrait of him."[22] Kunitz, who disapproved of the depiction of Jews in certain of Tolstoy's artistic works, believed that the writer himself thought that he was unable to portray a Jew sympathetically.

It remains, of course, entirely questionable whether all that Kunitz asserted really went through Tolstoy's mind while he was writing and revising *Resurrection*. In any case, it is very doubtful that the writer produced another draft of the novel in 1900, the year after it was first published. It is, however, true that Tolstoy wanted to write a sequel to the work which would have dealt with Nekhlyudov's life among the peasants. He referred to the plan in his diary—twice in 1900 and once in 1904—but never proceeded with it.

One can safely say that toward the end of the 1920s the interest that the Russians had in the revolutionaries of tsarist times, as portrayed by Tolstoy, was diminishing rapidly. The Stalinists who now ruled the country bore no resemblance whatsoever to the kind, self-sacrificing men, devoted to the working masses, that Tolstoy had written about. Yet *Resurrection* remained popular, and even today it is sold out the moment it is put on sale in Russian bookstores. In all probability, Katyusha's tragedy and Nekhlyudov's eagerness to atone for his "crime" never had a very strong grip on the feelings of Russian readers. After all, the dramatic sequence of commission of murder, sentencing by the judicial apparatus, exile to Siberia and spiritual rebirth there was familiar to them from Dostoevsky's *Crime and Punishment*. * One is, therefore, led to suspect that the interest of the Russians of the post-revolutionary period in *Resurrection* really lay in the fact that it portrayed something that was still part of their national

---

* The eminent prerevolutionary Russian critic, Nicholas Mikhailovsky, provided a brilliant analysis of *Resurrection* in which he asserted categorically that the novel was inspired by *Crime and Punishment*. He emphasized, however, that Tolstoy's ideas were opposed to those of Dostoevsky.

experience but which Soviet writers could not deal with openly as Tolstoy did. It was the penal and prison system as depicted in *Resurrection* that remained intact in Russia.

Opponents of the Revolution and "socially alien elements" were imprisoned, executed, and exiled in large numbers while the Bolsheviks were consolidating their hold on power. By about the mid-1920s it seemed that the worst was over and that it might indeed be possible to construct in Russia a socialist society free of violence and oppression. However, history had more trials in store for the Russians. Violence, instead of being eradicated, remained a common occurrence in their society for years to come.

At the time that the first five-year plan of industrialization was being put into operation at the end of the 1920s, the Soviet leaders embarked on the collectivization of agriculture. One reason was political: the fact that the millions of individual peasant households which then existed were not amenable to their control and so could constitute a danger to the very existence of the Soviet regime. The other reason was economic: the authorities had serious doubts as to whether their ambitious program of industrialization under the five-year plan could succeed without the creation of a modern, efficient agriculture based on collective farms. It was at the end of 1929 and the beginning of 1930 that collectivization started on a very large scale. Its organizers in many instances resorted to executions, beatings and deportations in order to break the resistance of the peasants. Feelings were bitter in the countryside and peasants often destroyed their livestock and equipment before being forced to join the collective farms. Then in March 1930, the authorities, fearing peasant riots on such a scale that they might be all but impossible to put down, relaxed their drive for collectivization, whereupon about half of the fifteen million peasant households that had joined collectives opted out of them. The drive was resumed in autumn of the same year and continued for about four years until peasant proprietorship had been effectively abolished.

The human cost of collectivization and the famines of 1932 and 1933 which arose out of it were enormous. The prosperous farmers, opprobriously referred to as "kulaks", who with their families numbered several million, were driven from the countryside. Some died in clashes with the authorities, but most of them were deported to the northern regions of Russia and very little is known of their subsequent fate. Those of the more numerous "middle peasants" who resisted collectivization also suffered grievously and there were great human losses due to starvation.

Soviet writers were silent about the atrocities that accompanied collectivization, the sole exception being Mikhail Sholokhov who, in his novel *Virgin Soil Upturned,* described shocking scenes of peasants and their families being evicted from their homes at a moment's notice. He represented such cruelties as the result of overzealousness on the part of local officials. The famine was not mentioned in Soviet literature until 1962,* since officially there had been none—only "food shortages"[23] in certain villages. The country's literature failed to reflect one of the greatest calamities in Russian history. As Adam B. Ulam of the Russian Research Center at Harvard University remarked: "Stalin did not have to fear that, as in tsarist times, a Leo Tolstoy would rise to denounce the regime's inhumanity."[24]

However, Tolstoy's books could still be read and given up-to-date interpretations. When he showed in *Resurrection* how the peasants were ground down by taxes and, if they attempted to stand up for their rights, were force-marched to Siberia, it was not the tsarist regime that was being indicted in the eyes of his new readers, but rather their own society. Tolstoy's voice demanding justice and the immediate cessation of the cruelties was the only voice in Russia at that time that was not muffled.

Mass deportations and the imprisonment of people with far less judicial sanctions than were customary in Tolstoy's day did not cease when peasant resistance to collectivization had been broken. A great purge commenced in December 1934, after the assassination of Sergei Kirov, head of the Leningrad party organization. Stalin (it has been suggested he may have authorized the deed) used it as a pretext for eliminating all those who might conceivably have challenged his position as supreme dictator. The first victims of the purge were party members. An extremely high proportion of those who played prominent roles in the Bolshevik revolution disappeared from view. Of the 139 members of the Central Committee in 1934 about a hundred were arrested, and most of them were executed or died in prison camps. Soon the whole of Russian society, the military included, became engulfed in the purge. Everyone was in the grip of animal fear. The great purge was over by the end of the 1930s, but various other purges occurred after the war. In 1949, for example, there was a purge of Jewish intellectuals, many of whom were executed. Most of the leading members of the Leningrad party organization were arrested and shot at about the same time.

The effects of the purges on Soviet society were so traumatic that in 1956 Nikita Khrushchev, then head of the Party, saw fit, in a "secret" speech to its twentieth congress, to denounce the excesses of the late dictator and thereby generate some measure of confidence for the future. Even though the number of Russians who perished or suffered exile or imprisonment during the purges of the Stalin era ran to millions,** no

---

* Soviet author, Ivan Stadnyuk, in his story, *People Are Not Angels* (Lyudi ne angely), published in the journal, *Neva* (1962 No 12), referred to the famine during the collectivization and to the dying masses of people. He wrote that it was generally observed that "the men died first, then the children, and finally the women".

** While the number of executions during the purges could only be verified from Soviet sources, one can obtain data on the population of prison camps from Western researchers

131

attempt had been made in any published Soviet work to provide an account of them. The only indignant voice from a not-so-distant past that condemned the arrest of innocent people, the crowded prison conditions, the harshness of Siberian exile and the executions, was Tolstoy's. It is unthinkable that the relatives of imprisoned or executed victims, upon reading the descriptions of the inhuman penal system in tsarist Russia in *Resurrection,* would not have drawn parallels to their own situation. Russian readers of the novel could also realize that the conditions under Stalin were immeasurably worse than the ones Tolstoy wrote about—not so much because life was valued less during the purges than at any time during Tolstoy's life,* but because most of the victims, as Khrushchev himself indicated, were innocent of any crime. Harrison Salisbury, an American authority on Soviet affairs, wrote:

> Stalin was using terror, the secret police, fabricated charges, false accusations of conspiracy and treason against his countrymen, and particularly against his fellow members of the Communist Party, on a scale that made the outburst of dictatorial terror by Nero in Rome, Ivan the Terrible in medieval Russia, and Hitler in Nazi Germany look like Sunday school exercises . . . Thousands were killed, thousands died of police brutality, hundreds of thousands were sent to the cruelest exile in Siberia."[25]

Resurrection to the Russians was not, until recent years, dealing with their prerevolutionary past, it was part of their very life. In the vacuum created by a censorship which forbade the discussion of mass arrests and imprisonments, the novel served to provide them with some idea of the likely fate of people who were taken away from among them.** It is

---

who have gathered them from former inmates and defectors from the Soviet security forces. One estimate of the prison camp population for the years 1935, 1936, and 1937 is between five and six million.[26]

* Dissident Soviet author, Roy Medvedev, has done some studies on the purges and according to his findings:

> During the revolutionary years 1905-7 and the subsequent years of reaction, the Tsar's executioners shot, over one year, the same number of workers, peasants, and tradesmen as the number of people either shot or who died in the camps in the course of one day in the Soviet Union of 1937-38.[27]

** The authorities no doubt had an inkling about the real reason for *Resurrection*'s popularity among the Russians. They could not possibly ban the book for exposing the unjust penal and exile system under the tsars but tried to give it a "low profile". For example, while other countries were making films based on the novel before and after the Revolution, it was only in the 1960s that Moscow finally decided to make one. The film *Resurrection* was made in two parts. The completion of the film occurred in 1962, the most liberal year of the so-called "thaw" that followed Stalin's death.

The following countries filmed *Resurrection* before the Russians:[28]

U.S.A.	1908, 1912, 1918, 1927, 1931, 1934
Italy	1915, 1917, 1958 (with France)
Denmark	1909, 1915
France	1908, 1958 (with Italy)
Germany	1923

understandable, therefore, that the greatest sensation in the history of Soviet literature was the appearance in 1962 of Alexander Solzhenitsyn's story, *One Day in the Life of Ivan Denisovich,* the first work ever to be published in the Soviet Union about life in Russian prison camps. The story was published in the journal *Novyi mir,* which had a circulation of some eighty thousand. Within hours the issue was passing from hand to hand at highly inflated prices. The demand for *One Day* was so great that it was printed in nearly a million copies over the next few months.

No less an authority than Vladimir Ermilov, a critic who usually represented the views of the Soviet establishment, wrote an article in *Pravda*[29] a few days after Solzhenitsyn's story appeared. In it he remarked that *One Day*'s quality called to mind Tolstoy's artistic power to depict the Russian national character.* As the "thaw" continued, and the Russians became adjusted to the fact that their country's prison and exile system had been exposed with official blessing, Solzhenitsyn was nominated for the highest Soviet literary award, the Lenin Prize—in December 1963. With the abatement and eventual ending of the "thaw" he never received the coveted award.

That the Russians still have a great interest in any writing about prison and exile in their country is indicative of the fact that the terror of the Stalin era has left a deep scar on the national psyche. Solzhenitsyn's subsequent writings about penal institutions were not permitted to be published in the U.S.S.R., but nevertheless many Russians—intellectuals especially—have managed to read them. *The Gulag Archipelago,* a monumental chronicle of the executions and mass deportations which took place during the years of Stalin's ascendancy, was broadcast from radio stations in West Germany and heard by millions of Russians, in spite of partial jamming. The impact of these broadcasts must have been significant since a spokesman of the Soviet government tried to counterbalance them by reading out letters on television from people who reacted to Solzhenitsyn's book with "outrage".[31]

There are many similarities between the messages Tolstoy and Solzhenitsyn conveyed to their readers through their respective works. When *Resurrection* appeared, many critics considered that, in spite of the horrors described in it, the work was optimistic in spirit. In their view,

---

* The eminent Marxist critic, Georg Lukacs, was also of the opinion that Solzhenitsyn continued the literary traditions of Tolstoy and of Dostoevsky as well.[30] Lukacs, of course, was aware of the fact that parallels had been drawn between *One Day* and Doestoevsky's *Notes from the House of the Dead,* which had been published exactly a hundred years previously, in 1862. Turgenev compared *Notes* to Dante's *Inferno,* and Tolstoy considered it the most beautiful piece of writing in nineteenth century Russian literature. Dostoevsky's work is basically the memoirs of a man serving a ten-year prison sentence for the murder of his wife. However, Dostoevsky, unlike Tolstoy or Solzhenitsyn, does not focus on the injustices of the prison system; his main interest lies in the investigation of the puzzling criminal psyche.

Tolstoy was demonstrating that not only Katyusha Maslova and Prince Nekhlyudov but also the whole of Russia could, by exercising spiritual strength, overcome adversity, be undaunted by the inhumanity of men and institutions, and in the end be resurrected. When Alexander Tvardovsky introduced *One Day* to the readers of *Novyi mir* as editor of that journal he expressed himself in strikingly similar terms. He referred to Solzhenitsyn's great service to his nation and the acclaim with which his new work was being received. Then, after acknowledging that the sufferings of innocent people which the author had set forth in *One Day* would fill readers' hearts with pain and bitterness, he went on to observe that "the author's greatest achievement, however, is that this bitterness and pain do not convey a feeling of utter despair. On the contrary. The effect of this novel, which is so unusual for its honesty and harrowing truth, is to unburden our minds of things thus far unspoken but which had to be said. It thereby strengthens and ennobles us."[32]

Tolstoy and Solzhenitsyn do indeed react in like manner* to the horrors committed in their respective societies. They hold a firm belief that the sufferings their nation has gone through have not been in vain, but will in the long run serve to benefit not only the Russians themselves but all mankind. In his later years Tolstoy repeatedly expressed the view that changes of great benefit to the world would occur in Russia, not in consequence of her military power but because in no other nation is the Christian faith so strong and pure as it is among the Russians. Solzhenitsyn believes likewise in the world mission of the Russian people. He is convinced that the trials and tribulations that his nation has gone through have served to purify the Russians and enable them to clearly see the path that mankind should follow—a path away from the frenzy of industrialization and technological innovations and back to fundamental values and religious principles. As that astute observer of the Russians, Hedrick Smith, has remarked, Solzhenitsyn speaks with the voice of a mystical apostle of Holy Russia.[33]

Both *Resurrection* and *One Day* caused great divergences of opinion in Russia. When Tolstoy's work appeared many of his readers considered that he had represented the institutions of his country in a deliberately morbid light because of personal dissatisfaction with his own life and surroundings. Others were indignant about the portrayal of members of certain social groups as either parasites or scoundrels. On the other hand, opponents of the tsarist regime welcomed the book and found every part of it as truthful as life itself. As for *One Day,* even while it was being tumultuously acclaimed, those who had opposed its publication began

---

* The American scholar, Kathryn Feuer, considers that one bond between Tolstoy and Solzhenitsyn is "their common understanding that the artist and the citizen are undivorceable."[34]

their counterattack. They considered that Solzhenitsyn should not have represented the camp authorities and the guards in such a totally unfavorable light, thereby giving ammunition to the enemies of the Soviet Union. As the months went by, the opponents of Solzhenitsyn became more sophisticated in their criticism, accusing him of having failed to provide a "philosophical assessment" of Stalin's Russia. Critics who had earlier written about Ivan Denisovich in glowing terms now began to represent him as a misfit and troublemaker, suggesting that even in a prison camp that simple man should have demonstrated unflinching loyalty to the Soviet state, rather than do nothing but think about his own survival. This suggestion caused revulsion among those who loved the story. For many Russians all the arguments and polemics surrounding it could be reduced to a simple proposition which began to circulate in the early 1960s, "Tell me what you think of Ivan Denisovich and I will tell you who you are."

It can be safely asserted that of all Tolstoy's works it was *War and Peace* which received the greatest amount of criticism from militant supporters of the new regime after the Revolution. This is no cause for surprise for, if one excludes his religious writings, this, the greatest of all Tolstoy's novels, was considered by many to be alien to the new Soviet spirit. Its pages are filled with glowing descriptions of the class enemies of the new order, who were killed by the thousands during the Revolution and the ensuing civil war. While hardly any indication is given in the novel that the Russian peasantry lived in appalling bondage, there is an abundance of idyllic scenes of landowners with their serfs. Tolstoy's contention that the Russians, completely oblivious to their class differences, became united under the impact of a foreign invasion in defence of the tsarist autocracy was incomprehensible to the fiery promoters of world revolution. They dismissed the philosophical passages of *War and Peace* as the ravings of one who had never learned to analyse historical events by the methods of dialectical materialism and thereby discover their true significance. The militant critics, led by Mikhail Olminsky and Vladimir Friche, who were also prominent in party affairs, advised the Russians to avoid reading Tolstoy's "reactionary" novel. Even the apolitical Formalists considered that it did such violence to historical accuracy that it could not be regarded as a useful depiction of the period and events it was concerned with. To be sure, *War and Peace,* unlike *Resurrection* with its gallery of revolutionaries, is lacking in characters which the politico-literary purists of the early Soviet period were prepared to regard as worthy sons of their land. Figures like the peasant Karataev and the dutiful artillery captain Tushin, hailed today as typical Russians, were not then looked upon with favor. Karataev was considered to be too meek and passive—a product of Tolstoy's idea of a God-fearing peasant with inner harmony. The brave Tushin, although humane to his men, was still a professional officer of the tsarist army, which was regarded in the early 1920s as a despicable reactionary force.

The Bolsheviks considered their victory in 1917 to be the prelude to a world-wide revolution and had no sympathy or tolerance for national loyalties. By the late 1920s, however, the greater revolution had for reasons of practical necessity ceased to be an active preoccupation of the Soviet leaders, and allegiance to Russia alone had become quite compatible with the official ideology. This development was probably the decisive factor in Tolstoy's acceptance in Soviet Russia. The alienation from the new order caused by collectivization, large-scale rapid industrialization, and the purges was another factor which contributed to the restoration of Russian national values and traditions. During World War II, particularly after the Germans invaded their country, the Russians were actually encouraged to eliminate the last stages of militancy toward their tsarist past.

In his first speech to the Russian people after the outbreak of hostilities, Stalin, instead of addressing them as "comrades", used the older and more familiar "brothers and sisters." He subsequently made a series of concessions to their national spirit. Churches were opened up for services, and heroes of the prerevolutionary past—saints, princes and generals— became respectable overnight. Even the dazzling uniforms of imperial Russia were reintroduced after the victory at Stalingrad—in place of the simple tunics which had been adopted in the civil war when distinctions of rank were deliberately underplayed. After victory had been achieved, Russian patriotism continued to be an acceptable emotion and has remained so ever since, provided it remains part of a wider Soviet allegiance. One result of the upsurge in Russian patriotic spirit both during and after the war years has been an increase in the popularity of *War and Peace*. Now that Soviet Russia has acquired overwhelming military strength, *War and Peace* by its former aristocrat, Count Tolstoy, has been proudly and unequivocally acknowledged by the present regime as a description of some of the most glorious events of the country's history.

At the time *War and Peace* first appeared it was, like today, its patriotic character which appealed to readers and critics alike. Nicholas Strakhov, the critic who edited the first eight-volume edition of Tolstoy's collected works, observed in a letter to the writer: "When Russian tsardom ceases to exist new nations will learn from *War and Peace* who the Russians were."[35] In Strakhov's view the novel was essentially a chronicle of heroic Russian behavior in all aspects of life. Tolstoy's great literary contemporary, Turgenev, did not have a very high opinion of the work's artistic qualities, and he found whole chapters "positively bad and boring". However, it was the Russian in him that spoke when, in recommending *War and Peace* to French readers, he described Tolstoy as "a Russian writer to the very marrow of his bones"[36] and the novel itself as "an accurate description of the character and temperament of the Russian people and of Russian life in general."*

It was not only the men of letters of tsarist times who regarded *War and Peace* as an expression of enthusiasm for everything truly Russian. The imperial authorities, although wary of Tolstoy as a writer, perceived the potential of the novel for inspiring patriotic feeling against Russia's enemies. Accordingly, after war broke out in 1914, *War and Peace* was reissued in cheap mass editions, and in 1915 alone three films based on the novel were made in Russia. The effect of these measures was minimal, since the situation was quite different from that described in *War and Peace.* Russia had not been attacked. It was the Russians who began hostilities by invading German and Austrian territory.

An entirely different situation existed in 1941 when the parallel between the fight against Hitler's invading armies and the resistance to Napoleon in 1812, as described in *War and Peace,* was quite obvious. Tolstoy's epic work took on new life and, as the writer Konstantin Simonov aptly remarked: "history came to resemble the novel."[37]

Both conflicts had been preceded by a political accord. In June 1807 Alexander I and Napoleon had conferred together at Tilsit, and concluded a treaty which facilitated Napoleon's conquest of Europe, and at the same time secured territorial gains for Russia in Poland and Finland. The treaty aroused the anger of many influential Russians who regarded Napoleon as a dangerous product of the French Revolution, totally incompatible with the spirit of imperial Russia. They sought to uphold the interests of French aristocrats, sworn enemies of the revolution, who had fled from that upheaval and were living as emigrés in Russia. Both the emigrés and their Russian friends were convinced that armed conflict between Russia and France was inevitable.

The pact concluded between Hitler and Stalin in August 1939 enabled Hitler to conquer one country after another, while Russia absorbed the Baltic republics and large areas of Poland and Rumania. The hitherto unthinkable accord came as a shock to many prominent communists in Russia who considered it damaging not only to their own country but to international communism as well. The fact that a high proportion of the victims of the great purge were army officers is often attributed to Stalin's awareness that any temporizing with Hitler would have been vigorously opposed by those officers. The most important of them, Marshal

---

* Turgenev died in 1883 before the artistic merits of *War and Peace* had been acknowledged by the leading French authors and critics. Of all the distinguished French literary figures who had received copies of the novel from Turgenev at the end of 1879, not one expressed any willingness to write a review about it. Flaubert, however, immediately praised the novel in a private letter to Turgenev:

> ... Quel peintre et quel psychologue! Il me semble qu'il y a parfois des passages a la Shakespeare. Je poussais des cris d'admiration pendant la lecture."

It should be added that Flaubert's enthusiasm did not extend to all parts of *War and Peace.*

137

Tukhachevsky, became a victim of the purge little more than a year after he voiced to the party leaders his conviction that Russia was in mortal danger from Nazi Germany. A group of high-ranking officers of the Red Army were secretly tried and executed along with him. After the pact between Hitler and Stalin was concluded, all who in any way opposed it—including a number of communist refugees from Germany who were living in Russia at the time—met the same fate.

Napoleon and Hitler both attacked Russia towards the end of June, and both had the capture of Moscow as a principal objective. Napoleon did capture Moscow but had to abandon it with the approach of winter. Hitler's soldiers were able to see the Kremlin's cathedrals through their field glasses, yet they could not capture the city, for they became immobilized. Not only their vehicles, but also their weapons, froze. The winter of 1941-42 in Russia was in fact one of the coldest of this century, the first snow arriving on the 7th of October—five days earlier than it did in 1812. But it was not the winter that defeated the two invaders—it was Russia itself. Tolstoy makes it abundantly clear in *War and Peace* that Napoleon lost his war against Russia the moment he invaded the country. And Hitler was also destined to be defeated, for he completely under-estimated the patriotic strength of the Russian people.*

In both wars the invaders had initial successes, but final victory eluded them. In *War and Peace,* Napoleon and his generals were overcome with alarm at Borodino when the Russians, after losing half of their number, fought with the same savage determination that they had demonstrated at the beginning of the battle. Hitler and his strategists must have experienced similar emotions. Red Army losses during the first months of the war were enormous. It has been estimated that its casualties in the battles at Smolensk and Kiev alone numbered over a million, and that by November 1941 over two million men were in German prisoner-of-war camps.[39] The German high command issued invitations to victory banquets in Moscow and Leningrad for the same winter but the celebrations never took place. The resistance of the Russians, instead of weakening, became stronger. The German staff officers who had planned the invasion of Russia were not fools, yet, once launched, their campaign followed a course which seemed to them to defy logic. Hitler bore a clear resemblance to Napoleon, as portrayed by Tolstoy, in being unable to comprehend the attitude of the Russians to the war. He became bewildered when the campaign that had seemed so simple to him at the beginning became incomprehensible and

---

* Even foreigners saw the parallels between the two invasions. Clifton Fadiman, in his introduction to *War and Peace* published in New York in 1942, remarked that "it is impossible to reread *War and Peace* in the Year of Death 1942 without being constantly reminded of the fact that history can at times be sensationally repetitious."[38] The London edition of *War and Peace* in 1943 was supplemented by maps showing the route of Napoleon's invasion in 1812 and that of Hitler's in 1941.

frightening. It seemed as if events were conspiring to vindicate the view, elaborated by Tolstoy in *War and Peace*, that the forces which direct human destiny are too complicated and mysterious for any man to understand.

The military tide turned due to the fighting qualities of the Red Army and also to the harrying of the Germans by armed civilians who answered the call of their government to fight a "patriotic war". The enemy suffered great losses in clashes with Russian combatants, who often attacked without waiting for orders from Moscow. From Tolstoy's account of the conflict between France and Russia in 1812 it is evident that the writer firmly believed that the decisive factor in the achievement of military victory is not the wisdom of governments or the leadership of generals but the attitude and morale of the person doing the actual fighting. The Russians of today fully share that view. They know that their leaders were demoralized by Hitler's initial successes, and that errors of enormous magnitude were committed by their generals in the conduct of the war. Some of the blunders made were so great that, after battles had been lost, the commanders concerned were recalled to Moscow, court martialed and shot. The Russians have every reason to believe that, although they had some talented military leaders during the fighting, they started winning the war only when the ordinary soldiers could see clearly who the enemy really was, and that the very existence of their country was at stake.

The great popularity of *War and Peace* among the Russians during the war was in large measure due to their realization that it was not the French that Tolstoy really detested, but rather the Germans. Although Napoleon, his entourage and some of his troops behave contemptibly in the novel, some individual Frenchmen are shown to have displayed human warmth and compassion. For the Germans, however, Tolstoy never has a good word,* even when they are trying to help the Russians against Napoleon. When, during the evacuation of Moscow by the Russians, Countess Rostov objects to leaving the family possessions behind in order to make room on their carts for wounded soldiers, her daughter, Natasha, remarks indignantly: "Are we Germans or something?"[40] The Germans in Tolstoy's novel are machine-like, angular creatures, narrow-minded and unfeeling**—the same types that are so often to be seen in Soviet war novels and films.

Upon reading *War and Peace*, the Russians were also able to perceive

---

* As unamiable characters the Germans are closely followed in *War and Peace* by the Poles. The Polish scholar, Waclaw Lednicki, dwells on this point in his book, *Tolstoy between War and Peace* (The Hague, 1965).

** The Germans either did not notice Tolstoy's prejudiced description of their forefathers in the novel or attributed no importance to it. *War and Peace* was published in Germany right up to the outbreak of war with Russia in 1941 and was generally well-received.

a resemblance between their society and that which had faced Napoleon. In Tolstoy's novel the great mass of Russians, who spent their lives in subjection to state officials and aristocratic landowners, resisted a formidable enemy with dogged determination and drove him out of their country. In the course of the fighting the ordinary people and the ruling classes got to know each other better. The former discovered that aristocrats were not all insensitive, cowardly parasites, but that some of them could be compassionate, heroic and self-sacrificing. The upper classes on the other hand had an opportunity to observe that their meek serfs could be an effective fighting force and that their endurance could match that of the world's best trained army. For a short period there was—according to Tolstoy—social harmony in Russia as the social classes joined together to expel the invader.

In 1941, following the violent social upheavals, there again existed a very wide gap in Russia between the rulers and the ruled. Indeed, this gap was one of the factors that Hitler took into account in deciding to attack Russia, for it seemed to him to guarantee victory for his armies within a few months. It appeared at first that he had calculated well, since hundreds of thousands of Russians surrendered to the invaders, refusing to fight for their Soviet rulers. However, when it became generally known how the Germans were behaving on Russian soil, and what the future would hold for the Russians in the event of a German victory, the Russian soldiers realized that they were fighting for the very survival of their nation. Thereafter, this social implication of the struggle caused it to resemble very closely that which took place against France in 1812.

The Russians could observe that many of the party leaders were making superhuman efforts to secure victory for Russia. Party commissars in the ranks are reputed to have so infuriated the Germans by their exploits that they were shot out of hand when captured. Casualties among party members were staggering; during the first months of the war, the party lost over a quarter of its membership. At the same time, the exigencies of the war obliged the party leaders to become more aware of the interests of the collectivized, industrialized and intimidated masses. They came to realize that appalling hardships were being suffered because of their failure to prepare adequately for the war, and they witnessed the sacrifices and heroism of ordinary people that eventually saved Russia. At the end of the war, in June 1945, Stalin acknowledged at a military banquet that victory had been brought about by the heroism of the "common people", by the dedicated efforts of "the cogs in the state machinery."

The Russians of the war years, in addition to perceiving great similarities between the military and social situation which then existed in their country and that described in *War and Peace,* also recognized enduring Russian traits in some of the principal characters of the novel. They were fascinated by Prince Andrei Bolkonsky, Pierre Bezukhov and

Natasha Rostov, even though all three were members of an aristocratic order which had vanished from their country. The fact that these characters represent people who had lived over a hundred and fifty years earlier in no way prevented their being close to the Russians of the 1940s. These heroes of *War and Peace* even today seem less remote to the Russians than, for example, the characters of Chekhov, which belong to the late nineteenth century and represent mostly the middle class, which is still in existence in Russia.

That Prince Andrei was a patriot, defended his country bravely, and died from wounds received in battle could have been related in one of countless war novels long forgotten by the Russians. It is the fact that he is in character such a very representative Russian that has caused him to be immortalized in his country's literature. He is preoccupied with the search for a way of life which would satisfy his analytical reasoning and his yearning for a higher purpose in his existence. The yearning to be involved in larger issues than those provided by one's immediate surroundings was never the exclusive privilege of the upper classes in Russia. It is part of the Russian national character, and Prince Andrei in this sense could easily be one of a group of present-day Russians concerned with the long-term effects of the technological revolution or the dangers of global nuclear conflict.

If Prince Andrei had remained throughout the novel a calm and intellectual figure, and not revealed that he was also an emotional human being, captivated by the charm and beauty of the young Natasha, he would not have endeared himself to the Russians. Like any true compatriot of his, Andrei expected absolute loyalty from his beloved. When Natasha became infatuated for a short time with Anatole Kuragin, he broke off all relations with her and displayed complete indifference to her illness. In doing so, he acted as most of his ordinary countrymen would have in the circumstances, and not in accordance with the refined unwritten code of the aristocracy. Furthermore, by not becoming reconciled to Natasha except on his death bed, he satisfied the great majority of Russian readers with their distaste for happy endings.

The slouching, bear-like Pierre is also a seeker. He is in search of a more humane order of things and of people with a sense of national responsibility. He is a much warmer human being than Prince Andrei, and, like any true Russian, seeks genuine relationships with those around him. He is also capable of real passion. When his initial admiration for Napoleon gradually turns to hate, he decides to kill the French emperor in order to save Russia. Frustrated in this intention, he achieves spiritual rebirth in captivity, as by tradition do protagonists of Russian novels from Dostoevsky to Solzhenitsyn. That the simple, uneducated peasant, Platon Karataev, meets the well-bred and widely-traveled Pierre in captivity and conveys to him by his personal example profound truths about life, may be incomprehensible to Westerners, but to the Russians it is perfectly natural. Pierre becomes a true Russian only after the battle of Borodino, when he unites with the ordinary people and is endowed by Karataev with purifying spiritual energy.

Natasha is never preoccupied with serious thoughts and does not search for the ultimate meaning of life, yet the reader does not take her for an empty-headed aristocratic girl. Her natural charm is irresistible; she is simple yet beautiful, pure and straightforward. She bubbles with love, and infects everyone around her with it. Her very appearance can change an atmosphere from dull to joyful. Critics who can wax eloquent about the lofty destinies of Prince Andrei, Pierre, Karataev and Kutuzov in *War and Peace* are often at a loss to suggest what Natasha represents in the novel,* yet this fact has never served to diminish the affection Russian readers have for her. Of all the characters in *War and Peace,* it is likely that it is she who has the largest retinue of admirers in Russia today, and even the most staunch guardians of Soviet values admit to no inconsistency in being captivated by the charms of the young Countess Rostov. Natasha is life itself to the Russians, and therefore transcends all theories about social classes.

The changing attitudes in Russia to *War and Peace* are well reflected in research on Tolstoy. In the first notable Soviet assessment of the novel,[41] published in 1928, Victor Shklovsky vigorously disputed the notion that it provided a true indication of popular feeling in Russia during the war of 1812. As has been mentioned earlier in this work, Shklovsky demonstrated that Tolstoy was unpardonably arbitrary and prejudiced in selecting the archival material he used in writing *War and Peace.* Shklovsky dismissed the idea of there having been a "people's war", and he quoted documents to the effect that Russian society at the time of the Napoleonic invasion was far from being united against the enemy.

It is significant that, although Shklovsky's contentions were subjected to occasional criticism, no work appeared in Russia in the years preceding Hitler's invasion in which any serious attempt was made to refute those contentions and prove that Tolstoy's portrayal of events in Russia in 1812 was an accurate one. It seemed as if either the Russians were not really interested in *War and Peace* or Shklovsky's allegations were valid. Actually, Shklovsky has never been answered satisfactorily, and the first post-war Soviet monograph on *War and Peace*, full of praise for the

_____

* Literary experts determined to explain Tolstoy's characters find themselves in the frustrating position of being unable to define *War and Peace* itself. Is it a novel? Is it a chronicle of Russia's fight against Napoleon? Is it a philosophical essay dealing with the causes of war, questions of life and death, good and evil? To the professional eye, the novel is shapeless, yet the Russians regard it as a literary work that has come the closest to depicting life.

novel's greatness, did not appear until 1954.[42] It was followed by a number of studies of the novel by acknowledged Tolstoy specialists.* Among these works, highly regarded by Western, as well as Russian scholars, are: Andrei Saburov's thematic analysis of the novel,[43] Sergei Bocharov's reflections on the real meaning of Tolstoy's writing,[44] and Evelina Zaidenshnur's monograph concerned with the process of writing *War and Peace.*[45] These works explain and interpret *War and Peace* from various points of view without attempting to criticize any of its possible short-comings.

The absence of criticism of *War and Peace* is a reflection not only of the Soviet government's changed attitude toward the country's past but also of the degree of emotion that the Russians feel for this novel today. It would not be surprising to discover that the Russians read *War and Peace,* not because they are attached to their distant past, but because the novel brings back the euphoric atmosphere of their victory over Germany—the most exciting time in their post-revolutionary history. This was the time when the rulers and the ruled were more united than at any time in Soviet Russia. The country's leaders have tried fervently to have that atmosphere eternalized by a present-day Soviet writer, but without success. Great hopes have been entertained that a popular and talented writer such as Konstantin Simonov or Mikhail Sholokhov might create a Soviet *War and Peace.* Their writings dealing with the war have so far failed to reach Tolstoyan heights. Another Russian author, Leonid Leonov, in a speech he delivered in 1960, acknowledged publicly the fact that everybody is aware of: "Tolstoy's seat stands empty" and there is no one "in present-day Soviet literature to compare with him."

The time when Tolstoy wrote *War and Peace* was separated from the military events of 1812 by over fifty years. Most of the participants in the war were dead by the time the novel was published, and so most of the emotions engendered by the hostilities were no longer active. Tolstoy could ascribe decent behavior to certain individuals in Napoleon's army without incurring the wrath of his compatriots. However, it would still be risky for a Russian writer to dwell on humane acts performed by members of Hitler's forces—deeds which no doubt occurred. The wounds of the 1941-45 war are still unhealed. There are still fresh flowers on the graves of the fallen, and crippled veterans are still a common sight in Russia today. At least another thirty years will have to pass before Russian writers will be able to contemplate the war with some degree of detachment without the possibility of adverse public reaction. Until a new Tolstoy arrives it is to *War and Peace* that the Russians will turn to recreate in their minds the

---

* In some bibliographical sources mention is made of Sergei Bychkov's study[46] published in 1949 as the alleged first Soviet monograph dealing with *War and Peace.* Bychkov's writing is not a monograph. It is a forty-page pamphlet based on his public lecture on Tolstoy's novel.

atmosphere and emotions of the years of their war with Germany.

144

Conclusion

Tolstoy's great authority made him often appear to be Russia's uncrowned tsar. Tolstoy's power did not rest on a large army or awesome state machinery, yet his words seemed to carry greater weight than those of the official rulers, for he was regarded as the very embodiment of Russia's noblest spiritual values. The crowned tsars, of which there were four during the writer's long life, were morally and intellectually inferior to Tolstoy. Captives of imperial ambitions, these rulers were oblivious to the plight of their subjects. Two of them were assassinated (Alexander II, and Nicholas II with his entire family), and when the other two died, the nation sighed with relief.

Tolstoy was above ambitions of political power. He detested the use of violence, and preached compassion and the principles of global brotherhood. He did not want his ideas to be represented in any movement or sect, yet he attracted many followers who were looking for moral redemption. Towards the end of Tolstoy's life, however, there were reports of his isolation in Russian society. Statements were issued to the effect that the number of people who loved Tolstoy and shared his views had been reduced to a handful. It seemed that Tolstoy and everything he represented had been a short-lived phenomenon in Russia. When the October Revolution triumphed and Tolstoyans were not anywhere in evidence, it was assumed that writers emphasizing the need for moral perfection in a violent and pragmatic world were doomed to fast oblivion.

Nevertheless, looking at Russia six decades later, it is evident that this prediction has turned out to be a false one. Tolstoy's influence on his compatriots is much greater today than it has ever been. While there are no groups of itinerant Tolstoyans in rags roaming the Russian countryside, Tolstoy is firmly established in a less spectacular way. Russian children who are only in kindergarten are already acquainted with his stories. In many instances, beginning readers are first inspired with love for Russian language and culture by Tolstoy's works. In universities, there are detailed programs for the study of Tolstoy's masterpieces. With literacy at almost a hundred per cent and Tolstoy as part of the universal curriculum, there are few Russian adults who have not read at least some of Tolstoy's major works. While it would be an exaggeration to state that Tolstoy's ethical writings are widely read in Russia, his artistic work is so saturated with the author's philosophy that any prolonged acquaintance with Tolstoy's stories inevitably results in some degree of appreciation of the writer's historical and moral views.

The Russians today know Tolstoy far more thoroughly than their predecessors did. The amount that has been written in Russia on Tolstoy during the past decades would fill whole libraries. A hundred years ago the Russians believed simply that Tolstoy was a talented national writer. The Russians of our time, better educated, insatiable purchasers of Tolstoy's works, perceive Tolstoy as a giant of world literature comparable only to Homer and Shakespeare. Tolstoy is regarded by them as Mother Russia's most precious gift to mankind, and they are immensely proud of him. Russians also observe that Tolstoy's moral stand and his involvement in the struggle for social justice have remained unsurpassed in their country. No one in modern Russian literature can write about the criminal activities of a corrupt government as passionately as Tolstoy did.

Tolstoy's impact on the Russians is a factor that no Soviet leader can ignore. High level comments on Tolstoy have always been complimentary, although what Tolstoy preached and represented is alien to the ruling establishment: the importance of spiritual values over materialistic ones, love of God over earthly authority, non-violence over class-hatred. During his pilgrimage to Yasnaya Polyana in January 1977, Leonid Brezhnev called Tolstoy's writings "a source of wisdom for all the generations to come."

To question whether the tribute the Soviet leaders have paid to Tolstoy is nothing but lip service to an internationally recognized author is irrelevant here. The important point, amounting to a paradox, is that in a country which has abolished titles and adopted atheism as state policy, no powerful Soviet political figure can show disrespect for the aristocratic and religious Tolstoy.

Tolstoy is perhaps the only figure in the social history of the Russians to become identified with Russia itself, and as a national symbol he transcends ideological barriers. There are indications that Tolstoy will remain with the Russians for a long time to come, since they need him more than ever. For the past sixty years the Russians have lived through more than their fair share of fundamental changes, many of them causing suffering, bewilderment, and alienation. Russian nationals observe with great concern that their percentage of the total population of the USSR is steadily declining. Russians need the protective warmth of their pre-revolutionary spiritual culture to endure the stress of the rapidly changing world and to understand the meaning of the sacrifices exacted of them.

Tolstoy is popular today because he understood the Russians better than any other writer. His work often dealt with Russia's destiny, which he regarded with profound optimism. His investigations into the lives of individual Russians and their place in society sound so contemporary that it seems unbelievable that Tolstoy is not among the living, that a political and industrial transformation has intervened. When a Russian reads

Tolstoy, he communicates with his forebears, he relates to his compatriots, and he understands himself better. It is to be hoped that the lofty ideals expressed in Tolstoy's artistic and ethical writings will surface one day in Russia and other countries as well, as guidance toward international brotherhood. Should this happen, mankind will be in Tolstoy's debt.

Notes

Introduction

1. L. Tolstoi, *Sobranie sochinenii*/ Collected works /, Moskva, 1960 vol.2 pp.108-9
2. I. Berlin, Conversations with Anna Akhmatova and Pasternak, *The New York Review of Books*, vol. XXVII No.18, p.27
3. L. Korneshov, Bol'she chem lyubov' /More than love/, *Otchizna*, 1978 No.9 p.3
4. Leonid Leonov, Thoughts about Tolstoy, *Reminiscences of Lev Tolstoi by his contemporaries*, Moscow, n.d. pp.8-34

Chapter 1.

1. H. Norman, *All the Russians*, New York, Charles Schribner's Sons, 1902 p.47
2. E. Steiner, *Tolstoy the man*, New York, The Outlook Company, 1904 p.22
3. S. Zweig, *Adepts in self-portraiture: Casanova, Stendhal, Tolstoy*, New York, The Viking Press, 1928 pp.218-9
4. R. Löwenfeld, *Graf Tolstoi: ego zhizn', proizvedeniya i mirosozertsanie* / Count Tolstoy: his life, works and world outlook / St. Peterburg, 1896 p.90
5. I. Tolstoi, *Moi vospominaniya*/ My reminiscences /, Moskva, 1969 p.27
6. S. Zweig, op. cit. pp.223-4
7. *Yasnaya Polyana*, Moskva, 1978 p.16
8. N. Riasanovsky, Afterword: the problem of the peasant, *The peasant in nineteenth-century Russia* ed. by W. Vucinich, Stanford, Stanford University Press, 1968 p.263
9. N. Berdyaev, *The Russian idea*, London, Geoffrey Bles, 1947 p.15
10. N. Gogol', *Sobranie sochinenii v semi tomakh*/ Collected works in seven volumes /, Moskva, 1967 vol.6 pp.316-7
11. C. Adler Jr. ed. Domestic Russia in 1801: A contemporary perspective, *Canadian Slavic Studies*, 1969 vol.3 No2 pp.343-4
12. N. Apostolov, *Lev Tolstoi i russkoe samoderzhavie*/ Leo Tolstoy and the Russian autocracy /, Moskva, 1930
13. N. Apostolov, *Zhivoi Tolstoi*/ The living Tolstoy / Moskva, 1928; *Lev Tolstoi nad stranitsami istorii*/ Tolstoy studying history /, Moskva, 1928; *Lev Tolstoi i ego sputniki*/ Tolstoy and his followers /, Moskva, 1928
14. A. Tolstoy, Tolstoy. *A life of my father*, London, Victor Gollancz Ltd., 1953 p.20
15. L. Tolstoi, *Sobranie sochinenii*/ Collected works /, Moskva 1965 vol.17 p.247
16. Ibid p.259
17. L. Tolstoi, *Polnoe sobranie sochinenii*/ Complete works /, Moskva, 1953 vol.61 pp.23-24

Chapter 2.

1. L. Tolstoi, *Polnoe sobranie sochinenii*/ Complete works /, Moskva, 1956 vol.37 pp.437-476
2. P. Birukoff, *The life of Tolstoy*, London, Cassel and Company Ltd., 1911 p.77
3. L. Tolstoi, *Voina i mir*/ War and Peace /, Moskva, 1960 p.596
4. Ibid p.478
5. Ibid p.478-9

6.   G. Krugovoy, *P'er Bezukhov i Platon Karataev: puti k pravednosti v "Voine i mire"* / Pierre Bezukhov and Platon Karataev : roads to righteousness in "War and Peace" /, Leo Tolstoy, 1828-1978; Transactions of the Association of Russian-American scholars in USA, New York, 1978 vol.11 p.150

7.   Sorokhin, *Tolstoy in prerevolutionary criticism,* Ohio State University Press, 1979 p.108

8.   D. Osipov, Geroicheskaya poema o 1812 gode / The heroic poem of 1812 /, *Pravda,* 1937 Sept. 8

9.   *Literaturnaya èntsiklopediya*/ Literary Encyclopedia /, Moskva, 1939 vol.11 p. 329

10. S. Bychkov, *Narodno-geroicheskaya èpopeya L.N. Tolstogo "Voina i mir"*/ "War and Peace"—the heroic epopee of Leo Tolstoy /, Moskva, 1949 pp.29-30

11. S. Leusheva, *Roman L.N. Tolstogo "Voina i mir"*/ Leo Tolstoy novel, "War and Peace"/, Moskva, 1957 p.168

12. D. Mirsky, *A history of Russian literature from its beginnings to 1900,* New York, Vintage Books, 1958 p.273

13. L. Tolstoi, *Sobranie sochinenii*/ Collected works /, Moskva, 1964 vol.16 pp.146-151

14. P. Birukoff, *The life of Tolstoy,* London, Cassel and Company Ltd., 1911 pp.103-4

15. A. Maude, *Tolstoy and his problems,* London, Grant Richards, 1901 p.103

16. *The novels and other works of Lyov N. Tolstoi,* New York, Charles Scribner's Sons, 1917 vol.18 pp.261-2

17. A. Goldenveizer, *Vblizi Tolstogo*/ Near Tolstoy /, Moskva, 1959 p.188

18. S. Tolstaya, *Dnevniki*/ Diaries /, Moskva, 1978 vol.2 p.527

19. A. Goldenveizer, *Talks with Tolstoy,* Richmond, The Hogarth Press, 1923 pp.57-8

20. *Utro Khar'kova*/ The Kharkov Morning /, 1911 April 24

21. A. Prugavin, *O L've Tolstom i o tolstovtsakh*/ Of Leo Tolstoy and the Tolstoyans /, Moskva, 1911 p.140

22. M. Gorky, *Untimely thoughts; essays on Revolution, culture and the Bolsheviks, 1917-1918.* Translated from the Russian with an introduction and notes by Herman Ermolaev, New York, Paul S. Eriksson, Inc., 1968 pp.111-2

23. L. Tolstoy, *The Kingdom of God is within you,* tr. by Leo Wiener, New York, The Noonday Press, 1970 p.286

24. L. Tolstoi, *Sobranie sochinenii*/ Collected works /, Moskva, 1964 vol.16 p.452

25. L. Tolstoi, *sobranie sochinenii*/ Collected works /, Moskva, 1965 vol. 18 pp.294-5

26. Ibid p.369

27. P. Birukoff, *The life of Tolstoy,* London, Cassel and Company Ltd., 1911 pp.154-5

28. E. Vysokomirnyi, *Yasnaya Polyana v gody revolyutsii*/ Yasnaya Polyana during revolutionary years /, Moskva, 1928 pp.12-14

29. E. Zaidenshnur, Yasnaya Polyana v gody sovetskoi vlasti / Yasnaya Polyana during the years of Soviet power /, *Yasnaya Polyana, Stat'i. Dokumenty.* Moskva, 1942 p.110

Chapter 3.

1.   V. Lenin, *Articles on Tolstoy,* Moscow, 1951 p.9

2.   L. Trotskii, *Leo Tolstoi,* Neue Zeit, 1908 Sept. 15

3.   L. Trotskii, Na smert' Tolstogo / On Tolstoy's death/, *Pravda,* 1910 Nov. 20

4.   A. Lunacharskii, Smert' Tolstogo i molodaya Evropa / Tolstoy's death and young Europe /, *Novaya zhizn',* 1911 No2 p.14

5.   M. Gor'kii, *Sobranie sochinenii*/ Collected works /, Moskva, 1951 vol.14 p.300

6.   N. Krupskaya, Tolstoi v otsenke frantsuzskogo pedagoga / Tolstoy in the evaluation of a French educator /, *Svobodnoe vospytanie,* 1916 No2

7.   H. Ermolaev, *Soviet literary theories, 1917-1934,* Berkeley, University of California

Press, 1963 p.149

8. *Literaturnoe nasledstvo*/ Literary heritage /, Moskva, 1961 vol.69 book 2 p.434

9. *Current opinion*, New York, 1919 Jan. vol.66 pp.49-50

10. C. Sarolea, Was Tolstoy the spiritual father of Bolshevism?, *The English Review*, London, 1925 Jan. vol.40 p.157

11. S. Zweig, *The living thoughts of Tolstoy*, London, Cassell and Company, Ltd., 1939 p.18

12. N. Berdyaev, *The Russian idea*, London, Geoffrey Bles, 1947 p.139

13. V. Bonch-Bruevich, Chto khotel chitat' V.I. Lenin po belletristike, iskusstvu i kul'ture v 1919 godu? / What did V.I. Lenin want to read in the field of fiction, art and culture in 1919 ?/, *Na literaturnom postu*, 1931 No8

14. *Pravda*, 1935 Nov.19

15. M. Gor'kii, Vladimir Lenin, *Russkii sovremennik*, 1924 No 1 p.231

16. Speech at the All-Russian meeting of village organizers, 1920, June 12; Speech at the meeting of the party workers of Moscow Province, 1920, Nov. 21; Speech at the planery session of the delegates to the Moscow Soviet, 1921, Febr. 28

17. A. Lunacharskii, *Sobranie sochinenii*/ Collected works /, Moskva, 1963 vol.1 p.315

18. F. Putintsev, *Politicheskaya rol' i taktika sekt*/ The political role and the tactics of sects /, Moskva, 1935 p.22

19. A. Lunacharskii, *Tolstoi i Marks*/ Tolstoy and Marx/, Leningrad, 1924 p.5

20. B. Eikhenbaum, *Molodoi Tolstoi*/ The Young Tolstoy /, Petrograd-Berlin, 1922

21. B. Eikhenbaum, *Lev Tolstoi. Kn.1.50e gody*/ Leo Tolstoy in the 1850s /, Leningrad, 1928

22. E. Zaidenshnur, *"Voina i mir" L.N. Tolstogo; sozdanie velikoi knigi* / "War and Peace" of Leo Tolstoy; the writing of the great book/, Moskva, 1966

23. E. Simmons, *Leo Tolstoy*, Boston, Little, Brown and Company, 1946 p.187

24. H. Troyat, *Tolstoy*, New York, Dell Publishing Co., 1969 p.339

25. R. Christian, *Tolstoy; a critical introduction*, Cambridge, University Press, 1969 p.159

26. B. Eikhenbaum, *Lev Tolstoi. Kn.1. 50e gody*/ Leo Tolstoy in the 1850s /, Leningrad, 1928 p.5

27. / B. Eikhenbaum, Tolstoi i Pol' de Kok / Tolstoy and Paul de Kock /, *Zapadnyi sbornik*, 1937 p.297

28. P. Popov, *Tolstoi i o Tolstom* / Tolstoy and about Tolstoy /, *Literaturnoe nasledstvo*, Nos.37-38 p.741

29. T. Motyleva, *"Voina i mir" za rubenzhom*/ War and Peace" abroad /, Moskva, 1978 p.392

30. L. Tsyrlin, Marshrut formalizma / The path of formalism /, *Literaturnyi Leningrad*, 1934 No5 p.70

31. N. Kornev, Rannii Tolstoi i "sotsiologiya" Eikhenbauma / Early Tolstoy and Eikenbaum's "sociology" /, *Literaturnyi kritik*, 1934 No5 p.70

32. K. Lomunov, Novye raboty o L've Tolstom /New works on Leo Tolstoy /, *Sovetskaya kniga*, 1947 Febr.2 pp.96-97

33. A. Karavaeva, Oruzhenostsy kosmopolitizma /The banner-bearers of Cosmpolitism /, *Novyi mir*, 1949 No9 pp.220-221

34. B. Eikhenbaum, O vzglyadakh Lenina na istoricheskoe znachenie Tolstogo / On Lenin's views on Tolstoy's historical significance /, *Voprosy literatury*, 1957 No5

35. K. Lomunov, *Lev Tolstoi v sovremennom mire*/ Tolstoy in our world / Moskva, 1975 p.460

36. V. Shklovskii, *Material i stil' v romane L'va Tolstogo "Voina i mir"*/ Material and style in Leo Tolstoy's novel, "War and Peace" / Moskva, 1928

37. Ibid p.27

38.   V. Shklovksii, *Zametki o proze russkikh klassikov*/ Notes on the prose of Russian classics /, Moskva, 1955 p.309

39.   I. Kubikov, *Lev Tolstoi,* Mosocw, 1928

40.   Ibid pp.144-5

41.   V. L'vov-Rogachevskii, *Ot usad'by k izbe. Lev Tolstoi,* 1828-1928 / From country mansion to peasant hut. Leo Tolstoy, 1828-1928/ Moskva, 1928 p.183

42.   V. Friche, *L.N. Tolstoi: sbornik statei*/ Leo Tolstoy; a collection of articles /, Moskva, 1929

43.   Ibid pp.19-20

44.   A. Lunacharskii, K predstoyashchemu chestvovaniyu L.N. Tolstogo / On the forthcoming celebration of Leo Tolstoy /, *O Tolstom; sbornik statei,* Moskva, 1928 p.53

45.   F. Raskol'nikov, Lenin o Tolstom / Lenin on Tolstoy /, *Na literaturnom postu,* 1928 No10 pp.16-17

46.   M. Ol'minskii, Nashe otnoshenie k L.N. Tolstomu / Our attitude toward Tolstoy /, *Na literaturnom postu,* 1928 No3 p.5

47.   *Ogonek,* 1928 No4 p.13

48.   M. Ol'minskii, Po povodu primechaniya Ogon'ka, *Pravda,* 1928 March 13

49.   V. Lenin, *Articles on Tolstoy,* Moscow, 1951 p.50

50.   M. Ol'minskii, Lenin ili Tolstoi / Lenin or Tolstoy /, *Pravda,* 1928 Febr.4

51.   P. Kogan, *Lev Tolstoi i marksistskaya kritika*/ Leo Tolstoy and the Marxist critics /, Moskva, 1928 p.64

52.   L. Averbakh, *Kul'turnaya revolyutsiya i voprosy sovremennoi literatury*/ Cultural revolution and problems of contemporary literature / Moskva, 1928

53.   Ibid p.85

54.   V. Lenin, *Articles on Tolstoy,* Moscow, 1951 p.9

55.   A. Fadeev, Stolbovaya doroga proletarskoi literatury / The main road of proletarian literature /, *Oktyabr',* 1928 No11 p.173

56.   A. Voronskii, *Iskusstvo videt' mir* / The art of looking at the world /, Moskva, 1928 p.28

57.   *Pravda,* 1928 Sept. 9

58.   A. Tolstaya, *Probleski vo t'me*/ Flashes in the dark /, Washington, 1965 p.209

59.   P. Krivorotenkov, Kak provesti tolstovskie dni v DRP i v "ugolkakh prosvesh-cheniya" / How to celebrate Tolstoy's jubilee in cultural centres /, B. Ol'khovyi ed. *Lev Tolstoi, 1828-1928;* sbornik statei, Moskva, 1928 p.98

60.   Ibid p.101

61.   A. Werth, The Bolsheviks and the classics, *The Slavonic (and East European) Review,* London, 1928-29 vol.7 p.757

Chapter 4.

1.   *Bibliografiya literatury o L.N. Tolstom, 1917-1967* / Bibliography of literature on Leo Tolstoy, 1917-1967 sost. N.G. Shelyapina / and others /, Moskva, 1960-1972 3 vols.

2.   A. Evlakhov, *Konstitutsional'nye osobennosti psikhiki L.N.* Tolstogo / The constitutional peculiarities of Leo Tolstoy's psyche /, Moskva, 1930

3.   Ibid p.12

4.   M. Gor'kii, *Sobranie sochinenii*/ Collected works /, Moskva, 1951 vol.14 p.265

5.   L. Zilov, *Novelly o Tolstom*/ Stories of Tolstoy /, Moskva, 1934

6.   Ibid p.163

7.   Ibid pp.9-10

8.   I. Éksler, V gostyakh u Sholokhova / A visit to Sholokhov's /, *Izvestiya,* 1937 Dec. 31

9.   H. Muchnic, Sholokhov and Tolstoy, *The Russian Review,* 1957 vol. 16 No2 p.25

10. D, *Stremya "Tikhogo Dona": Zagadki romana*/ The current of the Quiet Don: Riddles of the novel / Paris, YMCA Press, 1974

11. R. Medvedev, *Problems in the literary biography of Mikhail Sholokhov,* Cambridge, University Press, 1977 p.143

12. G. Kjetsaa, *The authorship of the Quiet Don,* Oslo, Universitetet i Oslo, 1978 p.6

13. Ibid p.23

14. R. Medvedev, op.cit. p.205

15. L. Averbakh, *Kul'turnaya revolyutsiya i voprosy sovremennoi literatury*/ Cultural revolution and problems of contemporary literature /, Moskva, 1928 p.130

16. V. Friche, Literaturnye zametki. O novom burzhua / Notes on literature. The new bourgeoisie /, *Pravda,* 1927 May 22

17. I. Nusinov, L.N. Tolstoi i V.I, Lenin / Leo Tolstoy and Vladimir Lenin /, *Lenin o Tolstom. Sbornik statei,* Moskva, 1928 p.58

18. I. Nusinov, Dvoryansko-burzhuaznyi i sotsialisticheskii realism / The noble-bourgeois and socialist realism /, *Novyj mir,* 1934 vol.5 p.252

19. *Soviet Writers' Congress 1934; the Debate on Socialist realism and modernism in the Soviet Union,* London, Lawrence and Wishart, 1977 pp.179-182

20. Ibid p.45

21. L. Nikulin, Stat'ya V.I.Lenina v biblioteke L'va Tolstogo /V. Lenin's article in the library of Leo Tolstoy /, *Komsomol'skaya pravda,* 1940 Nov.12

22. B. Eikhenbaum, *Lev Tolstoi. Kn 2. 60e grody*/ Leo Tolstoy in the 1860s /, Moskva, 1931

23. N. Gudzki, *Kak rabotal L. Tolstoi* / How Tolstoy worked /, Moskva, 1936

24. *Pis'ma grafa L.N. Tolstogo k zhene, 1862-1910 gg.* /Count Tolstoy's letters to his wife, 1862-1910/ Moskva, 1913

25. Ibid p.IV

26. *Literaturnoe nasledstvo,* Nos. 37-38 p.734

27. S. Tolstaya, *Dnevniki* / Diaries/, 1978 vol.1 p.25

28. Ibid p.27

29. Ot redaktsii / From the editors /, *Literaturnoe nasledstvo,* Nos.35-36 p.V

30. G. Lukacs, Tolstoi i razvitie realizma / Tolstoy and the development of realism /, *Literaturnoe nasledstvo,* Nos.35-36 Moskva, 1939 p.16

31. Ibid p.32

32. Ibid p.68

33. M. Khrapchenko, Mirovozrenie i tvorchestvo / World outlook and creativity /, *Voprosy literatury,* 1957 No9 p.75

34. Georg Lukacs, *Solzhenitsyn,* Cambridge, the MIT Press, 1971 p.35

35. K. Lomunov, *Lev Tolstoi v sovremennom mire*/ Tolstoy in our world /, Moskva, 1975 p.455

36. D. Zaslavskii, Sovremannaya istoriya/ Contemporary history /, *Literaturnyi kritik,* 1933 No1 p.73

37. V. Shklovskii, O staroi russkoi voennoi i sovetskoi oboronnoi proze / On old Russian military and Soviet war prose /, *Znamya,* 1936 1936 No1 p.220

38. P. Rahv, Introduction; *Leo Tolstoy, Sevastopol,* Ann Arbor, University of Michigan Press, 1972 p.X.

39. *The Novels and other Works of Lyof N. Tolstoi,* New York, Charles Scribner's Sons, 1917 vol.11 p.268; L. Tolstoy, *Sebastopol,* Ann Arbor, University of Michigan Press, 1972 p.109

40. L. Tolstoi, *Polnoe sobranie sochinenii*/ Complete works /, Moskva, 1935 vol.4 p.229

41. F. Mering, *Karl Marks. Istoriya ego zhizni* / Karl Marx. A history of his life /, Moskva, 1957 p.264; E. Tarle, *Sochineniya v 12-ti tomakh* / Works in twelve volumes /, Moskva, 1959 vol.11 p.157; S. Chubakov, *Lev Tolstoi o voine i militarisme* / Leo Tolstoy on

war and militarism /, Minsk, 1973 p.61

42. M. Friedberg, *Russian classics in Soviet jackets,* New York, Columbia University Press, 1962 pp.37-38

43. I. Kubikov, Ideya patriotizma v russkoi literature / The idea of patriotism in Russian literature /, *Istoricheskii zhurnal,* 1942 No3-4

44. A. Opul'skii, Vokrug imeni L'va Tolstogo / Around Leo Tolstoy's name /, *Grani,* 1978 pp.109-10

45. T. Motyleva, Mirovoe znachenie russkoi literatury / The world significance of Russian literature /, *Pod znamenem marksizma,* 1944 Nos.2-3

46. T. Motyleva, Mirovoe znachenie L'va Tolstogo / The world significance of Leo Tolstoy /, *Sovetskaya kniga,* 1946 no.1

47. T. Motyleva, Protiv nevernogo istolkovaniya romana "Voina i mir" / Against misinterpretation of *War and Peace* /, *Literaturnaya gazeta,* 1948 March 6

48. T. Motyleva, *O mirovom znachenii L.N. Tolstogo/* On Leo Tolstoy world significance /, Moskva, 1957 p.552

49. Ibid p.553

50. T. Motyleva, Burzhuaznaya kleveta na russkuyu literaturu / Bourgeois slander on Russian literature /, *Literaturnaya gazeta,* 1947 Febr. 8

51. A. Shifman, Lev Tolstoi—oblichitel' imperializma / Leo Tolstoy—the unmasker of imperialism /, *Tvorchestvo L.N. Tolstogo. Sbornik statei,* Moskva, 1954

52. V. Ermilov, *Tolstoi-khudozhnik /Tolstoy the artist /, Literaturnoe nasledstvo,* No69 Moskva, 1961 p.28

53. Ibid p.30

54. Ibid p.32

55. E. Zinner, *Tvorchestvo L.N. Tolstogo i angliiskaya realisticheskaya literatura kontsa XIX i nachala XX stoletiya* / Leo Tolstoy's literary career and the English realist literature of the end of the XIXth and the beginning of the XXth centuries /, Irkutsk, 1961 p.5

56. *Kur'er Yunesko /*UNESCO Courier /, 1957 Febr. p.13; *Kur'er Yunesko /* UNESCO Courier / 1965 Sept. p.34

57. N. Ardens (Apostolov), *Tvorcheskii put' L.N. Tolstogo /* Leo Tolstoy's literary career /, Moskva, 1962

58. B. Bursov, *Lev Tolstoi i russkii roman/* Leo Tolstoy and the Russian novel /, Moskva, 1963; V. Lakshin, *Tolstoi i Chekhov/* Tolstoy and Chekhov /, Moskva, 1963; V. Shklovskii, *Lev Tolstoi/* Leo Tolstoy /, Moskva, 1963

59. *Literaturnoe nasledstvo,* 1965 No75 vol.1 p.47

60. Ibid p.59

61. E. Kupreyanova, *Èstetika L.N. Tolstogo/* Leo Tolstoy's esthetics /, Moskva, 1966

62. Ibid p.19

63. Ibid pp.315-6

64. Ibid p.305

65. K. Lomunov, *Èstetika L.N. Tolstogo/* Leo Tolstoy's esthetics /, Moskva, 1972

66. K. Lomunov, *Lev Tolstoi v sovremennoi mire/* Leo Tolstoy in our world /, Moskva, 1975

67. K. Lomunov, *Nad stranitsami "Voskreseniya"/* On reading *Ressurection* /, Moskva, 1979

68. V. Gornaya, Tolstoi-myslitel' v sovremennom burzhuaznom literaturovedenii i filosofii / Tolstoy the thinker in contemporary bourgeois literary history and philosophy /, *Izvestiya Akademii nauk SSSR; seriya literatury i yazyka,* 1968 vol.27

69. Ibid p.521

70. V. Gornaya, L. Tolstoi v otsenke kritiki stran burzhuaznogo Zapada / Leo Tolstoy in the criticism of the bourgeois West / *Russkaya literatura i ee zarubezhnye kritiki; sbornik statei,* Moskva, 1974 p.160

71. D. Zhantieva, Angliiskoe literaturovedenie 50-60kh godov o Turgeneve, Tolstom i

Dostoevskom / English literary criticism of the 1950s and 1960s on Turgenev, Tolstoy and Dostoevsky /, *Russkaya literatura i ee zarubezhnye kritiki; sbornik statei,* Moskva, 1974

72. Ibid p.233

73. S. Zhislina, *Dobryi svet izdaleka/* A friendly light from afar / Moskva, 1978

74. N. Prutskov, L.N. Tolstoi, istoriya, sovremennost' / Leo Tolstoy, history and present /, *Russkaya literatura,* 1978 No3 p.18

75. N. Shneidman, Soviet approaches to the teaching of literature. A case study: L. Tolstoy in Soviet education, *Canadian Slavonic Papers,* 1973 vol. XV No3 p.345

Chapter 5.

1. L. Leonov, Thoughts about Tolstoy, *Reminiscences of Lev Tolstoi by his contemporaries,* Moscow, n.d. p.8

2. E. Walsh, *The Fall of the Russian Empire,* New York, Blue Ribbon Books, 1931 p.73

3. L. Averbakh, *Kul'turnaya revolyutsiya i voprosy sovremennoi literatury* / Cultural -evolution and problems of contemporary literature /, Moskva, 1928 pp.8-14

4. A. Fet, *Moi vospominaniya* / My reminiscences /, Moskva, 1890 pt.2 p.7

5. L. Tolstoi, *Sobranie sochinenii* / Collected works /, Moskva, 1965 vol.17 p.269

6. | N. Gusev, *L.N. Tolstoy. Materialy k biografii, 1855-69/* Leo Tolstoy. Materials for a biography, 1866-69 /, Moskva, 1957 p.610

7. P. Gromov, *O stile L'va Tolstogo; stanovlenie dialektiki dushi* / On Leo Tolstoy's style; the shaping of dialectics of the soul /, Leningrad, 1971; P. Gromov. *O stile L'va Tolstogo; "dialektika dushi" v "Voine i mire"* / On Leo Tolstoy's style; "dialectics of the soul" in the "War and Peace" /, Leningrad, 1977

8. L. Tolstoi, *Sobranie sochinenii/* Collected works /, Moskva, 1964 vol.16 p.600

9. Kh. Abrikosov, Dvenadtsat' let okolo Tolstogo (1898-1910) / Twelve years with Tolstoy (1898-1910) /, *Letopisi Gosudarstvennogo Literaturnogo muzeya,* Moskva, 1948 vol.2 p.454

10. V. Zhdanov, *Poslednie knigi L.N. Tolstogo/* Leo Tolstoy's last books /, Moskva, 1971 pp.97-98

11. N. Lerner, Ob odnom "plagiate" L'va Tolstogo / On one of Leo Tolstoy's "plagiaries" /, *Zvezda,* 1928 No11

12. H. Williamson, *Farewell to the Don; the Russian Revolution in the journals of Brigadier H.N.H. Williamson* ed. by John Harris, New York, The John Day Company, 1971 p.81

13. R. Luckett, *The White Generals: An account of the White movement and the Russian Civil War,* New York, The Viking Press, 1971 p.237

14. L. Shestov, The last judgement: Tolstoy's last works, *Tolstoy: a collection of critical essays,* ed. by Ralph E. Matlaw, Englewood Cliffs, Prentice-Hall Inc., 1967 p.162

15. H. Troyat, *Tolstoy,* New York, Dell Publishing Co., 1969 p.111

16. H. Troyat, *Tolstoi,* Paris, Fayard, 1965 p.108

17. E. Simmons, *Leo Tolstoy,* Boston, Little, Brown and Company, 1946 p.521

18. J. Bayley, Introduction, *Great short works of Leo Tolstoy,* New York, Harper and Row, 1967 p.XVI

19. N. Dobrolyubov, *Polnoe sobranie sochinenii/* Complete works /, Moskva, 1937 vol.4 p.149

20. V. Shklovskii, *Lev Tolstoi* / Leo Tolstoy /, Moskva, 1963 p.751

21. T. Cain, *Tolstoy,* London, Paul Elek, 1977 p.185

22. T. Redpath, *Tolstoy,* Bowes & Bowes, 1960 pp.83-84

23. *L.N. Tolstoi v vospominaniyakh sovremennikov/* Leo Tolstoy in the reminiscences of contemporaries /, Moskva, 1978 vol.2 p.242

24. G. Orwell, Lear, Tolstoy and the Fool, *Polemic,* 1947 March No7 pp.11-12

25. N. Losskii, Nravstvennaya lichnost' Tolstogo / Tolstoy's ethical personality /, originally published in the Russian journal *Logos,* 1911 No1. It was reprinted in the *Transactions of the Association of the Russian American scholars in U.S.A.,* New York, 1978 vol.9 pp.21-22

26. L. Kiseleva, O stilevykh traditsiyakh Tolstogo v russkoi sovetskoi klassike /, Tolstoy's stylistic traditions in Soviet Russian classics /, *Tolstoi v nashe vremya,* Moskva, 1978 pp.122-159

Chapter 6.

1. A. Derman, Gallereya revolyutsionerov / A gallery of revolutionaries /, *Nedelya narodnogo slova,* 1918 April 22

2. P. Biryukov, *Biografiya L.N. Tolstogo*/ A biography of Leo Tolstoy /, 3rd ed. Moskva, 1923 p.317

3. L. Tolstoi, *Voskresenie* / Resurrection /, Moskva, 1967 pp.137-8

4. G. Steiner, *Tolstoy and Dostoyevsky. An Essay in the Old Criticism,* New York, Alfred A. Knopt, 1959 p.92

5. E. Heier, Tolstoy and the Evangelical Revival among Russian aristocracy, *Russian Literature,* The Hague, 1971 No1 p.44

6. R. Christian, *Tolstoy, A critical introduction,* Cambridge, University Press, 1969 pp.221-2

7. E. Simmons, *Tolstoy,* London, Routledge & Kegan Paul, 1973 pp.193-4

8. *Saturday Night* 1980 July p.49

9. *The Athenaeum,* London, 1900 April 7

10. Constance Garnett and Edward Garnett, Tolstoy and "Resurrection," *The North American Review,* New York, 1901 vol.172 pp.512-13

11. G. Chesterton, G. Perries, etc., *Leo Tolstoy,* New York, James Pott and Company, 1903 pp.21-22

12. G. Kennan, *Siberia and the Exile System,* New York, The Century Co., 1891 2 vols.

13. Ibid vol.1 pp.376-8

14. L. Tolstoi, *Voskresnie*/ Resurrection /, Moskva, 1967 p.333

15. G. Kennan, op. cit. vol.1 p.382

16. L. Tolstoi, op. cit. p.386

17. G. Kennan, op. cit. vol.1 p.383

18. L. Tolstoi, op. cit. p.390

19. N. Bilichenko. Obraz Simonsona v romane L.N. Tolstogo "Voskresenie" (k vorposu o prototipe) / The portrayal of Simonson in Leo Tolstoy's novel, "Resurrection"(on the question of prototype) /, *Russkaya literatura,* Leningrad, 1972 No4 pp.161-5

20. G. Kennan, op.cit. vol.1 p.194

21. J. Kunitz, *Russian literature and the Jew,* New York, Columbia University Press, 1929 p.140

22. Ibid p.140

23. P. Yudin, Nasha literaturnaya kritika / Our literary criticism /, *Literaturnaya gazeta,* 1934 Aug. 12

24. A. Ulam, *Stalin; the man and his era,* London, Allen Lane, 1974 p.348

25. H. Salisbury, *The Soviet Union: The fifty years,* New York, Harcourt, Brace & World, Inc., p.19

26. D. Dallin and B. Nicolaevsky, *Forced labor in Soviet Russia,* New Haven, Yale University Press, 1947 p.58

27. R. Medvedev. On Solzhenitsyn's The Gulag Archipelago, *Aleksandr Solzhenitsyn: critical essays and documentary materials,* New York, Collier Books, 1975 pp.465-6

28. L. Anninskii, *Lev Tolstoi i kinematograf*/ Leo Tolstoy and the cinematograph /, Moskva, 1980 p.284

29. V. Ermilov, Vo imya pravdy, vo imya zhizni / In the name of truth, in the name of life /, *Pravda* 1962 Nov. 23

30. G. Lukacs, *Solzhenitsyn,* Cambridge, The MIT Press, 1971 p.35

31. H. Smith, *The Russians,* New York, Ballantine Books, 1976 p.394

32. A. Tvardovsky, Instead of a Foreword, *A. Solzhenitsyn, One day in the life of Ivan Denisovich,* tr. by Max Hayward and Ronald Hingley, New York, Praeger Publishers, 1970 p.XXIII

33. H. Smith, op. cit. pp.570-1

34. K. Feuer, Introduction, *Solzhenitsyn; a collection of critical essays* ed. by Kathryn Feuer, Englewood Cliffs, Prentice-Hall, Inc., 1976 p.14

35. *Perepiska L.N. Tolstogo s N.N. Strakhovym*/ Leo Tolstoy's correspondence with Nicholas Strakhov /, San-Petersburg, 1913 p.27

36. I. Turgenev, *Sobranie sochinenii v desyati tomakh*/ Collected works in ten volumes/, Moskva, 1962 vol.10 p.298

37. K. Simonov, *Segodnya i davno*/ Today and long ago /, Moskva, 1974 p.165

38. L. Tolstoy, *War and peace,* tr. by Louise and Aylmer Maude, with a Foreword by Clifton Fadiman, New York, Simon and Shuster, 1942 p.XXXIX

39. G. Fisher, *Soviet opposition to Stalin,* Cambridge, University Press, 1952 p.3

40. L. Tolstoi, Voina i mir / War and peace /, Moskva, 1960 vol. 3-4 p.335

41. V. Shklovskii, *Material i stil' v romane L'va Tolstogo* "Voina i mir" / Material and style in Leo Tolstoy's novel," War and Peace /, Moskva, 1928

42. S. Leusheva, "Voina i mir" L.N. Tolstogo / Leo Tolstoy's "War and Peace" /, Moskva, 1954

43. A. Saburov, *"Voina i mir" L.N. Tolstogo. Problematika i poetika*/ A thematical analysis of Leo Tolstoy's "War and Peace" /, Moskva, 1959

44. S. Bocharov, *Roman L. Tolstogo "Voina i mir"*/ Leo Tolstoy's novel, War and Peace" /, Moskva, 1963

45. É. Zaidenshnur, *Voina i mir" L.N. Tolstogo : sozdanie velikoi knigi* / "War and Peace" of Leo Tolstoy : the writing of the great book /, Moskva, 1966

46. S. Bychkov, *Narodno-geroicheskaya èpopeya L.N. Tolstogo* "Voina i mir" / Leo Tolstoy's "War and Peace"; a heroic epopee /, Moskva, 1949

Biographical Notes

Afanasev-Chuzhbinsky, Alexander (1817-1875): Russian author. Many of his stories portrayed Russian military life at the time. Wrote poems in Ukrainian.

Alexander I (1777-1825): Russian emperor, reigned from 1801. Son of Paul I. He ruled Russia during Napoleon's invasion, best described artistically in Tolstoy's *War and Peace.*

Alexander II (1818-1881): Russian emperor, reigned from 1885. Son of Nicholas I. He abolished serfdom in 1861. Was assassinated by terrorists.

Alexander III (1845-1894): Russian emperor, reigned from 1881. Son of Alexander II. He is remembered chiefly as a great opponent of liberalization in his country.

Alexander Nevsky (ca. 1220-1263): Russian statesman and saint. Grand Prince of Vladimir from 1251. Defeated the Swedes in 1240, and two years later, the Teutonic Knights. His policy toward the invading Tartars resulted in the winning of important concessions for Russia. Was canonized by the Orthodox Church.

Alexei Petrovich (1690-1718): Son of Peter the Great. Was arrested as a conspirator against his father. Died during the interrogation.

Apostolov (Ardens from 1934), Nicholas (1890-1974): Russian literary historian. Graduated from Kiev University. The author of major contributions to research on Tolstoy.

Auchincloss, Louis (1917-   ): American novelist and critic. Received law degree from the university of Virginia. His legal practice was interrupted by war service in the U.S. navy. Regarded as a major writer, his stories deal with the world of the wealthy.

Averbakh, Leopold (1903-1937): A leading figure in the Association of Russian Proletarian Writers. Lost his influence when his association was dissolved in 1932 to give way to the Writers' Union. He is presumed to have been executed during the purges.

Babel, Isaak (1894-1941): Russian writer. Took part in the civil war in the Red cavalry. Was a professional author from 1923. During the purges, in 1937, he was arrested and later executed. His collections of stories, *Red Calvary* (Konarmiya, 1926) and *Odessa Tales* (Odesskie rasskazy, 1926-31), have become classics in Soviet literature.

Balzac, Honoré de (1799-1850): French novelist. In 1819 obtained a law degree, but switched to literature. One of the most prolific authors of all time, he was considered twice for election to the French Academy but was refused. His major undertaking, *La comédie humaine* (The Human Comedy), consists of nearly one hundred novels.

Bayley, John (1925-   ): British scholar. Received his education at Eton and Oxford. Served in the army from 1943 to 1947. Has been teaching at Oxford since 1951. The author of numerous artistic and scholarly works which include *Tolstoy and the Novel* (1966).

Bazin, René (1853-1923): French novelist. Wrote mainly about the life of peasants. Was elected to the French Academy in 1904.

Berdyaev, Nicholas (1874-1948): Russian philosopher. Was arrested and exiled by the tsarist authorities in 1898 for his Marxist views. In 1922 he was expelled from Soviet Russia as a thinker alien to Marxist philosophy. His main philosophical interest was the religious concept of freedom.

Berlin, Sir Isaiah (1909-   ): Professor of social and political theory at Oxford. He was knighted in 1957 and was president of the British Academy between 1974 and 1978. Among his numerous books if *The Hedgehog and the Fox; An Essay on Tolstoy's Views of History* (1953)

Berlioz, Louis (1803-1869): French composer.

Bervi-Flerovsky, Wilhelm (1829-1918): Russian sociologist. Graduated in law from Kazan University, and was a participant in the Russian Populist movement. Was arrested several times for his activities. He allegedly served as the prototype for Simonson, the revolutionary, in Tolstoy's *Resurrection.*

Bibikov, Alexei (1837-1914): Tolstoy's estate manager in the Province of Samara.

Biryukov, Paul (1860-1931): Tolstoy's collaborator and biographer. A graduate of the St. Petersburg Naval Academy. He met Tolstoy in 1884 and became one of his followers. Took a very active part in Tolstoy's publishing house, *Posrednik* (Intermediary). His four-volume biography was compiled with Tolstoy's assistance. In 1927 he left his country to live among the Dukhobors in Canada. Died in Switzerland.

Bocharov, Sergei (1929-   ): Russian literary historian. Graduated in arts from the University of Moscow. His popular book on *War and Peace,* originally published in 1963, was in its third edition by 1978.

Bonch-Bruevich, Vladimir (1873-1947): Lenin's personal secretary during the early years of Soviet power. Was active in the Marxist movement from 1892. Knew Tolstoy well and collaborated with him to transport the Dukhobors to Canada. Was firmly convinced that Tolstoy was suitable for Soviet readers. Removed from his party posts by the end of the 1930s, he was appointed director of the Moscow Literary Museum.

Brahms, Johannes (1833-1897): German composer.

Brezhnev, Leonid (1906-1982): Soviet statesman. Graduated from an institute of metallurgy. Served in the army from 1941 to 1945. A party worker from 1937, he became the General Secretary in 1966. Was appointed President of the Supreme Soviet in 1977.

Bukharin, Nicholas (1888-1938): Communist party official. Participated in the Marxist movement from the age of eighteen. Edited the communist newspaper, *Novyi mir* (New World) in New York in 1916. Rose rapidly in the Party after the Revolution becoming member of the Politburo in 1924, but was expelled five years later. Was arrested and shot during the purges.

Bulgakov, Valentin (1886-1966): Tolstoy's biographer, and during the writer's last year, in 1910, his secretary. His best-known work, *The Last Year of Leo Tolstoy,* has been published in a number of editions in several languages.

Bursov, Boris (1905-   ): Russian scholar. Taught literature in Leningrad institutes of higher learning until 1966. His publications include two books on Tolstoy.

Catherine II, the Great (1729-1796): Empress of Russia, reigned from 1762. A princess from Germany, she was married to Grand Duke Peter of Russia,who died under mysterious circumstances soon after he became emperor. Russia was greatly enlarged during her rule, mostly by the conquest of Turkish territories. An educated person, she corresponded with Western thinkers and in the early years of her reign she showed great interest in liberal ideas. Was the author of literary and historical works.

Cervantes Saavedra, Miguel de (1547-1616): Spanish novelist, poet and playwright. Educated by the Jesuits, he served in the army and saw action against the Turks. In 1575 was captured by pirates and spent five years as a slave in Algeria. After being ransomed, he worked in the Spanish civil service for over twenty years. Of his literary works the best-known is *Don Quixote* (1605-15).

Chernyshevsky, Nicholas (1827-1889): Russian critic. Graduated from the University of St. Petersburg in 1850. Five years later he was invited to work on the journal *Sovremennik* (Contemporary). In 1862 was arrested for revolutionary propaganda and sentenced to prison and exile. He was released twenty years later.

Chertkov, Galina (1859-1927): The wife of Vladimir Chertkov.

Chertkov, Vladimir (1854-1936): Tolstoy's collaborator and publisher. Member of a Russian aristocratic family, he chose a military career. In 1881 he underwent a spiritual crisis which led him to embrace Tolstoy's religious and ethical principles. In 1897 he was expelled from Russia and settled in England. There he published Tolstoy's writings, originally banned or mutilated by tsarist censorship. Returned to his country in 1908 and continued his publishing activities, eventually becoming editor-in-chief of the jubilee edition of Tolstoy's works.

Chesterton, Gilbert (1874-1936): British author. Appeared in print in 1900. Was a prolific contributor to newspapers and journals. Wrote several novels and with his *Father Brown* detective stories, became very popular. Was the author of a number of essays dealing with literary criticism.

Christian, Reginald (1924-   ): British scholar. Graduated from Oxford. Was attached to the British Embassy in Moscow in 1949-50. Taught at Birmingham and since 1963 has been the head of the Russian Department at the University of St. Andrews. He is one of the foremost Western Tolstoy specialists.

Defoe, Daniel (1660-1731): English novelist. Studied in a puritan theological seminary then entered business. Was active in politics. Began his literary career in 1697 and his most widely read novel is *The Life and Strange Surprising Adventures of Robinson Crusoe, of York, Mariner* (1719).

Dillon, Emile (1855-1933): British author. Knew Tolstoy personally and visited him in Yasnaya Polyana in 1890. Wrote several books on Russia. His work, *Count Leo Tolstoy; a New Portrait by his Contemporary and Critic,* appeared posthumously in 1934.

Dmitry Donskoi (1350-1389): Grand Prince of Moscow from 1363. The first Russian statesman to seriously challenge the Tartar rule in Russia. In 1380 he defeated the Tartar forces at Kulikovo by the Don River.

Dmitry Ivanovich (1582-1591): Son of Ivan the Terrible. Died mysteriously, and it was rumored that Boris Godunov, then the Regent of Russia, had him murdered. The alleged crime is the topic of Alexander Pushkin's dramatic play, *Boris Gudonov,* put to music by Modest Musorgsky.

Dobrolyubov, Nicholas (1836-1861): Russian radical critic. Studied at a teachers' institute and from 1859 was attached to the journal *Sovremennik*. Died of tuberculosis.

Dostoevsky, Fedor (1821-81): Russian novelist. Studied at a military engineering school but soon after graduating decided to be a writer. In 1849 he was arrested for belonging to a utopian socialist circle. Received a death sentence but it was commuted to four years in prison and exile. He was only allowed to return to European Russia ten years later. His prison experiences are described in his book, *Notes from the House of the Dead* (1862), which was highly regarded by Tolstoy. His most read book is probably *Crime and Punishment* (1866).

Eikhenbaum, Boris (1886-1959): Russian scholar, a prominent Formalist in the 1920s. Taught at the University of Leningrad for over thirty years, and made important contributions to research on Tolstoy.

Ermilov, Vladimir (1904-1965): Russian critic. Graduated from Moscow University. Was one of the leaders of the Russian Association of Proletarian Writers. In the late 1940s edited *Literaturnaya gazeta* (The Literary Gazette). Among his books on Russian authors there is a monograph dealing with *Anna Karenina.*

Ermolaev, Herman (1924-   ): Russian-born American scholar. Received his Ph.D. from the University of California at Berkeley. Has been teaching at Princeton since 1959. He is the author of several major contributions to Russian studies.

Estaunié, Edward (1862-1942): French novelist. An engineer by training, he appeared in print in 1891. Was elected to the French Academy in 1923.

Evlakhov, Alexander (1880-   ): Russian critic. Held degrees in the humanities and psychiatry. Was greatly interested in the relationship between esthetics and the psychology of authors.

Fadeev, Alexander (1901-1956): Russian novelist. Fought as a youth in the civil war on the Red side. Was one of the leaders of the Russian Association of Proletarian Writers. From 1939 he headed the Writers' Union. Committed suicide. Appeared in print in 1923 and established his reputation with the novel *The Rout* (Razgrom, 1927).

Fadiman, Clifton (1904-   ): American author. Studied at Columbia University. Worked for many years as an editor, free-lance writer and lecturer. Has a particular interest in children's literature.

Fedin, Konstantin (1892-1979): Russian novelist. Spent World War I in Germany as a civilian prisoner. A prolific writer, he was elected to the Soviet Academy in 1958. Was active in editing literary journals and headed the Writers' Union from 1971. Contributed significantly to Tolstoy's acceptance in Soviet Russia.

Fedor Ivanovich (1557-1598): Son of Ivan the Terrible. Russian tsar, reigned from 1584. He was a weak-willed sovereign and it was actually Boris Godunov, his brother-in-law, who ruled the country. He was the last monarch of the Rurik dynasty.

Fet, Alexander (Real name: Shenshin, 1820-1892): Russian poet. Graduated from Moscow University. Fought in the Crimean War and retired in 1856 as an army captain. His estate was often visited by Turgenev and Tolstoy and he developed close ties with both writers. Regarded as a major poet, he left highly-acclaimed translations from German and Latin.

Feuer, Kathryn (1926-): American scholar. Received her Ph.D. from Columbia University. Taught Russian literature in California and was chairperson of the Russian Department at the University of Toronto from 1966 to 1971. She is the author of numerous studies dealing with Russian literature.

Fielding, Henry (1707-1754): English novelist and playwright. Studied at Eton and had a degree in law. Appeared in print in 1728—wrote a number of novels and about twenty-five comedies. His well-known work is *The History of Tom Jones, a Foundling* (1749).

Filaret (1782-1867): Metropolitan of Moscow from 1821. He wrote Alexander II's manifesto emancipating the serfs in 1861.

Flaubert, Gustave (1821-1880): French writer. Studied law in Paris but did not graduate. From 1844 lived almost continuously on his estate near Rouen. He wrote a large number of novels, the best known of which is *Madame Bovary* (1857). Was an admirer of Tolstoy and gave an enthusiastic welcome to *War and Peace*.

France, Anatole (Real name: Thibault, 1844-1924): French author. Started his literary career as a poet, subsequently writing a large number of novels, plays and volumes of literary criticism. Was elected to the French Academy in 1896 and received the Nobel Prize in 1921. Took an active part in social issues and was an enthusiastic supporter of revolutionary Russia.

Friche, Vladimir (1870-1929): Russian critic. A trained philologist, he took part in the Marxist movement from the beginning of the century. After the Revolution he held high positions in cultural institutions and editorial offices of numerous journals. He was a resolute opponent of Tolstoy's acceptance in Soviet Russia.

Gamzatov, Rasul (1923-): Daghestani poet, writes in Avarian and Russian. Studied at the Gorky Literary Institute. Appeared in print in 1937 and his poetry collection, *Distant Stars* (Vysokie zvezdy, 1962), was awarded the Lenin Prize.

Garnett, Constance (1862-1946): English authoress, translator of Russian literature. Wife of Edward Garnett. Visited Russia twice and met with Tolstoy. Her translations of Tolstoy's books were highly regarded by the author.

Garnett, Edward (1868-1937): English critic and playwright. Husband of Constance Garnett. Was instrumental in the popularization of Russian writers, mainly Turgenev, Tolstoy, and Chekhov, in English speaking countries.

Gay, Nicholas (1831-1894): Russian painter. A friend of Tolstoy, he shared many of the writer's religious principles.

George, Henry (1839-1897): American economist. In his book, *Progress and Poverty* (1879), he developed the idea of a single tax based upon land values. Tolstoy was greatly influenced by the single tax idea regarding it as a possibility of establishing equal rights to land by all those who cultivated it.

Godunov, Boris (ca.1551-1605): Russian tsar, reigned from 1598. The first Russian ruler to effect meaningful orientation towards the West. He was deposed by a pseudo-Dmitry (a person masquarading as Ivan the Terrible's son who died in 1591) backed by the Poles. After his death followed "the time of troubles" the most confused period in Russian history, lasting until the first Romanov's reign in 1613.

Goethe, Johann Wolfgang von (1749-1832): German author. Studied law at the universities of Leipzig and Strasbourg. From 1775 lived at the court of the Duke of Weimar. He is considered to have been Germany's greatest poet. Of his works which have been collected in 133 volumes (the Weimar edition) the most famous is his dramatic poem, *Faust* (1808-31).

Gogol, Nicholas (1809-1852): Russian author. Appeared in print in 1829 and within a decade he became a leading writer. After the staging of his comedy, *The Inspector-General* (1836) he left for Italy where he spent nearly twelve years. His story, *The Overcoat* (1842) and his novel *Dead Souls* (pt. 1, 1842) influenced generations of Russian writers. Toward the end of his life his mental state deteriorated and he burnt the manuscript of the second part of *Dead Souls.*

Goldenveizer, Alexander (1875-1961): Russian pianist, professor of Moscow conservatory. Was Tolstoy's confidant and favorite chess partner. The author of reminiscences dealing with the writer.

Gorchakov, Prince Nicholas (1823-1874): Russian general. Was related to Tolstoy. He commanded the garrison in besieged Sevastopol, which he surrendered to the Allies in September, 1855.

Gorky, Maxim (Real name: Peshkov, Alexei, 1868-1936): Russian writer. Self-educated. From 1889 he was under police surveillance for his participation in the revolutionary underground. Appeared in print in 1892 and ten years later he was elected honorary academician but Nicholas II vetoed it. In 1906 he visited the U.S.A. where he finished his famous novel, *Mother.* His initial reaction to the Bolshevik capture of power in October 1917 was a negative one but by 1919 he had come to support the new regime. Lived abroad between 1921 and 1931. Was an admirer of Tolstoy whom he considered the greatest figure in Russian literature.

Grigorovich, Dmitry (1822-1899): Russian writer. He was one of the first to be openly critical of serfdom.

Gromov, Paul (1914-): Russian literary historian. Graduated from Moscow University. A specialist in Russian poetry, he has written two books on Tolstoy's style.

Gudzy, Nicholas (1887-1965): Russian scholar. Was appointed professor at Moscow University in 1922. A specialist in ancient Russian literature, he became interested in Tolstoy by the end of the 1920s. Prepared a number of Tolstoy's texts for publication.

Gusev, Nicholas (1882-1967): Russian literary historian. Became Tolstoy's secretary in 1907 but was arrested and exiled two years later for revolutionary propaganda. Was the author of voluminous biographical studies of Tolstoy.

Hadji Murat (died in 1852): A prominent figure in the Caucasian resistance movement against the Russian advance. After a disagreement with Shamil's leadership he went over to the Russians. Later escaped from them but was caught and killed. He was the subject of a novel by Tolstoy.

Hardy, Thomas (1840-1928): English novelist and poet. Studied architecture but became a professional author. After having written over a dozen novels he switched to poetry in 1898. His best known work is *Tess of the d'Urbervilles* (1891).

Heier, Edmund (1926-): Canadian scholar. Received his Ph.D. from the University of Michigan. Has been teaching in the Department of German and Russian at the University of Waterloo since 1960.

Hellman, Lilian (1905-): American playwright. Studied at Columbia and New York Universities. Was active in the anti-Fascist movement of the thirties. Visited Russia several times and edited Chekhov's letters for a New York edition in 1955. She is a member of the American Academy of Arts and Letters. One of her popular plays is *Watch on the Rhine* (1941).

Hingley, Ronald (1920-): British scholar. Received his Ph.D. from the University of London. Served in the army between 1940 and 1945. Has been teaching at Oxford since 1955. He is the author of several books dealing with Russia and its literature.

Hitler, Adolf (1889-1945): German statesman, leader of the German National Socialist

Workers Party. Became chancellor of Germany in 1933. Unleashed World War II by attacking Poland in September 1939. Committed suicide.

Homer (Presumably lived in the second half of the 8th century B.C.): Greek poet. Author of the epic poems, *The Iliad* and *The Odyssey*.

Howells, William (1837-1920): American author. Appeared in print with poems in 1860. Served as the American consul in Venice between 1861 and 1865. Was active in journalism; edited *Atlantic Monthly* and *Harper's Monthly*. Became president of the American Academy of Arts and Letters in 1909. Wrote a large number of novels, critical studies, and collections of poems. He was an enthusiastic admirer of Tolstoy.

Ivan the Terrible (1530-1584): Was proclaimed Grand Prince of Moscow at the age of three, and the first tsar of Russia in 1547. Used savage methods to eliminate any real or imagined opposition to his power. Conducted successful campaigns against the Tartars. It was during his reign that the conquest of Siberia was largely accomplished.

James, Henry (1843-1916): American author and critic. Studied law at Harvard. Settled in England in 1876 and became a British subject a year before he died. A prolific writer and influential critic, his works were published in thirty-five volumes in 1921-23.

Joyce, James (1882-1941): Irish writer. Studied medicine and music. In 1912 he left his country and lived mostly in Paris. Became well-known for the introduction of new literary devices in his works. His most famous novel is *Ulysses* (1922) which was banned in many countries for a number of years following its publication.

Kalinin, Mikhail (1875-1946): Soviet statesman. Was arrested and exiled several times by the tsarist authorities for participating in underground activities. Took part in the October Revolution, then held high positions in the state apparatus. In 1938 he became president of the Supreme Soviet.

Kant, Immanuel (1724-1804): German philosopher. Studied at the University of Königsberg and was appointed professor of logic and metaphysics in 1770. The greatest figure in German classical philosophy, he was concerned mainly with the problems of rational understanding. The basic tenets of his investigations are expressed in *Critique of Pure Reason* (1781), *Critique of Practical Reason* (1788), and *Critique of Judgement* (1790). Tolstoy read him fairly thoroughly and was in accord with his discussions on esthetics.

Karamzin, Nicholas (1766-1826): Russian author and historian. Appeared in print in 1783. Widely traveled in Europe and visited France during the Revolution. In his artistic works he introduced the Western literary trend, sentimentalism, into Russian literature. Published twelve volumes of *History of the Russian State*.

Kennan, George (1845-1924): American author. Wrote the fundamental book, *Siberia and the Exile System* (1889-90) which was used as a source book by Tolstoy for the writing of the Siberian scenes of *Resurrection*. Met Tolstoy in 1886. Visited Russia again in 1901, but was expelled by the tsarist police.

Kennan, George Frost (1904-   ): American diplomat and historian. After graduating from Princeton in 1925 he joined the foreign service. In 1952 was appointed ambassador to the U.S.S.R. but was soon recalled under Soviet pressure. Was appointed professor at the Institute for Advanced Study in 1956. He is the author of numerous books dealing with the history of Soviet-American relations.

Kerensky, Alexander (1881-1970): Russian statesman. Received a law degree from the University of St. Petersburg. After the abdication of Nicholas II he became minister of justice and in July of 1917, the premier of Russia. Was ousted by the Bolsheviks. Fled to Paris and eventually settled in the United States. Died in New York.

Khrapchenko, Mikhail (1904-   ): Russian literary historian. Worked for many years as a govenment official dealing with cultural affairs. In 1966 became a member of the Soviet Academy and the following year the secretary of its literary section. For his book dealing with the development of literature he received the Lenin Prize in 1974. He is the author of the study *Leo Tolstoy as an Artist* (Lev Tolstoi kak khudozhnik, 1963)

Khrushchev, Nikita (1894-1971): Soviet statesman. In 1939 was elected to the Politburo,

164

and in September 1953 became first secretary of the Party. In 1958 he was appointed chairman of the Council of Ministers but was forced to resign all his positions in 1964. Visited the United States in 1959.

Kirov, Sergei (Real name: Kostrikov, 1886-1934): Communist party official. Was trained to be a mechanic. Took part in the Bolshevik underground from 1904 and was arrested several times. Participated in the October Revolution and in the civil war. Elected to the Central Committee in 1923 and to the Politburo seven years later. Was the secretary of the Leningrad party organization when he was assassinated.

Kirpotin, Valery (1898-   ): Russian scholar. Fought on the Red side in the civil war. Worked for many years in the party apparatus, and in 1956 was appointed professor at the Gorky Literary Institute. Has published numerous works on Dostoevsky.

Kock, Paul de (1793-1871): French novelist and playwright. His humorous adventure stories were greatly popular in the second quarter of the nineteenth century.

Kogan, Peter (1872-1932): Russian Marxist critic. Graduated from Moscow University and after the Revolution was appointed professor there. Wrote numerous studies dealing with Russian and Western authors.

Koni, Anatole (1844?-1927): Russian lawyer. Received his law degree in 1865 and was elected honorary academician in 1900. Was a friend of Tolstoy's.

Korolenko, Vladimir (1853-1921): Russian writer. Studied mining engineering and was exiled twice to Siberia for criticism of the tsarist regime. Allowed to work in St. Petersburg from 1895, he was active in journalism. Was elected honorary academician in 1900. Tolstoy had high regard for him.

Kramskoi, Ivan (1837-1887): Russian painter.

Kropotkin, Prince Peter (1842-1921): Russian revolutionary and philosopher of anarchism. Came from a wealthy family and was trained for a military career. From 1872 participated in the anarchist movement. Was arrested several times, spent three years in prison in France between 1883 and 1886. Visited the United States twice, where he was given a friendly reception. Returned to Russia in 1917 but took no part in politics after the Revolution.

Krugovoy, George (1924-   ): Russian born American scholar. Received his degrees in philosophy in Salzburg, Austria. He has been teaching Russian literature at Swarthmore College since 1974. Writes mainly on Old Russian literature.

Krupskaya, Nadezhda (1869-1939): Lenin's wife. Married him in 1898 in Siberia while in exile for participation in the revolutionary movement. Was active in educational work after the Revolution.

Kryukov, Fedor (1870-1920): Russian writer. Was a school teacher between 1893 and 1905, then became involved in politics, and later in journalism. Most of his creative writing deals with the life of the Don Cossacks.

Kubikov, Ivan (Real name: Dementev, 1877-1944): Russian critic. Took part in the revolutionary movement and was exiled twice. After 1917 he became a university professor in Moscow. Was the author of a number of books on Russian writers including Tolstoy. His works are officially described today as having been written in the spirit of "vulgar sociology.".

Kuez, Maurice (1890-   ): Swiss author. Was tutor to one of Tolstoy's grandsons. Published a book on Tolstoy in 1945.

Kukolnik, Nestor (1809-1868): Russian writer and playwright. A popular author of the mid-nineteenth century, with interest in Russian life under Peter the Great.

Kunitz, Joshua (1896-1980): American author. For many years edited the journal, *New Masses*. Published several studies dealing with Russian history and literature.

Kupreyanova, Elizabeth (1906-   ): Russian literary historian. Graduated in art history and wrote her doctoral dissertation on Tolstoy's aesthetics. A specialist in Russian literature of the first half of the nineteenth century, she has also written several studies on Tolstoy.

Kuprin, Alexander (1870-1938): Russian writer. Studied in a military school and served for four years as a commissioned officer in the imperial army. From 1894 on he was a professional author. Emigrated after the Revolution but returned to Russia a year before dying of cancer. His most successful story was *The Duel,* (Poedinok, 1905) which describes the brutalities of life in the tsarist army.

Kutuzov, Prince Mikhail (1745-1813): Russian general. After serving as Russia's embassador to Turkey and Prussia he retired to his estate. Was recalled to active duty by Alexander I and commanded the Russian army against the French invasion led by Napoleon. Was made a field marshal after the battle of Borodino.

Lakshin, Vladimir (1933-   ): Russian literary historian. Graduated from Moscow University and was appointed to teach there in 1958. In 1962 he joined the editorial board of the journal *Novyi mir.* His books include *Tolstoy and Chekhov* (1963)

Lanoux, Armand (1913-1983): French writer. After trying painting and journalism he became a professional author in 1943. Was the president of the French Pen Club between 1972 and 1975. Author of a large number of novels.

Lavrin, Janko (1887-   ): British scholar born in Austria. Studied at universities in Russia, France, and Norway. Worked as a journalist in Russia between 1910 and 1947. Taught Russian language and literature at the University of Nottingham from 1918 to 1952. An extremely prolific writer, his works include two books on Tolstoy.

Lenin, Vladimir (Real name: Ulyanov, 1870-1924): Soviet statesman. Studied at Kazan and St. Petersburg universities. Active in the revolutionary movement, he was exiled to Siberia. Left Russia in 1900 and three years later became leader of the Bolshevik faction of the Russian Social Democratic Labor Party at a congress held in London. In 1912 the Bolsheviks became a separate party and five years later they captured the power in Russia. After the Revolution, Lenin became the head of the Soviet government.

Leonov, Leonid (1899-   ): Russian novelist and playwright. Appeared in print in 1915 and his most famous novel is *The Thief* (Vor, 1927—ideologically corrected edition, 1959). His voluminous novel *Russian Forest* (Russkii les) was awarded the Lenin Prize in 1957.

Lermontov, Mikhail (1814-1841): Russian poet. Was given military education and became an officer of the Guard. In 1837, for his poem which alluded to the regime's complicity in Pushkin's death, he was sent to the battle zone in the Caucasus. Was killed in a duel. He is considered to have been one of Russia's greatest poets and his best-known prose work is *A Hero of Our Times* (Geroi nashego vremeni, 1840).

Lerner, Nicholas (1877-   ): Russian critic. Received a law degree and worked in the tsarist juridicial apparatus. Was active in the Russian press before and after the Revolution. Wrote a number of scholarly studies on Pushkin.

Leskov, Nicholas (1831-1895): Russian writer. Received little formal education and became a civil servant at the age of sixteen. His works, first printed in 1862, established his reputation as a first-class narrator. Knew Tolstoy well and was influenced by his ethical views.

Löwenfeld, Raphael (1854-1910): Tolstoy's German biographer and translator.

Lomunov, Konstantin (1911-   ): Russian scholar. Graduated from Moscow University. Taught in a teacher's institute and since 1969 had been a department head at the Gorky Institute of World Literature. In print since 1930, he is the most widely published Soviet expert on Tolstoy.

Lossky, Nicholas (1870-1965): Russian philosopher. Taught philosophy at Petrograd University. In 1922 was expelled from his country by the Soviet authorities as an ideologically alien person. Settled in Czechoslovakia and in 1946 moved to the United States. Died in France. His philosophy and esthetics are deeply permeated by religion.

Lukacs, George (1885-1971): Hungarian Marxist philosopher and literary critic. Studied law in Budapest and Berlin. Participated in the international communist movement and was a cultural commissar in the short-lived Hungarian Soviet republic in 1919. Lived in Moscow between 1933 and 1945 and was attached to the Institute of Philosophy of the Academy of Sciences. After World War II he returned to Hungary; became professor of Budapest University and was elected to the Academy. In 1956 he was a member of the Hungarian revolutionary government. After its liquidation he was imprisoned until April the following year. His books, numbering more than forty, were written mostly in German.

Lunacharsky, Anatole (1875-1933): Soviet cultural figure. A professional revolutionary from 1897, suffered a number of arrests and exiles. Lived abroad between 1906 and 1917, and after the Revolution was a commissar of education for twelve years. Was appointed ambassador to Spain but died on the way to his post. He played a major role in securing Tolstoy's place in Soviet Russia.

Lvov-Rogachevsky, Vasily (1874-1930): Russian critic. A leading member of the Soviet sociological school which attributed primary importance to the author's class position in the evaluation of literary works.

Maistre, Joseph de (1753-1821): French author and philosopher. Served between 1803 and 1817 as ambassador of the King of Sardinia to St. Petersburg. Was greatly opposed to the French Revolution and advocated the principles of spiritual absolutism.

Makovitsky, Dushan (1866-1921): Tolstoy's Slovak physician. Was a member of the writer's household from 1904 to 1910. A convinced Tolstoyan, he left Russia in 1920 and the following year committed suicide.

Matlaw, Ralph (1927-   ): German-born American scholar. Received his Ph.D. from Harvard. After teaching in several universities he has joined the Department of Slavic Languages at the University of Chicago. He is the author of the book *Tolstoy* (1967).

Maude, Aylmer (1858-1938): English author and translator. Received his schooling in Russia and lived there until 1897. Knew Tolstoy personally and translated his major works into English. Was Tolstoy's first English biographer.

Mayakovsky, Vladimir (1893-1930): Russian poet. As a youth participated in the revolutionary underground and was arrested several times. Studied at an art school but was expelled. Appeared in print in 1912 and eventually became a leading figure of the Futurist literary trend. After the Revolution, he was an ardent and talented supporter of the Bolshevik rule. Visited the USA in 1925 and gave a highly critical description of it in *My Discovery of America* (Moe otkrytie Ameriki). Towards the end of his life wrote two plays, *Bedbug* (Klop) and *Bathhouse* (Banya) in which criticized certain aspects of Soviet reality. Committed suicide.

Medvedev, Roy (1925-   ): Russian dissident author. Was division head in a Moscow educational research institute and has been a free-lance writer since 1971. Has authored many books dealing with the current problems of the U.S.S.R. and the effects of Stalin's rule in the country. His writings, except the ones on education, have been published abroad but not in Russia.

Menshikov, Prince Alexander (1673-1729): Russian statesman. A soldier in one of Peter the Great's regiments, he became a friend and close associate of the tsar. In 1705 he was made a prince, and became field marshal after the victory over the Swedes at Poltava in 1709. Following the death of Peter, during the reign of Catherine I, he virtually ruled Russia. In 1729 he was deposed and exiled to Siberia where he died.

Merezhkovsky, Dmitry (1866-1941): Russian novelist. A graduate of St. Petersburg University, appeared in print in 1883 with poems. Opposed to the tsarist regime, he was forced to live abroad between 1906 and 1912. Left Russia after the Revolution and lived mostly in Paris. Was a leading figure in the Russian symbolist movement and his major work is a trilogy, *Christ and Antichrist* (Khristos i Antikhrist, 1896-1905).

Mikhailovsky, Nicholas (1842-1904): Russian critic and thinker. Studied law and began publishing in 1860. Contributed to the Russian press and from 1892 edited the radical journal *Russkoe bogatstvo* (Russian wealth). He is considered to have been a major thinker whose ideas greatly influenced the Russian Populist movement. Was the author of penetrating analyses of Dostoevsky's and Tolstoy's works.

Mirsky, Prince Dmitry (1890-1939): Russian literary historian. Graduated in arts from the University of Petersburg. Lived in England between 1922 and 1932—taught at universities and published two books dealing with Russian literature. After his return to his country he was an active participant in intellectual life. Was arrested during the purges and later executed.

167

Moskvin, Ivan (1874-1946): Russian actor.

Motyleva, Tamara (1910-   ): Russian literary historian. Graduated from Moscow University and was later appointed to teach there. Was barred from teaching in 1948 for being a "cosmopolite", but was reinstated later. Between 1956 and 1963 she was a department head at the Gorky Institute of World Literature. Has written a number of works dealing with Tolstoy's international reputation.

Muchnic, Helen (1903-   ): American scholar. Received her Ph.D. from Byrn Mawr College and taught Russian literature from 1947. Has written several books on Russian writers.

Murat—see Hadji Murat

Napier, Sir Francis (1819-1898): British diplomat. Was ambassador at St. Petersburg between 1860 and 1864.

Napoleon I (1769-1821): French emperor. Had spectacular military victories in Italy for which he was named First Consul of France in 1800. Four years later he became emperor. Attacked Russia in June 1812 and took Moscow three months later but retreated due to the lack of supplies and the approaching winter. In 1814 his foes entered Paris, forced him to abdicate, and sent him to the Island of Elba. Returned the following year, gathered an army, but was defeated at Waterloo. Spent the rest of his life in exile on the Island of St. Helen.

Ney, Michel, Prince de la Moscova (1769-1815): Marshal of France. Made his military career under Napoleon I, and was made prince after the battle at Borodino. When Napoleon abdicated Ney swore allegiance to Louis XVIII but sided again with Napoleon on his return from the Island of Elba. After the battle at Waterloo he was captured, tried for treason, and shot.

Nicholas I (1796-1855): Russian emperor, reigned from 1825. Son of Paul I. Believed in strong autocracy and ruled Russia as if it were a military camp. His ambitions to expand Russia's influence to the Balkans resulted in the Crimean war.

Nicholas II (1868-1918): Russian emperor, reigned from 1894 to 1917. Son of Alexander III. Suffered a humiliating defeat from the Japanese which greatly fuelled the revolutionary discontent in his country. In March 1917 he was forced to abdicate and was put under house arrest. Was executed with his entire family by a Bolshevik firing squad in 1918 in Ekaterinburg (now Sverdlovsk).

Norman, Sir Henry (1858-1939): British author. Was active in journalism. Traveled extensively and published a number of books describing his experiences. Was knighted in 1906 and nine years later became a baronet. In the book *All the Russias* (1902), he describes a visit to Tolstoy's estate.

Nusinov, Isaak (1889-1950): Soviet literary historian. Took part in the revolutionary underground; lived abroad between 1905 and 1917. Was arrested in 1949 during the purge of Jewish intellectuals and executed the following year. He wrote many books in Yiddish which contain studies on prominent Russian writers including Tolstoy.

O'Connor, Frank (1903-1966): Irish writer. Joined the Irish Republican Army in his teens and participated in the civil war from 1919 to 1921. Was jailed for about a year after hostilities ended. Worked as a theatre director in Dublin during the 1930s. Published several essays in England dealing with Russian authors.

Olminsky, Mikhail (Real name: Aleksandrov, 1863-1933): Communist party official. Was expelled from the University of St. Petersburg for revolutionary activities. Endured several arrests and exiles; spent five years in solitary confinement. Was a close collaborator of Lenin and after the Revolution held responsible positions in the party apparatus. Had a thoroughly disapproving attitude toward Tolstoy.

Orwell, George (Real name: Eric Blair, 1903-1950): British writer. Was educated at Eton. Served five years in the imperial police force in Burma. Became a professional author in 1935, and the following year was badly wounded in the Spanish civil war. Suffered from tuberculosis for years before his death.

Ozerov, Vladislav (1769-1816): Russian playwright. His plays, mostly written in a sentimental style, were very popular in his lifetime.

Panaev, Ivan (1812-1862): Russian writer. In 1847 he founded, with the poet Nicholas Nekrasov, the prestigious literary journal, *Sovremennik*. Was one of the first authors to write about women's emancipation in Russia.

Pasternak, Boris (1890-1960): Russian poet and novelist. Son of the artist Leonid Pasternak. His first collection of poems, *The Twin in the Clouds* (Bliznets v tuchakh, 1914) was followed by others establishing his reputation as a leading poet. He was awarded the Nobel Prize after the publication of his novel, *Doctor Zhivago*. The novel was published abroad, and it upset the Soviet authorities so much that Pasternak decided to decline the prize.

Pasternak, Leonid (1862-1945): Russian artist. Was elected to the Petersburg Academy of Arts in 1905. Was well-known for his illustration of Tolstoy's *Resurrection*. Left Russia in 1921; died in England.

Paul I (1754-1801): Russian emperor, reigned from 1796. Son of Catherine the Great. (His alleged father, Peter III, never recognized him as his son.) Was considered despotic and unbalanced. A group of Russian nobles assasinated him in his fortified St. Petersburg palace.

Paustovsky, Konstantin (1892-1968): Russian writer. Studied law at Moscow University. Appeared in print in 1912 and was a professional writer from 1929. He was the author of many colorful stories and his major work *The Story of a Life* (Povest' o zhizni, 1945-1963) has been translated into many languages.

Peter I, the Great (1672-1725): Russia's first emperor, reigned from 1696. (Between 1682 and 1696 he shared the throne with his brother, Ivan.) He was determined to eliminate Russia's social, technological and military backwardness by introducing large scale reforms. Successfully challenged the Swedish supremacy of the Baltic and built his new capital St. Petersburg on captured territory.

Plekhanov, Georgi (1857-1918): A prominent figure in the Russian Marxist movement, and the founder of its first organization, the Emancipation of Labor, in 1883. When, in 1903, the Russian social democrats split into Bolsheviks and Mensheviks, he became the leading figure of the latter. He rejected the October Revolution but stayed out of the politics afterward. Died in Finland. Was recognized as the finest Russian Marxist theoretician. Among his numerous works there are valuable essays on Russian literary figures, including Tolstoy.

Pobedonostsev, Konstantin (1827-1907): Procurator of the Russian Holy Synod from 1880 to 1905. He was the prime figure behind Tolstoy's excommunication from the Orthodox Church.

Prokofiev, Segei (1891-1953): Russian composer.

Proudhon, Pierre-Joseph (1809-1865): French radical economist. Advocated the principles of philosophical anarchism. He believed that ownership of property was unjustifiable and that the power of the state should be eliminated. Tolstoy was allegedly influenced by Proudhon's *War and Peace* (La guerre et la paix), published in 1861.

Prugavin, Alexander (1850-1920): Russian author. Wrote several books dealing with Russian religious sects.

Prutskov, Nikita (1910-   ): Russian scholar. Since 1951 he has been attached to the Academy's Pushkin House in Leningrad.

Pugachev, Emelyan (1740-1775): Leader of a Russian peasant uprising. In 1773 proclaimed himself Peter III, Catherine the Great's husband. After gathering a large number of peasants to his banner he took a number of cities, among them Kazan and Nizhni Novgorod. Was captured by the imperial forces and brought to Moscow, where he was executed.

Pushkin, Alexander (1799-1837): Russian poet. Was educated at a lycée for children of the nobility. In 1817 he began working in the civil service but three years later he was exiled to the south of Russia for writing political epigrams. Pardoned in 1826 by the Emperor Nicholas I, he subsequently became a well-known figure in the capital's social life. Was killed in a duel by a Frenchman. First achieved fame with his fairy-tale poem, *Ruslan and Lyudmila* (1820) but his major work is a novel in verse, *Eugene Onegin* (1823-1831). He is regarded as Russia's greatest poet.

Radishchev, Alexander (1749-1802): Russian writer and liberal thinker. Studied at the University of Leipzig and in 1771 began his career in the civil service. In 1790 he privately published his work *Journey from Petersburg to Moscow* (Puteshestvie iz Peterburga v Moskvu) in which he criticized serfdom. Was condemned to death for his writing but the sentence was commuted to exile in Siberia. Was permitted to return to European Russia in 1796 but was under police surveillance until 1801. The following year he committed suicide.

Raevsky, Ivan (1835-1891): Russian landowner. Was Tolstoy's friend and collaborator in feeding the hungry during the famine in 1891.

Raskolnikov, Fedor (Real name: Ilyin, 1892-1939): Communist party worker. Was the Bolshevik leader of the sailors at Kronstadt during the Revolution. After 1917 he carried out important military and diplomatic missions. Was adamantly against Tolstoy's acceptance in Soviet Russia. Defected in 1937 while abroad and allegedly committed suicide two years later.

Razin, Stepan (ca. 1630-1671): Leader of a Russian peasant uprising. Started his rebellion in 1670 in the lower Volga region. Since the serfs joined him in great numbers, his movement soon spread to other areas of Russia. Nevertheless, the peasant army was stopped and defeated at Simbirsk the following year by the imperial troops. Razin was later captured, brought to Moscow, tortured and executed.

Redpath, Theodore (1913-   ): British scholar. Received his Ph.D. from Cambridge. Served in the army during World War II. Has been teaching English at Cambridge since 1954. He is the author of the book *Tolstoy* (1960).

Repin, Ilya (1844-1930): Russian painter. Was the best known member of the realist school. His most famous canvas is probably *The Volga Boatsmen* (Burlaki na Volge).

Riasanovsky, Nicholas (1923-   ): American historian born in China. Received his Ph.D. from Oxford. Has been teaching at the University of California at Berkeley since 1969.

Rolland, Romain (1866-1944): French writer. Was educated at Ecole Normale Supérieure in Paris, then taught history of music at the Sorbonne. Appeared in print in 1897 and by 1915 his works had earned him the Nobel Prize for literature. He is mainly known for his fictionalized biographies of famous composers and novels dealing with the French Revolution. Had a great interest in Russian culture and was the author of a book on Tolstoy.

Roosevelt, Theodore (1858-1919): Became the 26th president of the United States in 1901 following the assasination of President William McKinley. In 1906 he was awarded the Nobel Prize for peace for his diplomatic efforts to end the Russo-Japanese War.

Rousseau, Jean-Jacques (1712-1778): French author and philosopher. An important figure in French romanticism, he became famous for his essays commenting on social inequality. These works, especially *The Social Contract* (Du contrat social, 1761) and *Emile* (Emile; ou de l'éducation, 1762), greatly influenced the development of social thought in a number of countries. Rousseau's essays and artistic works were very popular in the nineteenth century. Tolstoy's deeply felt kinship with the French philosopher was well-known.

Rurik, Prince (died in 879): The reputed founder, allegedly of Scandinavian origin, of the Russian state. Invited by the Slavs to rule, he first established himself in the area near Ladoga Lake then, in 862, became grand prince of Novgorod. His descendants reigned in Russia until 1598.

Saburov, Andrei (1902-1959): Russian literary historian. Graduated from Moscow University. Appeared in print in 1930 and became known as an expert on Gorky. He published a book on *War and Peace* in 1959.

Salisbury, Harrison (1908-   ): American author. Studied at the University of Minnesota. Started his career as a journalist in 1928. Was *The New York Times* correspondent in Moscow between 1949 and 1954. He is the author of numerous books on Russia.

Sarolea, Charles (1870-1953): Taught French for many years at Edinburgh University.

Was the author of a number of books dealing with Russia. He had a great interest in Tolstoy.

Serebryansky, Mark (1900-1941): Russian critic. Participated in the civil war, then was employed in the Soviet press. From 1932 he taught Soviet literature in Moscow. Died in action in World War II.

Shamil, Imam (1797-1871): Leader of the religious movement known as Muridism, originating in Daghestan. From 1834 he headed the armed resistance against Russia's advance in the Caucasus. In 1859 he was captured by the Russians but later released. He died in Medina while on a pilgrimage.

Shchedrin, Rodion (1932-   ): Russian composer.

Shestov, Leo (Real name: Schwarzmann, 1866-1938): Russian philosopher. Received a degree in law from Kiev University. Left Soviet Russia in 1920 and later settled in Paris. His writings focused on the questions of religion and existentialism. Knew Tolstoy personally and wrote essays about him.

Shklovsky, Victor (1893-   ): Russian writer and critic. Studied arts at the University of Petersburg. Was a major figure in the Russian Formalist school in the 1920s. He is the author of numerous works of fiction and movie scripts. His scholarly publications include several studies of Tolstoy.

Sholokhov, Mikhail (1905-   ): Russian novelist. First published in 1925 and within a decade he became a recognized author. In 1939, he was elected to the Soviet Academy and in 1961 to the Central Committee of the Party. In 1965 he received the Nobel Prize for his novel *Quiet Flows the Don* (Tikhii Don, 1928-1940).

Sholom Aleichem (Real name: Sholom Rabinovich, 1859-1916): Yiddish writer. From the mid 1880s onward he was an estate manager while engaged in literary activities. In 1905 he was a victim of the pogrom in Kiev—left his country but returned three years later. In poor health, he settled in New York in 1914 where he died two years later.

Shukshin, Vasily (1929-1974): Russian writer. Studied at the Moscow Institute of Cinematography. Appeared in print in 1958 and soon became a very popular author. His highly acclaimed writing *Snowball Berry Red* (Kalina krasnaya, 1973) was made into a film which was awarded the Lenin Prize. The film was directed by Shukshin himself and he also played the leading role in it. Died of a heart attack.

Simmons, Ernest (1903-1972): American scholar. Received his Ph.D. from Harvard. Taught at Harvard and Cornell, and was chairman of the Department of Russian Literature at Columbia University between 1946 and 1959. His numerous contributions to Russian studies include several books on Tolstoy.

Simonov, Konstantin (1915-1979): Russian writer. Graduated from the Gorky Literary Institute. Was an immensely popular author during World War II—his writings received several Stalin prizes. Visited the U.S.A. in 1945 and wrote a play, *Russian Question* (Russkii vopros), dealing with American political life. Held high positions in the Writers' Union and during various periods he edited leading Soviet literary periodicals. His works include poetry collections, a number of novels and plays.

Singer, Isaak (1904-   ): Yiddish writer. Was born in Poland and came to the U.S.A. in 1935. Has written several novels and collections of stories. His work was awarded the Nobel Prize in 1978.

Smith, Hedrick (1933-   ): American journalist. Born in Scotland, spent his graduate years at Oxford. Served in the U.S. Air Force between 1956 and 1959. Held major posts in various locations for *The New York Times* and was the chief of its Moscow bureau from 1971 to 1974. His book *The Russians* (1976) was a highly acclaimed bestseller.

Solzhenitsyn, Alexander (1918-   ): Russian writer. Received a degree in mathematics from the University of Rostov. He was an artillery captain in the Red Army when in February 1945 he was arrested and sentenced to eight years in prison for derogatory references to Stalin. His first published work, *One Day in the Life of Ivan Denisovich* (Odin den' Ivana Denisovicha, 1962), was a great sensation in Russia. In 1970 he was awarded the Nobel Prize and four years later he was expelled from Russia. Moved to the United States in 1976.

Speirs, Logan (1938-   ): American scholar, Received his higher education at Cambridge. Teaches in the Department of English at the University of California, Santa Barbara. Author of the book *Tolstoy and Chekhov* (1971).

Spence, Gordon (1936-   ): British scholar. Received his Ph.D. from Cambridge in 1968. The following year he became a lecturer in English at the University of Canterbury, New Zealand. He is the author of the book *Tolstoy the Ascetic* (1967).

Sreznevsky, Vsevolod (1867-1936): Russian literary historian. Was elected to the Imperial Academy. Wrote numerous biographical studies of Tolstoy.

Stadnyuk, Ivan (1920-   ): Russian writer. Was trained as an officer and served in the army between 1939 and 1958. He is the author of several novels and plays.

Stalin, Joseph (Real name: Dzhugashvili, 1879-1953): Soviet statesman. Took part in the Marxist revolutionary movement from the age of nineteen. Was arrested and exiled several times. In 1917 he was elected to the Party's Politburo. From the end of the 1920s he was the all-powerful leader of the Soviet Union.

Steiner, Edward (1866-1956): Was a professor of Applied Christianity at Iowa College. In 1903 he spent several months in Russia on assignment from *The Outlook* publishing firm. Was the author of the books *Tolstoy the Man* (1904) and *Tolstoy the Man and his Message* (1908)

Steiner, George (1929-   ): French-born American scholar. Received his postgraduate degrees from Harvard and Oxford. Taught literature at several American and European universities. Fellow of the Royal Society of Literature and professor at Cambridge University. His numerous books include *Tolstoy or Dostoevsky. An Essay in the Old Criticism.* (1958)

Strelnikov, Nicholas (Real name: Mezenkampf, 1888-1839): Russian composer.

Stendhal (Real name: Marie Henri Beyle, 1783-1842): French writer. Served in Napoleon's army as an intendant and accompanied the Grande Armée to Russia. Was appointed French consul in Trieste in 1830. Wrote books dealing with art and eminent musicians but he is remembered mostly for his fiction such as *The Red and the Black* (Le rouge et le noir, 1830).

Strakhov, Nicholas (1828-1896): Russian critic. Was trained in natural sciences. From the early 1870s he was Tolstoy's close friend and wrote enthusiastic reviews on *War and Peace*. Was opposed to the influence of the West on Russian literature.

Strauss, Richard (1864-1949): German composer.

Suvorov, Prince Alexander (1729-1800): Russian field marshal.

Syutaev, Vasily (1829-1892): Russian peasant. Refused to follow the official church and formed his own congregation based on brotherly love. He maintained that hard physical labor on the land was essential for salvation. He first met Tolstoy in 1881, and they were drawn to each other during the latter's spiritual crisis.

Timkovsky, Nicholas (1863-1922): Russian writer. Graduated in arts from Moscow University and started his literary career in 1891. His writings mostly deal with the lives of urban intelligentsia.

Timofeev, Alexei (1812-1883): Russian writer. Held a law degree from the University of Kazan. His stories and poems, written in a romantic mood, were very popular among his contemporaries.

Tolstoy, Alexandra (1884-1979): Leo Tolstoy's youngest daughter. Served as a nurse in World War I and was decorated for bravery. After the Revolution she suffered arrests and imprisonment. Left Russia in 1929 and eventually settled in the United States where she was granted citizenship in 1941. Published books of reminiscences dealing with her family.

Tolstoy, Countess Alexandra (1817-1904): Leo Tolstoy's first cousin once removed. Was for many years a maid of honor to the Great Duchess Maria, daughter of Nicholas I.

Tolstoy, Andrei (1877-1916): A son of Leo Tolstoy.

Tolstoy, Count Dmitri (1827-1856): Leo Tolstoy's brother.

Tolstoy, Ilya (1866-1933): A son of Leo Tolstoy. Died a pauper in New York. Published reminiscences of his father.

Tolstoy, Marya (1871-1906): A daughter of Leo Tolstoy.

Tolstoy, Mikhail (1879-1944): A son of Leo Tolstoy. In the early 1920s he left Russia. Lived in France until 1935, then he moved to Morocco, where he later died.

Tolstoy, Count Nicholas (1794-1837): Leo Tolstoy's father. At the age of eighteen he entered the Russian army to fight Napoleon. Was captured by the French in 1813, but was liberated the following year. He retired from the army in 1819 with the rank of lieutenant-colonel and entered the civil service. In 1822 married Princess Maria Volkonsky and settled down on his wife's estate, Yasnaya Polyana. There is a strong probability that he was killed and robbed by his servants on a business trip.

Tolstoy, Count Nicholas (1823-1860): Leo Tolstoy's eldest brother.

Tolstoy, Count Peter (1645-1729): Russian statesman. Served as Russia's ambassador to Turkey between 1701 and 1714. His services were highly appreciated by Peter the Great and he was appointed head of the Secret Chancellery in 1718. Two years after Peter's death he was banished to a monastery where he died.

Tolstoy, Sergei (1863-1947): The eldest son of Leo Tolstoy. He was a musician. Wrote a book of reminiscences of his father.

Tolstoy, Count Sergei (1826-1904): Leo Tolstoy's brother.

Tolstoy, Countess Sophie (1844-1919): Leo Tolstoy's wife. In 1861 received a degree in education from Moscow University and the following year she married Tolstoy. She bore thirteen children and was an invaluable help in preparing Tolstoy's writings for publication.

Tolstoy, Tatyana (1864-1950): Leo Tolstoy's eldest daughter. Left Russia in 1925 and died in Rome. Published several volumes of reminiscences of her life in Yasnaya Polyana.

Trotsky, Leon (Real name: Bronstein, 1879-1940): Soviet statesman. Participated in the revolutionary movement from the age of nineteen; was arrested and exiled several times. Played a prominent role in the Russian revolution of 1905. In 1917 he became commissar for foreign affairs in the Soviet government and five months later he was appointed head of the Red armed forces. In 1929 he was expelled from Russia and after trying a number of countries settled in Mexico. Was assassinated by an alleged Stalinist agent.

Troyat, Henri (Original name: Lev Tarasoff, 1911-   ): Russian-born French author. A professional writer since 1941, he was elected to the French Academy in 1959. The large body of his writings includes a book on Tolstoy published in 1965.

Trubetskoi, Paolo (1866-1938): Russian impressionist sculptor. From 1906 he lived abroad. Died in Italy.

Tsyavlovsky, Mstislav (1883-1947): Russian literary historian. Graduated from Moscow University and taught literature at various Soviet universities. Was a leading specialist on Pushkin.

Tukhachevsky, Mikhail (1893-1937): Soviet marshal. Was born into a noble family and given military training. Fought in World War I, volunteering for the Red Army in 1918. Rose rapidly in the ranks and was made marshal in 1937. Was executed during the purges on false charges.

Turgenev, Ivan (1818-1883): Russian author. Studied at the universities of Moscow and Petersburg. Established his reputation with his work, *A Sportsman's Sketches* (Zapiski okhotnika, 1852). His best known novel is *Fathers and Children* (Ottsy i deti, 1962). Spent the last twenty years of his life abroad to be near the object of his adoration, the French singer Pauline Viardot.

Tvardovsky, Alexander (1910-1971): Russian poet. Graduated from the Moscow Institute of Philosophy, Literature and History. Achieved fame with his long poem, *The Land of Muravia* (Strana Muraviya, 1936) for which he received a Stalin prize in 1941. Another poem, *Horizon beyond Horizon* (Za dal'yu—dal', 1960) earned him the Lenin Prize in 1961. As editor-in-chief of the journal *Novyi mir,* he was instrumental in publishing Solzhenitsyn's work *One Day in the Life of Ivan Denisovich* in his periodical in 1962.

Ulam, Adam (1922-   ): Polish-born American scholar. Received his Ph.D. from

Harvard. Began teaching there in 1947, eventually rising to the directorship of Harvard's Russian Research Center. Has written a number of books dealing with the Soviet Union.

Velichkina, Vera (1868-1918): Wife of Bonch-Bruevich. Was Tolstoy's assistant during the famine of 1891-92.

Volkonsky, Prince Fedor (died in 1380): Russian aristocrat. Died on the battlefield at Kulikovo.

Volkonsky, Princess Maria (1790-1830): Leo Tolstoy's mother. Wedded Count Nicholas Tolstoy in 1822 and during her brief marriage she gave birth to four boys and a girl. After the birth of her last child, Maria, in March 1830, her health was rapidly declining, and she died four months later.

Volkonsky, Prince Mikhail (died in 1610): Russian aristocrat. Died defending Moscow against invaders.

Voltaire (Real name: Arouet, François-Marie, 1694-1778): French author and philosopher. Was educated by the Jesuits in Paris. Lived in England between 1726 and 1728. Spent three years at Potsdam following the invitation of Frederick the Great of Prussia in 1750. From 1758 to his death he lived in Switzerland near the French border. A major figure in French literature, he was the author of poetry collections, numerous prose works, philosophical treatises, and pamphlets.

Voronsky, Alexander (1884-1943): Russian Marxist critic. Took part in the revolutionary underground; was arrested and exiled several times. Between 1917 and 1920 he was a member of the Soviet government, then edited journals until 1927 when he was expelled from the Party. Was arrested during the purges and presumably died in a prison camp.

Wagner, Richard (1813-1883): German composer.

Wasiolek, Edward (1924-): American scholar. Served in the U.S. Navy during World War II and ten years later received his Ph.D. from Harvard. He has since been teaching Slavic and comparative literature at the University of Chicago. An expert on Dostoevsky, he has also written a book on Tolstoy's major fiction.

Werth, Alexander (1901-1969): Russian-born British journalist and author. Studied at the University of Glasgow. Between 1941 and 1947 he was the Moscow correspondent for *The Sunday Times* and the BBC. Wrote a large number of books dealing with Russia.

Wrangel, Baron Peter (1878-1928): Russian general. Trained as a military officer, he commanded a Cossack division in World War I. In 1918 he joined the Whites in the civil war and was put in charge of an army. In April 1920 he became the leader of the White movement. After a series of defeats he left Russia with the remains of his forces. Died in exile in Belgium.

Zaidenshnur, Evelina (1902-): Russian literary historian. Was employed by the Tolstoy Museum in Moscow from 1924.

Zaslavsky, David (1880-1965): Russian journalist and critic. Was on the *Pravda* staff from 1928 until his retirement. Published studies on Russian writers.

Zhantieva, Dilyara (1902-1975): Russian literary historian. Her doctoral dissertation *The English Novel of the Twentieth Century, 1918-1939* (Angliiskii roman XX veka, 1918-1939) was published in 1965. This was followed by other works dealing with English literature.

Zhdanov, Andrei (1896-1948): Communist party official. In 1934 he became head of the Leningrad party organization and five years later was elected to the Politburo. Directed the defence of besieged Leningrad during World War II. In 1946 he was appointed President of the Supreme Soviet and given full power over the cultural affairs of the U.S.S.R. He imposed strict controls over literature, purged journals, and launched verbal attacks on well-known literary figures.

Zilov, Lev (1883-1937): Russian writer. Appeared in print in 1904; some of his stories were devoted to Tolstoy.

Zweig, Stefan (1881-1942): Austrian writer. Studied literature at the universities of Berlin and Vienna. Was known for his pacifist views in World War I. In 1928 he visited Russia to take part in the celebration of the one hundredth anniversary of Tolstoy's birth. Left

Germany in 1934 as a protest against the established Fascist regime. Committed suicide in Brazil. Apart from novels, he also wrote highly popular biographies of eminent authors and artists.

No dates have been found for the following persons mentioned in the main text:

Bychkov, Sergei: Russian scholar. Committed suicide.

Gornaya, Victoria: Russian scholar. Published studies on Tolstoy's influence abroad.

Kiseleva, L: Russian critic.

Kjetsaa, Geir: Member of a Swedish-Norwegian research group of scholars and computer experts.

Leusheva, Sofya: Russian scholar. Published a monograph on *War and Peace* in 1954.

Rubin, V: Russian composer.

Shelyapina, Nina: Co-author of a three-volume bibliography on Tolstoy.

Shifman, Alexander: Russian critic.

Popov, Pavel: Russian scholar.

Sorokin, Boris: Author of the book, *Tolstoy in Prerevolutionary Russian criticism,* published by the Ohio State University Press in 1979.

Zinner, E: Russian scholar.

Zhislina, Susanna: Russian authoress.